FINDING CENTER:

Strategies to Reveal Strong Girls and Women

FINDING CENTER:
Strategies to Reveal Strong Girls and Women

MAUREEN D. MACK

NEW HORIZON PRESS
Far Hills, New Jersey

Copyright © 2007 by Maureen D. Mack

All rights reserved. No portion of this book may be reproduced or transmitted in any form whatsoever, including electronic, mechanical or any information storage or retrieval system, except as may be expressly permitted in the 1976 Copyright Act or in writing from the publisher. Requests for permission should be addressed to:

New Horizon Press
P.O. Box 669
Far Hills, NJ 07931

Maureen D. Mack
Finding Center: Strategies to Reveal Strong Girls and Women

Cover Design: Norma Rahn
Interior Design: Susan Ramundo

Library of Congress Control Number: 2006923965

ISBN 13: 978-0-88282-280-8
ISBN 10: 0-88282-280-2
New Horizon Press

Manufactured in the U.S.A.

2009   2008   2007   2006   2005   /   5   4   3   2   1

Dedication

To Rebecca Sue Baumgartner Wyss, my daughter,
Bradley Leo Baumgartner, my son,
And Lauren Christina Maureen Wyss,
Hannah Jane Noreen Wyss, my granddaughters,
And Jack Wyss, my grandson.
All strong girls and boys.
Finally, in memory of Helen and Victor Mack,
whose life spirits are with me always.

Author's Note

This book focuses on women's issues, particularly adolescents, and ways to build and maintain strong core values. Research is drawn from experience counseling patients, as well as my clients' own real life experiences. Fictitious identities and names have been given to all characters in this book in order to protect individual privacy and some characters are composites.

Table of Contents

Acknowledgments		viii
Introduction		ix

Chapter 1:	Forging a Path	1
Chapter 2:	Mother and Daughter Attachment	5
Chapter 3:	Limited Life Experience	22
Chapter 4:	Alcohol in the Family	36
Chapter 5:	Dangers of Early Dating and Mating	58
Chapter 6:	Models and Mentors	74
Chapter 7:	Sensuality and Sexuality	93
Chapter 8:	Women as Assets	111
Chapter 9:	New Age Schooling	129
Chapter 10:	Teens Off Track	159
Chapter 11:	Choosing Her	167
Chapter 12:	A Beautiful Girl—A Beautiful Woman	187

General References	193
Index	217

Acknowledgments

I am indebted to many people who assisted and supported me with this project. The University of Wisconsin-Eau Claire, specifically the Office of Research and Computer Networking Systems, provided technical and research funding for projects which supported this work as well as the University Sabbatical Program, which provided me time to revise, promote, and reflect. Special thanks to Katherine Rhoades, Dean of the College of Education and Human Services, who believed in the book's message and supported my efforts to complete it.

I extend appreciation to James Johnson for his permission to use his poem, "My Father Drinks" and to Patsy Grandberg for her permission to use her drawing "Reflection." Both of these creative works add emotional strength to my message.

Thanks to the careful work of Jennifer Berchem, my writing assistant, who built the index, kept a running record of chapter references and put them in top notch form, and performed a host of other activities to move the book along. Katherine Bowman, a very talented English major and writer, contributed to the content in the chapter on new-age schooling.

For spiritual guidance and affirmation, I am especially indebted to my friend Carol Mazur, who has watched, coached, and inspired me for the last five years as the work has taken form. She was never in doubt about the project reaching fruition. In a similar vein, thanks so much to Liz Ryder, who read an early book proposal of the project and gave me a deadline to report to her regarding acquiring both an agent and a publisher. To both Carol and Liz, I am so thankful for your inspiration and friendship.

To Maryann Karinch, thanks so much for representing me. You delivered exactly what you promised, and to New Horizon Press and editor Joan Dunphy, thanks for taking a chance on this work.

To Lud Nordahl who served as my production coach and who has heard more than one person ever needs to know in such a short amount of time about girls and women, but who has listened and provided the kind of coaching I missed out on as a girl and young woman proving that it is never too late for any of us to find a coach.

Finally, to Dave Hancock, national business leader and inspirational human being.

Introduction

Current researchers, including myself, have listened to many girls and young women during personal interviews, group "sister to sister" forums, and counseling sessions speaking of their four main struggles: the silencing of girls and women, schooling, sexual harassment and violence, and believing in themselves.

Silencing of Girls and Women

Some believe the silencing of young females is a result of growing up in a sexist society. However, silencing is not a girl-only malady. The silencing strategy in many countries, for instance, has long been in effect as a way to control adult women. Some European immigrant women lived as second-class citizens in their country of origin and were considered to be the property of their fathers and, later, if married, their husbands. When they immigrated to the United States, customs employed in their countries of origin were transplanted to America. Practices common in male dominant European cultures included limiting a women's ability to acquire money and other assets, excluding women from leadership roles in religious practice, forcing women to work for no or meager pay in intolerable work conditions, forbidding or restricting health care, and restricting a woman's right to choose for herself in nearly all community, legal, and personal affairs. White European women often viewed themselves as far superior to Native Indian women in North America. The truth was that Native Indian women enjoyed more freedom and cultural rights than did most white women who immigrated to the Americas.

Girls and young women have maintained time and time again that they encounter a wide variety of aggressive and passive-aggressive behaviors directed at them in order to keep them in their place. Their place is quiet, submissive, and reticent at demanding that their voices be heard around the table or in the classroom in a serious manner. Other writers maintain that girls and women who are tough, strong, or outspoken may be viewed as less feminine by the adults in their families and their peer groups and, thus, are less valued. When a young girl or woman detects this devaluing, it often threatens her ability to develop and maintain close interpersonal relationships. Girls report that speaking up gets them into trouble with peers and teachers who prefer quiet, compliant, "nice" girls.

Girls did not get to this silent state of affairs on their own. They have been in a long training program, beginning with their families before ever stepping into elementary schools at the age of five, or middle schools at the age of eleven. Their mothers are now armed with bank accounts, legal rights and high school and college diplomas of their own. They and their daughters live in an enlightened society with respect to domestic abuse, equal education, and employment opportunities. Yet many of these civil rights rich women put up with behaviors in their homes that they would litigate if the same behaviors were wielded at their daughters in school.

I believe, and my research has confirmed, that many girls learn to be submissive, neurotic, and self-hating from poor mothering. Regardless of race, ethnicity, and social class, girls learn the cultural conventions of womanhood from their mothers and other significant women in their early lives. Many young women report that they receive very early messages from their mothers that "some" man is better than "no man at all" even if that man is abusive and controlling. A great number of young women believe that if their mothers were to have talked honestly and openly to them, it would have required their mothers to break the pattern of idealizing marriage or from covering up frequent patterns of control and abuse which were common in their own marriages. When this doesn't happen, girls and young women are then raised with blinders on their eyes and mufflers on their ears. Their collected experiences taught them to remain submissive to patterns of hostile, aggressive behavior in marriage relationships; though eventually they learn life under these conditions is difficult.

Today's realities of society and economic change have leveled the playing field for a great many white women as well as for women of color. Women have increased their participation in the labor force as well as in higher education in impressive numbers. Sadly, for many women, this success has been met with mixed messages by men in the domestic scene. Many men have come to expect that they are responsible for providing for the economic means of the family and, thereby, be afforded the same rights and privileges of being the dominant force in one's domicile, much as their fathers had. Jean Anyon, who studied social class and schools wrote, "girls are meant to be subordinate, even submissive" in their homes where fathers are expected to be the authority figure. This may contradict the reality of their own mother's role and importance in the world outside of the family. In the Hispanic family, machismo traditionally means men are to exhibit courage and honor and to respect women and other family members as well as to provide for the economic needs of the family. In modern culture, where women have made gains in both educational and economic status, many men experience serious difficulties in letting go of the world of their fathers for a more egalitarian model of family roles with their female partners and children. This inability to let go and acquire new relationship skills provides for a ripe environment where control, abuse, and violence breed.

While interviewing high school girls, I became more acutely aware of how intolerable the word "nice" was for young women today. This was not the first time I obtained negative feedback on "nice." As a professor reading a hundred student papers, (primarily female) for a class I taught, I occasionally wrote "nice work" on a paper or two. When reviewing my student evaluations, more than one student indicated how she hated the word *nice* used in the context of either her work or her performance. I shared my experience with the word *nice* when I was teaching a women's studies class. Both women and men students confirmed the negative connotation they held for *nice women.* They associated *nice* with girls and women who prefer to give power away rather than stand up for themselves and ask for more attention and feedback even though they may experience ridicule and/or rejection by an authority figure or in an interpersonal relationship. Writer J. Taylor tells of a woman named Olivia who had an aversion to her "nice" mother who she believed was a doormat to everyone other than her daughter and who could not say no to anyone. Olivia regarded her mother's niceness as inauthentic. She saw her mother as powerless to express herself honestly and to make choices in her own life. Her mother chose to preserve the curtain of niceness and took out her anger on her daughter, Olivia, in a very "unnice" manner. It is still another way that adult women teach girls and young women to accept the realities of a female life.

In her book, *The Body Project: An Intimate History of American Girls* (Random House, New York, 1997), Joan Brumberg reports that girls want more social interactions with their teachers about all kinds of "real-life" issues. However, I believe the people girls want to take their life lessons from are their mothers. Mother, and specifically mother's choices, and the sense of her own value, weighs in as paramount to the way a girl, and eventually the grown woman, negotiates her own battles over a lifetime.

Negative Schooling

Some scholars argue that in America the educational system reinforces existing social status and does not equalize opportunities for all students. In *School-Smart and Mother-Wise: Working-Class Women's Identity and Schooling* (Routledge, New York, 1997), Wendy Luttrell maintains that schools are a primary territory where loss of female self-worth occurs with the silent permission of school professionals.

> *"In one sense, the women's stories support a view of schools as trading posts where students bring different sorts of "cultural capital" i.e., different kinds of knowledge, dispositions, linguistic codes, problem-solving skills, attitudes, and tastes, only some of which get rewarded or valued by school authorities. Those with the "right" (i.e., legitimated) cultural capital fare the best in school."*... *"students of higher social standing were automatically viewed by the teachers as smart. Similarly, those students with obedient or submissive behavioral styles and attitudes were the "teachers' pets" and were understood to be "going places."* Luttrell, 1997, page five.

The 1990s provided firsthand evidence of the psychological and physical distress of girls and young women. I believe that a state-of-the-art school that meets the "whole" female person's needs is rare. While some writers believe that much has been made about nothing with respect to public schools shortchanging girls, schools have made little substantive changes to meet the emotional, physical well-being and future employment needs of the majority of girls and young women. Sexual harassment in schools, both public and private, is still an everyday occurrence. Little has been done to address hostile hallways where girls and young women put up with sexual harassment and abusive language.

Introduction

Curriculum content and instructional methodology in the secondary high school, aside from word-processing skills, looks much as it did decades ago. Young women are passive in science and mathematics, and many teachers do not connect curriculum to women's future lives and career paths. In too many middle and high schools, science, math, history, and technology classes are still taught by a majority of male teachers (some of whom sideline as coaches) and who have little or no recent education in meeting the needs of female and minority female students in their curriculums. While the mission of Title IX was to enhance the inclusion of women in boys/men traditional curriculum, the law's primary effect has been in athletics. While it is true that there are now many more opportunities for girls and women to compete in sports, there are still far too few female coaches. And while white female teachers comprise eighty percent of the public school K-12 teacher workforce, curriculum which includes women's roles and contributions in society in a substantive manner is rare indeed.

There is still an appalling lack of inclusion of the contributions women have made and the roles of women in social sciences, history, and mathematics. Visible signs of girls and women in the curriculums and in the classroom settings (posters, visual displays, internet cites) are still by and large missing. Many girls are still clustered in the traditional female occupations in school-to-work and vocational education programs. They do not have substantial choices within the public school curriculum in the sciences, computer technology, and environmental technology. In many cases, girls must choose to leave the public schools for private all-girls' school or be home schooled where it is possible to put together a state-of-the art curriculum by tapping into a host of educational choices such as technical colleges, college courses and on-line courses. While 21st century industries clamor for students prepared in computer science, biotechnology, and environmental science, there is a pronounced gap between young women's and men's level of preparedness in these areas.

Finally, strong female leaders who are knowledgeable about alternative curriculum for girls and young women are a rare commodity in our schools. I recently attended a regional meeting of about one hundred public school administrators and principals. The room was filled with men of all ages, young and old. There were less than a handful of women. How does a lone female leader take the political heat that is needed to fight for equal resources and inclusion of girls and young women into advanced mathematics, sciences, and technology courses?

Girls and women should be encouraged to take as many mathematic, science, and technology courses as possible, regardless as to whether the student is considered to be a "math" student or whose post-secondary plan includes college. It is simply not acceptable to allow archaic standards to dictate student access to curriculum that will make the difference for both girls and boys to compete in today's and tomorrow's economy which is less and less defined by national borders.

Sexual Harassment and Violence

Sexual harassment in our schools is a serious and continuing problem. The American Association of University Women (AAUW) study, "Hostile Hallways: Sexual Harassment In America's Schools," provides a stinging view of what the life of many girls under the age of eighteen in schools is like. Eighty-five percent of all girls surveyed in this study report being sexually harassed. Seventy six percent of these girls had been the targets of sexual comments, jokes, gestures, or looks, while two-thirds of them had been touched, pinched, or grabbed in sexual ways. Girls who had been the targets of sexual harassment indicated they had been harassed in the hallways (most common place) or in the classroom (second most common place). In a document supplied to all students, a Wisconsin university reported that "as many as seventy percent of undergraduate students at that university indicated they had been the target of discrimination or harassment because of their sex." Most studies document that twenty to thirty percent of undergraduate women have experienced sexual harassment (leering, unwanted touching, direct or indirect threats, etc). It is common belief that the actual numbers are much higher due to the reluctance of women to admit to or to report such an experience.

I interviewed approximately fifty high school seniors who had recently graduated and discovered firsthand the appalling number of girls who experienced sexual harassment in my own community. When I asked, "Did you experience any instances of students/adults talking inappropriately about girls' bodies, sexual suggestions, etc., during your schooling?" two-thirds of the young women whom I spoke reported yes. When I asked the question, "Did you personally experience any instance of inappropriate physical touching?" one-quarter of the young women to whom I interviewed indicated yes. When I asked, "If /when you encountered difficult times relating to these issues of sexuality, who did you turn to most often for support and guidance?" two-thirds of the young women named their mothers, while seventeen percent said they kept it to themselves. Given the track record of many girls and teenage mothers, the fact that the majority said they turned to their mothers is certainly good news. We can only hope that the mothers provided them with positive messages that supported their daughters and that they spoke out against such negative behaviors in their daughters' schools. However, it is upsetting, to say the least, that seventeen percent of the young women kept their bad experiences to themselves.

Sexual harassment results in an exceedingly negative effect on a girl's academic participation and performance. It creates poisonous emotions and feelings. It alters her focus from searching for positive experiences in school to focusing on avoidance behaviors: avoiding harassers, avoiding classrooms where teachers do not protect and stop such behaviors from occurring, or even worse, avoiding teachers who engage in such behavior. Simply put: it negatively alters the girl, the young woman. It moves her life from the light to a psychological darkness.

Believing in Self

The majority of girls and young women report tension between what they want to accomplish and how they intend to get there. They report deep feelings of insecurity, frustration, and disappointment surrounding the issues of sexuality, acceptance, and self-identity. Young women report that they know that they can be anything they want to be when they graduate from high school. As one high school woman I interviewed put it—that is exactly the problem. They have opportunities their mothers never had. But where is the roadmap—the mentoring, the new curriculum to assist with the choices? That is the enormous unknown. It is the rare high school curriculum and not enough family dialogues where serious discussions occur concerning the choices that girls and young women can now make and the impact those choices will have on their life goals, family roles, dating partners, or use of their time. Girls and women function in societies that more than ever shape their image of who they ought to become by television and media that overwhelmingly sends women messages that they are sexual objects, ornaments, and background players in life's most important scenes.

So what is the problem? It is one of staying focused, having a plan, and setting goals for themselves. It requires girls and young women to integrate the best of their mothers' lives with their own. Their own plans for their lives must include setting their own time lines instead of the ones their mothers used.

Many girls and young women go through their formative years without a mentor to assist them with the changing roles of women and men in today's society. In my interviews with young women, most could not accurately define a mentor. We don't directly address role changes for boys. The culture has not changed very much regarding the primary message given to boys and young men. Men are the providers. Men's value will be determined by their abilities to pay for and sustain acceptable lifestyles and livelihoods, which they choose. Their prestige will be partly determined by their abilities to attract and retain beautiful and sought-after women. The prettier, the better; those messages have not changed.

Some messages have changed for girls and young women. They are told they can and should work inside and outside of the home. College is the door to professional careers, expression of their talents and the mechanism to focus on their personal development. Young women of today are getting into college with greater success than their male counterparts. For the first time in the history of American undergraduate institutions about sixty percent of all undergraduates are comprised of women. Their completion rate is also impressive. However, without mentors and role models, young women report that they struggle with how to accomplish it all. One young woman told me that she intended to pursue at least the first level of graduate school, be married, and begin a family by the age of twenty-five. She believes if she is not married by twenty-two, she will be delaying her family beyond what is desirable. After all, she commented, I don't want to be one of those old mothers who started having children in their thirties!

The first time I heard the "need to do everything before age thirty" scenario, I thought to myself, I did that. Should I tell her? And what would I say? I graduated with an undergraduate degree at twenty-two, married the fall after graduation, and finished my master's degree two weeks before my first child was born when I was twenty-five. I finished my Ph.D. at the age of thirty. My son was born in the second of three full-time years of my doctoral studies at a major university where I experienced both sexual discrimination (when my motherhood and pregnancy was discovered by a male professor) and sexual harassment by another professor in one of my courses. I either worked full-time teaching in the public schools or was a teaching and research assistant in graduate school. Didn't I do it? And what would I have said if I had told her? That I was unusually gifted and talented? That I was independently wealthy? That I received unexpected and unconditional support from many of my professors who wanted to see a female, who was also a mother, succeed? Nothing could be further from the truth.

Like many girls, I established being "good at school" at an early age. Not to mislead the reader, I was not an exceptionally accomplished student. However, I was an early reader. That in itself garnered favor with my primary teachers. I had an insatiable desire to write everything down (even when I was too young to really know how to write) and to just "do" those things those adults did that I loved.

I wanted to play the piano. There was a piano in my family home and I knew my father both played piano and had written songs. But due to the family dynamics that occur when a mother is ill who has four small children, my father could not focus on obtaining piano lessons for me. It is hard to remember if he even heard me ask. Even so, as a child of five in kindergarten, I studied my teacher playing the piano to my class as if my very life depended on me being able to repeat the patterns her fingers made across the keys. I can still remember running out of my kindergarten classroom, across the road and up the hill where we lived, tearing into the living room and sitting at the piano determined to play as my teacher had played. After repeated trials, I did learn some things on my own. Certain patterns resulted in song-like tunes. I learned to plunk out the notes to songs that I could sing, such as *Silver Bells*. However, without instruction and an adult guide, I became frustrated and turned my attention instead to my grandfathers' books. I still remember trying to solve the code found on the pages of his books and how amazed I was that I could find some words I knew.

Even as a young child, I had a strong intuitive sense that I would need to do things for myself. My mother, who had serious mental and physical problems, was not able to be a part of my five- to seven-year-old life in the way my little friends' mothers were. Shortly before my seventh birthday, my mother took her life rather than face the aftermath of electroconvulsive shock therapy and a latent diagnosis of tuberculosis which required isolation and confinement to a sanitarium. (I will talk more of how this relationship affected me in a later chapter.) On an instinctual level, I knew I had to make things okay for myself as my father and other adults in my family were having trouble coping with their own lives at that point. I never once thought acting like a princess would help me.

Chapter 1
Forging a Path

"Courage doesn't always roar. Sometimes courage is the quiet voice at the end of the day saying, 'I will try again tomorrow.'"
MARY ANNE RADMACHER

Some women learn to forge a path and stay on it to survive. Early life trauma teaches many of us lessons those living a normal life would miss. When you lose one parent as a very young child, you keep very close track of the one who remains. My father worked outside of the home selling insurance. I was scared to death each morning he left the house that he would not return. I made enough of a nuisance of myself that I did travel with him, up and down rural Wisconsin highways, to farms, taverns and houses along the way as he sold insurance. Going with him during summer and school vacations I learned at a very early age that working outside of the house was fun. I loved school and loved some of my classmates, but I loved leaving the house and traveling down the hill and over the next one even better.

Years later, my Aunt Margie, then in her eighties, and I discussed the events that surrounded my mother's death and the years to follow. Having lived in our home (it was her childhood home as well) and having assumed the responsibility of caring for her family and mine, she was surprised to learn that I remembered so vividly the scenes surrounding my mother's death. She was even more surprised to learn that I had experienced adult post traumatic stress disorder due, in part, to flashbacks about those early, painful years. Margie said she recalled thinking, at the time my mother died, that I was doing well in coping, being busy, figuring out reading and learning to write, and, yes, she remembered my relentless plunking on the piano. She said she never worried about me in the same way she was concerned for my male siblings.

Finding Center: Strategies to Reveal Strong Girls and Women

Despite my outward appearances of being adjusted, which can be deceiving, early loss is profound. As I struggled to move ahead, I was not to know that my "girlness" would bring me back for years to the morning of my mother's death. Negotiating a country life, and then at age nine one in suburbia, without my mother and without a protector (father), more damage was heaped upon me, eroding my "I am okay today" feeling and "I can make things okay" confidence.

Centering myself and forging a path took many years and carried me down many roads. My struggles, I have come to realize, are ones many young girls and women must confront if they too are to grow after traumas to become the strong individuals they were meant to be. In this book we will undertake the journey together but, just as I have, you alone must reach for your star and embrace your own dream. Don't be discouraged if this endeavor takes time and persistence. You can do it.

One day in the mid 1990s May Sarton's commanding voice jumped out of my car radio and wired a permanent connection in my brain. I was commuting to my university office and listening to Jean Faraca's morning show on Wisconsin Public Radio.

The host introduced the poet, fiction writer, and essayist as the people's poet—someone that speaks to us all. Her published journals, which describe her struggles with solitude, depression, and recovery from a major illness, hit an intimate cord with the general reading public. When I first heard Sarton that morning, she was eighty-something and experiencing the success as a published author that she had yearned for from the time of her first publication at age seventeen.

Speaking from her home in Maine, where she lived alone, she described her life as being a battle between the need for solitude and creativity and her insatiable desire for social companionship, affirmation, and acceptance. While she was clearly in the twilight of her life, she transmitted such life force that as a listener, I conjured up an image of a strong, forceful woman.

As if the tenacity of her spirit and the intoxication of her voice were not enough, she cemented my attention when she spoke of her lifelong search for her identity. May Sarton was born in the countryside north of the ancient village of Wondelgem, Belgium, in 1912. Her parents, and May, an only child, lived in a picturesque two-story home adorned by large window casements draped with climbing Jasmines and vines over glass entrance doors and a roofed porch. Her father, George Sarton, was a gifted and ambitious scholar determined to rank as a premier science historian. Her mother, Mabel Elwes Sarton, a painter of miniature portraits, was as equally determined to have a career as her husband.

May tells the story of living an idyllic, princess-like life that she was ripped from when she was two years old. In 1914, German troops invaded and occupied both Belgium and the Sarton residence. The family fled to Mabel's mother's home in England. May's family was poor due to her father's regal demeanor that he be freed from the drudgery of providing an income for the family; free to work on his scholarship full-time. George sailed to America leaving his wife and the toddler May without funds, a home, or a secure life. Mabel relied on a network of comfortable family friends in England and Europe and later in the States to provide her and the baby May with food and housing until such a time May's father could find a suitable university position. When her father accepted a position at George Washington University in Washington D.C, Sarton's mother worked menial jobs to put food on the family's table. She eventually abandoned her own income-bearing artistry to deal with the increasing difficulties of living in poverty with a husband whose attention neither May's mother nor May could sustain.

While poor, in a way, Sarton's parents lived the life of aristocracy. After their relocation to America, they traveled extensively to Europe allowing their wealthy friends and sponsors to provide them with food, shelter, and entertainment. At times, May was included in their travels. More often, she was left behind as the Cinderella border with her parents' friends who had young children. Her early post-Belgium life can be described as parent-starved, for she never seemed to be able to garner either her mother's or her father's attention.

Between the ages of nineteen and twenty-five, May emulated her parents in journeying to Paris, England, and Belgium as much as she could. She connected with her parents' European friends. Through their connections, she was able to meet and be hosted by some of the most prolific and notorious writers of that era: Virginia Woolf, Elizabeth Bowen, Vita Sackville-West, Julian and Juliette Huxley, and S.S. Koteliansky, to name a few. She ignored her father's strong advice that she get a university education to secure her future. Instead, she pursued New York repertory theatre as both an actress and a producer. Until her father died, she was successful in obtaining money from him to support a lifestyle she modeled after his. She did not believe she had to earn an income necessary to support her if it meant giving up her theatrical pursuits and then, later on, her writing endeavors.

In an autobiographical account, Sarton describes a trip back to the family home in Belgium when she was seven years old. It had been five years after the family's escape from the Nazis. Her father returned to Wondelgem to finalize the sale of the family home and land to the sexton of the local parish. The home was to be demolished soon after the transaction of the sale.

Seven-year-old May walked with her parents room by room through their former lives. Troop occupation and the absence of care for the home had damaged some rooms. Yet other rooms remained amazingly intact. Sarton describes her mother's surprise when she retrieved a favorite glass she had buried deep in the ground for safekeeping until she could return. It was unaltered!

Sarton lived with her parents in their New England home until after their death. At the age of forty-six, Sarton sold the family home and bought an eighteenth century Maine house that had a strong semblance to her beloved Belgium childhood castle. May Sarton's published journals contain frequent entries referring to her struggles to restrain friends and fans from encroaching on her solitude. In reality, she was always running. If she was not flying to Europe and London to meet friends, she was crisscrossing the United States to read her poetry at colleges and universities. She yearned for Belgium and London when she was not in Europe. When in London, she pined for Maine or for the New York theatre. As Margot Peters' biography of Sarton documents, from the time she left Belgium as a child, May never found home.

I frequently think about May Sarton, her lifelong struggle to overcome her loss of family and home and perhaps her greatest loss—never having found herself. Much like the unbroken, beautiful glassware uncovered by May's mother at the Sarton Belgium home, I was able to find, in a dark period of my own life, a piece of myself hidden away, in the inner core of my being.

It is for May and for all of us females, young and not so young, who still search for ourselves, and home, that this book is written.

Chapter 2
Mother and Daughter Attachment

> "She was the archetypal selfless mother: living only for her children, sheltering them from the consequences of their actions—and in the end doing them irreparable harm."
>
> MARCIA MILLER

Sixteen-year-old Melissa, writing for *Teen Voices Online*, says, "We say that we would jump at the chance to rule a country and wear a crown and have people bow to us, but is this really what want? Is it merely a cry to be noticed? Do we really want to be Princess Mia in *The Princess Diaries*?" She cries out, "Young women are talented; they are beautiful and independent, but no one tells them that they are. So, they lapse into the latest Princess Diaries book and wish they were actually adopted and someone would take them away to a mythical country to make them a queen."

I sense the anger in these girls who dwell in princess land. I see them peer into their looking glasses to find the images that stare back at them are girls that are inadequate and who have allowed themselves to be manipulated and deceived by the outside world. Sadly, while this teen writer condemns her girl pack for being so easily waylaid, she ends her column by lamenting, "I know that I would love to find out that I'm really the long lost heiress to a throne—and I am the one writing this article. What does that say about young women?"

Popular culture would have us believe that girls and young women look toward their peers and to the media for input on how to lead their lives. I believe that the person a girl wants to take her life lessons from is her mother.

Some women are born with strong mothering capital; the rest of us must learn effective mothering. Quality mothering is no accident. The primary mother skill is that of creating a strong sense of attachment before the child is age two and building on that attachment as the daughter faces developmental milestones and the evidential challenges that follow. However, in order for a mother to be successful in preparing her daughter for a sound future, she must know what she is preparing her daughter for.

In post World War II United States and other countries, mothers raised their daughters to get married and to find their princes as the only avenue to secure their futures. As Patricia Beard writes in her book, *Good Daughters,* in 1960 *Glamour* magazine sent the ten best-dressed college girls to Washington, D.C. to ask the senators from their home states for one piece of advice they would offer to young women. A future president of the U.S., Senator John F. Kennedy, advised women that if they wanted interesting lives, they should marry politicians. Sam Ervin, senator from North Carolina, suggested that women be beautiful, natural, and holy. And Senator Harry Byrd of Virginia told young women to get married; you will never have any problems.

Today the path for girls and young women has expanded from the one-way lane to marriage to a superhighway with multiple lanes, exits, and destinations. How important is the role of mother-daughter attachment to a girl's ability to forge a path that is flexible but yet remains true to her own dreams, talents, and aspirations?

How Secure Attachment Looks and Feels

Many of us admire women who just naturally appear confident and at ease regardless of the situation. We find ourselves believing that girls and women are born with this kind of confidence. For a few, this is true. But more often, such self-confidence comes from the quality of mothering a woman experienced during the stages of childhood and adolescence. It has much to do with the qualities of emotional caretaking and open communication that was delivered to her by her mother or mother substitute. A mother who is there for her daughter generally has a life of her own characterized by warmth, constructive communication systems and resiliency, rather than a day-to-day struggle to survive.

A major feature of attachment is emotional sensitivity or the appropriate mother presence, emotional expression, and reception. It has to do with the ability of the mother to observe and make an explicit positive response to the needs expressed by her daughter at any given moment. It means that a mother has constructed her own world in a way that she is also giving and receiving the same emotional support from significant others in her own life.

The quality of a mother's emotional sensitivity forms a deep and long-lasting emotional attachment in a girl that will carry her into adulthood. Secure attachments influence her mind-body connection and her emotional states, as well as the way she will conduct her relationships with others over a lifetime. A girl, and then later the young woman, who has a strong, healthy attachment with her mother and her family of origin, develops the foundation upon which positive self-esteem, independence, and compassion grows. She becomes resilient in the face of the inevitable setbacks and losses that life sends her way.

The primary feature of an emotionally sensitive mother is a warm, open language style coupled with affirming verbal communication. A child begins to trust in the mother's actions and reactions, which over time, leads to a sense of security and safety. These emotional bonds develop rapidly in infants and are critical to the child's sense of belonging. A mother's eyes that connect and lock on the child's eyes, hugging and touching accompanied by warm supporting words in the face of a hurt or challenge, or the joyful, smiling eyes of a mother when her child engages in a behavior that pleases her all combine to promote a daughter's sense of trust and security and, later, help build her identity.

How Poor Attachment Looks and Feels

When a small infant or girl is raised in an environment where the mother is unable to respond to her needs, a break in attachment occurs. This often results in a girl being unable to secure long-lasting relationships later in life, no matter how hard she may try. How does a mother create a child who does not possess a strong sense of belonging?

Most of us do not have to search far in our families or friends to find a story similar to this one. When I first met Jasmine she was seven years old. I had committed to being her mentor after a mentor organization had a hard time matching her.

She was a bouncy, sunny, and somewhat hyper-vigilant child whose father was not in her life and whose mother had a long history of problems with substance abuse and men. Her mother gave birth to her when she was in the armed services during her twenties. The mother married the father of her child but the marriage broke up when Jasmine was a toddler. The small girl moved around a lot with her mother as mother continued to make new starts to her life without much success. Jasmine once shared with me when she was ten years old, "my mother has a lot of problems, but for as long as I can remember; it has been just me and her. Without my mother, I would have no one."

My small student exhibited many symptoms of being an anxious child who was never sure that her mother would be home when she returned from school. As a very young child, Jasmine had taken on the role of watching out for her mother and engaging in many troublesome arguments over her mother's bad choices regarding men in her life. Her energy was used primarily to try to get and keep her mother's attention. It was nearly impossible for her to make friends at school as she was constantly moving from one place to another. When at school, her attention was still on her mother and if she was going to be either alright or even there when she retuned.

If you do not know a childlike student, perhaps you know someone like Stephanie. Stephanie's young years were spent with a stay-at-home mother. When Stephanie went to middle school her mother returned to school to complete her college degree. Her father and his family had a long history of alcohol dependency. Her parents' communication style was passive, hostile, and argumentative. Her father interacted with her mother primarily in a way that either made fun of her, dismissing her, or not taking her seriously. If that did not work, his verbal demeanor became disrespectful.

Stephanie's mother had family issues of her own, having lost her mother at a very young age. Stephanie's mother had spent her life avoiding the stuffed feelings she carried with her from her own story of loss.

Stephanie could not get enough attention from her mother even as a very young child. When her mother entered the workforce and hammered together a successful career that required her to be away a significant amount of time, Stephanie seemed frozen in a child-like stage of dependency. She avoided making decisions regarding her own life, and when she did, she made them impulsively and seemingly in direct conflict to what her mother wanted her to do. She experienced a depressive panic episode during her first year after high school when she was away from home. She commented at that time that it was her wish to return to her hometown, have her own life, but have her mother pay the bills to support her life. That is exactly what she did.

Mothers Who Are Attachment-Wise

A baby and young child possess a strong built-in drive to connect to his or her primary caregiver, ordinarily the mother. Upon birth, the infant sends out signals that keeps its mother at its side, insures the child's safety from harm, and keeps him or her fed. If the mother responds to her child in a sensitive, warm, and regular fashion, the child learns she can depend upon her mother for support, warmth, and closeness. The child, and later on the adolescent, will continue to ask for and receive support from her mother, especially during times of stress.

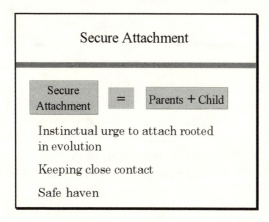

This feeling of belonging and attachment will also extend to a child's father and, later on, to teachers, close friends, and eventually to life partners. Professionals who have studied attachment for many years maintain that if the primary attachment is strong, infants and toddlers will use their parents as a secure base from which to explore their world and become confident, independent women. Secure attachment allows a child, adolescent, and then later an adult, to trust that her needs will be met in a consistent fashion. She will take her cues from a mother who is both warm and open that others will respond to her in the same way. The girl, in turn, begins to mirror those same behaviors back to her mother, family, and to others she meets along the way. She begins to take risks using her mother as a secure base from which to explore. She knows she can come back for continual open and caring support for her choices and be reassured that a certain amount of uncertainty and discomfort is both okay and expected.

> **Definition of Secure Attachment**
>
> Secure attachment is an enduring affective bond characterized by a tendency to seek and maintain proximity to a specific person, particularly when under stress.
>
> – Ainsworth and Bowlby

Not all attachment bonds are the same. Mothers who create strong security in their daughters find effective ways to respond to them when they are in distress. Attachment-wise mothers use their eyes, vocal tones, and words to comfort. They communicate, "You will be okay—this too will pass" with both their words and their non-verbal signals. When their daughters are not in distress or in crisis, they remain emotionally open and available. They do this by listening, questioning, and sharing. Mothers, who are strong in attachment skills, do not give ultimatums nor do they engage in intrusive and upsetting behaviors to their daughters. Perhaps the most significant thing an attachment-wise mother does is to live her own life in such a way that it is void of enduring conflict, hostility, and defensiveness. These qualities, perhaps more than anything else, derail feelings of security and confidence in women and mothers. When left to survive in a setting of pervasive unresolved conflict over time, women and mothers acquire defensive strategies along with a learned helplessness profile. This is counter-intuitive to sending strong messages of attachment and security to any child they are raising, daughter or son.

Role of Father in Attachment

Several young mothers in my university class that focuses on the education of girls and women have related similar scenarios: I am totally immersed in the daily care of these children, the diaper changes, the meals, laundry, transporting to nursery school, the doctor appointments, and the constant bathing, wiping faces, reading the books, etc. My husband gets up, leaves for work, and is gone ten to twelve hours a day. When he hits the back door, the children run from wherever they are to greet him, knocking whatever is in their path aside. He is the king and I am just the mother, the caretaker, the laundress, and the cook that is always with them.

Fathers are, indeed, major players in the lives of their children. Whether effective, available, healthy or unavailable, controlling or unhealthy, it is clear that a father's influence follows a child into adulthood. When children's fathers were never present in their lives, many of these children will be placed on the defensive to explain how they can be okay in the face of this clear disadvantage.

While some women may like to hold on to the belief that fathers are not necessary to raise strong, emotionally healthy sons or daughters, the evidence stacks up on the opposite side of the argument. Fathers play instrumental roles in developing a sense of self-worth and social competence in their children. Children and adolescents who feel the presence of strong father support in their lives are less likely to be rejected and victimized by their peers. Father-supported children display less anxiety, depression and social withdrawal (internalizing behaviors), as well as rule-breaking, aggression and antisocial behaviors (externalizing behaviors). Most fathers do spend less time interacting with their children throughout childhood and adolescence than their mothers do. When they do interact, many father contacts tend to involve physical activities and outdoor play. Father playtime appears to be very important to the development of social skills and a child's sense of social competence outside of the home.

In addition to playtime, involved and supportive fathers provide children with role models when it comes to dealing with separating from mother and the home. While a mother's primary role is to secure connectedness, the role of the father in a child's life is to achieve autonomy—to separate from home, the father and especially the mother.

Fathers who encourage independence but who do not also provide the warmth and social support of a secure base raise children and adolescents that may have difficulty dealing with their own social problems. They have more difficulty separating from their mothers and making their own decisions. The characteristics of securely attached fathers are similar to those of mothers with a few key differences. Fathers who form strong emotional bonds with their children are more likely to share their outside interests (work or play) with their daughters. They are more likely to provide a strong leadership model and engage in effective problem-solving strategies with her in order to help her solve her own problems. Over time, a daughter with a secure attachment to her father learns the process of solving problems but also experiences the success in doing so on her own. The adolescent girl acquires both the confidence and the skills to make decisions, articulate her choices, and solve her own problems as she moves her life circle further away from her home.

It is a common belief that an intact family (when the mother and father live together with their children) is by and large healthier for children than a single-mother family. One study, "Back to School 1999—National Survey of American Attitudes on Substance Abuse V: Teens and their Parents" asserted that children parented by single mothers who demonstrated the behaviors of secure attachment had children and adolescents with fewer school-related problems and who were less likely to drink alcohol and abuse drugs than were children whose fathers were living in the home but were not emotionally or physically available. These fathers who come and go and use the home primarily as a residence, but are not supportive, active, healthy co-parents are more likely to raise both daughters and sons who engaged in drinking alcohol, abusing drugs, and other behaviors counter productive to success in school.

A very important message that comes from the attachment research on fathers is that quality mothering may not be enough for a young girl or woman if it is not followed by either a positive father interaction or at least by a neutral fathering effect. Even when girls are raised away from their fathers, many develop father-hunger and may be at risk for early dating and mating in middle or high school. Intrusive overmothering is not an antidote for the regular occurrence of negative fathering behavior.

Characteristics of Fathers of Securely Attached Children

Secure Attachment Father Attributes	Insecure Father Attributes
Shows physical affection to child	Makes little positive physical contact
Plays with child	Avoids play and appropriate child activity
Possesses authoritarian parenting style	Possesses autocratic or absentee parenting style
Knows important details of child's life	Avoids learning details of child's schedule, significant friends' names
Meets child's teachers, coaches, leaders and communicates expectations	Makes little contact with significant adults in child's life
Attends important events	Engages in argumentative, ordering, one-way dialogue with child and/or child's mother
Engages in warm, open communication with child and others	Shows preoccupation with own life, desires and activities
Shows warmth, openness and availability to child's mother	Relates to child as an equal or childlike
Problem solves with child placing himself as leader and adult	Demonstrates unhealthy habits that lean towards physical and emotional instability
Holds significant adults in child's life accountable for actions and behaviors	Does not take personal responsibility for own parenting and/or does not hold significant adults in child's life accountable
Demonstrates healthy habits that lean towards wellness and emotional stability	

Strategies to Build Feelings of Attachment

At the start of this chapter, I mentioned that some mothers and fathers are born with strong attachment capital; the rest of us must learn effective mothering as well as ask for strong attachment skills in the fathers of our daughters as well. Life is not fair! We come with a host of family histories and experiences—some positive, some negative. The good news is that there is ample information available to both mothers and fathers on how to develop securer bases for ourselves and to acquire skills in parenting which lead to secure daughters (and sons).

Attachment Styles

Effective Attachment Strategies	Non-Effective Attachment Strategies
Sees distress as temporary	Feels anger and resentment frequently and for long duration
Uses support systems	Self Consciousness
Expresses personal thoughts	Isolates; is lonely
Seeks comfort from parents or partner	Uses distancing strategies
Highly resilient; feels that things will be okay	Engages in risky behaviors
Behaves in gentle fashion	Uses threats and personal insults
Engages in calm discussion; listens	Autocratic one-way dialogue
Compromises	Shows less constructive behavior
Exchanges positions without dominance	Shows negative emotions during conflict
Shows constructive behaviors-emotions	Encourages, develops dependence upon parents
Encourages, develops independence from parents	

As I've said earlier, I believe you cannot give to others that which you cannot provide for yourself. The first step in providing a more effective relationship with your daughter is to build a strong relationship with yourself. For mothers, this means focusing on building a richer, well-balanced life that includes rest, relaxation, a support group of friends and a variety of professionals from which to draw strength and healing. These include exercise leaders at health clubs or the YWCA, regular visits to physicians for yearly checkups and mental health screenings, and experienced healers whether they be well-trained counselors, ministers, or wellness specialists. Support groups assist women in building effective communication and problem-solving skills and help individuals to establish appropriate boundaries within their lives. For many women and mothers, and indeed men and fathers, the concept of boundary setting—that is knowing what is your responsibility and what is not: when to intervene, when not to intervene, when to let others involve you in their problems, when to say no—is new territory. In some circumstances, mothers may need to take temporary or permanent vacations from their life partners so they can focus on their own emotional and physical well-being if partners are too intrusive and demanding. It is impossible to heal oneself if a partner insists you stay put and in place.

INCREASING SECURE ATTACHMENT: FOR MOTHERS
- Give yourself what you did not get from your own mother
- Construct your own professional attachment team
- Have a plan to address anxiety, learned helplessness, and compulsive care-giving
- Increase comfort with and skills in living independently
- Choose high-quality female friends and interact regularly
- Become visible in your child's school/to your child's teachers
- Ask for and obtain warmth, reciprocity, caring in your life

While many of the strategies recommended for women and mothers are also effective for men and fathers, men and fathers have their own unique needs. Because of the differences in both cultural expectations and the presence of higher levels of testosterone, men oftentimes have difficulties in communicating their feelings, expressing and controlling anger, and dealing with feelings of rejection and isolation. As they become husbands and fathers, their lives may become out of balance, with work consuming a larger portion of their waking hours. More than ever, a father requires connections with healthy men in his life from which to gather support and share similar challenges and ways to deal with conflict and problems. Some men are resistant to using their time to forge male bonds that do not center on outdoor activities, sports events, or television viewing. However, the most effective men and fathers demonstrate positive skills in family dynamics and provide positive physical presences in the lives of their partners and daughters.

INCREASING SECURE ATTACHMENT: FOR FATHERS
- Give yourself what you did not get from your own mother
- Give yourself what you did not get from your own father
- Construct your own professional attachment team
- Have a plan to address acting out, feeling of rejection and vulnerability and letting go
- Choose high-quality male friends and interact regularly
- Increase physical presence in your daughter's life
- Show leadership, accountability and caring to child's mother and to daughter whether living together or apart

While parents are the primary sources from which a girl and young woman gathers her strength, there are other sources which can foster confidence in girls and can moderate the effects of negative or insecure parental attachment. High-quality friendships and schools that promote interpersonal development and team camaraderie are powerful influences. Later on, in late adolescence, a dating partner who has experienced a secure attachment to both his mother and father will contribute to the resilience and future development of a girl and young woman.

Friends matter but not all friends are alike. Many girls feel that what is most desirable is to be the most popular girl with many friends. However, studies demonstrate that it is far better to have a few friends who are well socialized and can express warmth and acceptance. High-quality friendships cannot buffer the negative effects of a girl or young woman who is insecurely attached to her mother. However, a friend who is open and who is securely attached to her own parents can provide a model to a girl who needs exposure to warm validating parents. In addition, high-quality friends can buffer the effects a girl or young woman is experiencing due to family adversity or to low maternal support due to a host of reasons.

As friendships are not all alike, neither are schools. Superb information is available that documents the role that teachers and other school personnel can play in teaching social and emotional growth and conflict resolution skills. Schools that promote girl connectedness are committed to fostering climates where the feelings of students matter, where bullying, sexual harassment, and exclusion of children are not tolerated and where teachers actively demonstrate that the social and emotional well-being of children are as important as their academic

Increasing Secure Attachment in Girls and Young Women

Friendship Bonds When it comes to friends...	School Bonds Work with daughter's school to...	Pair Bonds Parents and school discuss regularly with daughter-girls that she...
Choose friends who express warmth and validation	Provide opportunities for involvement	Recognize that sexual maturity propels girls to seek opposite sex partners
Encourage friends who are well-socialized	Teach social and emotional growth, refusal skills, and conflict resolution skills	Talk about difference between comfort and sexual satisfaction
High-quality friends can buffer effects of family adversity or low maternal support	Show how social growth is linked to academic competence	Talk about relationship between chronic anxiety and use of sex to address these feelings
Friends do not buffer effects of daughters insecurely attached to mothers	Balance social-emotional focus with academic success	Be on lookout for anger and fighting as way of expressing love and sex
Children with a few high-quality friends are better adjusted	Use positive management techniques that minimize interruptions	Acknowledge that a daughter's sexual desire is a strong motivator of behavior and provide strategies to cope while attending to more important psychological needs
Friends who are securely attached to parents can provide model to daughters who need experiences of warm, validating parents	Visibly include parents in school, class and curriculum, especially mothers in elementary grades	Acknowledge and talk on ongoing basis why sexual intercourse is dangerous for adolescent girls (and for boys)

progress. Within these superior kinds of schools, girls build positive attachments and relationships to their teachers and classmates. They develop social skills and, at the same time, learn how to inhibit the development of antisocial or inappropriate behaviors for their ages. Schools that are sophisticated in their understanding of the importance of child attachment and emulate those behaviors that secure mothers and fathers use toward their own children play central roles to girls' and young women's development. These state-of-the-art schools have significant influences in how girls regard themselves and what they expect of things. Perhaps the most important function a strong school bond provides to secure and insecure girls alike is that of protector.

Cost of Low Self-Regard to Girls and Women

Five experiences create the vast majority of childhood pain that when left untreated persist into adulthood and often interfere in appropriate attachment bonds in life. These experiences are abuse, neglect, addiction, multiple home placements, and parental death or loss. Life-changing events result in immense trauma and, thus, a substantial decrease in the quality of mother-daughter attachment and appropriate attachment to fathers, friends, and school bonds. If these events are not handled with the appropriate degree of emotional sensitivity especially by a mother or mother substitute, a girl will grow up missing a major piece of her identity.

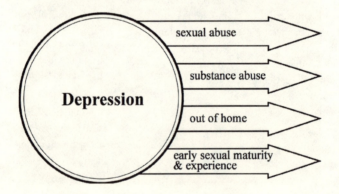

Depression is often a trigger response in girls and women who have experienced victimization, prolonged physical abuse or sexual harassment and substance abuse. For women with early histories containing one or more of these devastating experiences, it is critically important that they address their own healing. If women become mothers before they heal, they will unknowingly pass on their anxieties, insecurities, and weak choice-making abilities to their children. However, research in the fields of sexual abuse, substance abuse, depression, as well as attachment disorder, all demonstrate that it is never too late to heal a child or an adult from these devastating experiences. Healing and treatment that focuses on both the strengths of the woman or girl and is holistic in nature can alter neural connections in the brain, restore a better balance of brain chemistry, as well as promote the development of proactive behaviors and choice-making repertoire.

What is of imperative importance is that a survivor of any of these life events needs to heal herself first before she can provide a maternal relationship to her daughter that is characterized by a secure attachment. Mothers of insecure daughters are usually themselves products of insecure experiences. Insecure attachment is passed on from one generation to the next unless healing occurs.

PRINCIPLES OF EFFECTIVE HEALING FOR DEPRESSION AND TRIGGERING EVENTS
1. Hire a healing team and services that matches needs of individual girls-woman's story.
2. Choose well-trained, experienced professionals; include significant proportion of female healers.
3. Effective healing treatment attends to the whole girl or woman; medication alone is rarely enough or appropriate.
4. Counseling and other behavioral therapies are essential components of a healing approach. Care must be taken to allow the girl-woman to have input into the selection of the professional.
5. Holistic healing requires time, commitment, and patience.

Ways of Knowing
There are two ways of knowing about an issue such as mother attachment. One is what I have tried to do within this chapter; that is, condense and share expert opinion on the topic. The other way of knowing is by firsthand experience. As I've revealed earlier, shortly before my seventh birthday, I lost my mother to suicide. She was misdiagnosed after the birth of her last child and subjected to multiple rounds of

electroconvulsive shock therapy. It devastated her on the most profound level. I have written her story in an essay entitled, "A Better Ending" which can be found on my website at *http://people.uwec.edu/mackmd/*.

Before the loss of my mother, I was a confident, feisty, outdoor girl running the woods of northern Wisconsin by daylight when not in school, and trying to decipher the words in my grandfather's books in the evening. Two women, my mother and a paternal aunt, Margie, kept the large white house on a towering hill functioning as I ran in and out, free as the wind. Years later I would recognize that it was Margie who kept the household together as my mother was already damaged from the "treatments" for what medical professionals believed to be depression. The image of my mother lying on a stretcher covered in her own blood hardwired on my brain where it remained for years. Like many families faced with the choice to survive or collapse under the pressure of a tragedy, my family slowly moved on in silence. I was left on my own to decipher the meaning of how and why mother died as she did as well as how to stop the image of her death from popping up continually during the day.

Within a few years, I moved from the freedom of a hilly rural Wisconsin countryside to the cement streets of suburban Milwaukee to live with one of my mothers' many sisters. Within a few years, I also lost my father. Reeling from the loss herself, my aunt thought it best for me and for her to silently leave the tragedy in the past and move on. She obtained a court order barring my father from contact as to see him triggered her own unresolved feelings about the loss of her sister. She transferred all responsibility of my mother's death squarely on my father's shoulders. She believed any contact I would have with my father would work against my acclimation to my new life. What she did not know is that the path to recovery from such profound losses requires survivors to release both the energy and the toxic chemicals produced from the survival moments or carry it inside where it will wreak havoc and increase in pressure to be released. As a child, you look for others to lead the way in making order of a chaotic loss and to assist you in retaining the memory of your loved one. When that did not happen, I held on to the only memory that remained of my mother: her moment of death.

That process of hanging on resulted in early episodes of depression and anxiety. I went from a rather securely attached child to an anxious, traumatized one without the assistance of a healer. As I continued to grow and regain my footing, I chose to forget my mother, to dismiss any memory or reference of her. In a way, I acted as if my mother never existed. Other girls had mothers; I did not.

What mothers and mother substitutes must accept and act upon is that the most important relationship for a young girl or woman is that between her and her mother, and then her father. The road to gaining, or in my case to regaining, security and confidence in the feeling and belief that you can take care of yourself first leads back to understanding and knowing mother.

Chapter 3
Limited Life Experience

> *"I think that what we're seeking is an experience of being alive, so that our life experiences on the purely physical plane will have resonances within our own innermost being and reality, so that we actually feel the rapture of being alive."*
> JOSEPH CAMPBELL

In Victorian England, girls and young women who expected to marry well were kept housebound. Lower class girls certainly worked outside of the home oftentimes at hard labor at tender ages with little to no pay. But women who wanted to improve their security and stature did so by living through men's success and identity. First they attached to their fathers. Later, if they were lucky to marry and marry well, their attachment came at the good will of their husbands.

Today most parents of girls and young women hold much more progressive expectations. They desire their daughters to be educated, independent, and able to provide for their own financial security in later years. At the same time, the message that both the culture and oftentimes parents provide to young girls is in direct opposition to what many hold in our minds for them. A common message a little girl child gets from both her culture and often from her parents is the princess message. Along a similar vein, the most frequent message an adolescent girl and a woman gets from her culture and perhaps her family is that her worth is directly proportionate to her sexual body image. We should not be surprised when we hear about the pervasive problem girls and women still have with eating disorders, depression, middle school sexual acting out, and drug and alcohol experimentation at an earlier and earlier age.

Women all over the world spend millions of dollars each year in the cosmetic surgery industry slicing away their bodies and/or smoothing away the lines in their faces in order to hide that they are mature, smart women. Millions of women's identities are based upon what they look like and not on what they do, what they believe, or who they are. Sadly, while most mothers and daughters are now too sophisticated to believe that once they marry they will not have any problems, a case can be made that what society imparts as important to young women really has not changed all that much.

The wedding day craze is yet another way to live out the princess lifestyle with little to no serious thought given to how couples will negotiate the complex world of marriage. In America, couples are willing to spend an average of $22,360 for their wedding day according to Conde Nast Bridal Infobank. In New York City, a typical ceremony will average $33,500. Yet, it is not just in the circles of Hollywood or international celebrities, where people marry and break up at a dizzying pace, that couples never discuss what the post-honeymoon life will be like. Just recently I heard a story about Alicia, a young woman I know. She and her husband of just two years had reached a serious impasse. He wants to have at least one child and she does not wish to have any. How is it that a young woman spends large amounts of time discussing her wedding day, yet the prospective bride forgets to discuss whether she and her future husband will have children together? As Dr. Phil McGraw is fond of saying, that's a deal breaker for sure!

Here is the challenge: You can coach a girl to become a princess or you can coach a girl to be a performer. The romantic notion of a "princess-perfect-lifestyle" lives only in mythology; a performer reaps benefits in the real world. A princess's legacy, including the Germanic princesses of early medieval Europe, was often murder or accidental death as, it was for the most famous princess of our time, Princess Diana. A girl-woman performer develops her own skills and talents, makes choices for herself, and grows identity capital of her own. In my opinion you cannot have it both ways.

Let's go back in history to expose the real life of a princess from medieval times. Medieval girls and women were taught from birth that they were inferior to boys and men. Girls were not given personal freedom and were taught that their only purpose in life was to marry and to bear children. Most were illiterate, including princesses. Education of girls, when it did occur, was for the privileged and the rich. It was not intended to develop the girl's independent thinking or problem solving. Skills taught to girls had to do with managing a household and the care and feeding of their husbands. Marriages of princesses were arranged by their fathers or other male relatives for the sole purpose of land acquisitions, military purposes, trade advantages, or to merge wealth between two families. Princesses did not marry for love.

There was no legal age for the marriage of a princess. Marriage of children was commonplace. A princess's chance of getting married depended more on her wealth and social position rather than upon her beauty or accomplishments (and it was assumed the princess did not have any accomplishments, being a girl!). In most cases, a princess never met her future husband before the wedding as she lived much too far away. Romance did not exist as we know it today. Courtship consisted of formal letters from the court asking the princess's father for her hand in marriage. A dowry agreement made on behalf of a princess looked very much like a legal contract would look today to buy goods and services. Once married, the princess or queen was totally dominated by her husband, who was often a domestic brute. (There were, as always, exceptions to these unhappy unions; Queen Victoria, for one, was happily married.)

A princess's marriage was by no means jovial, glamorous, or enviable. She often traveled a long, dangerous trip from her home to a new land and into the hands of a total stranger who had every power over her. She left her home, her family, and her native land in most cases never to see any of them again. Her entire life was put at the mercy of a male court to accomplish financial objectives and progeny, primarily the birth of a son. If sons were not forthcoming, many princesses found themselves dead within a respectable amount of time, and in some cases, in a very short period of time due to any number of unlucky circumstances—sudden illness, accident, poisoning. Once the unlucky princess or queen was dead, the way was cleared for the entrance of yet another child princess with more fortunes to offer the Prince/King.

Many girls think of a closet filled with Cinderella-like dresses when they think of a princess. However, the truth is that the clothes of both princesses and queens were also determined by the court. They were few in number and were long, bulky, heavy, and long-sleeved even in the hot summers. Sometimes undergarments were made of leather and/or wood to compress the breasts. Other times breasts were displayed in squared-off necklines by being shoved upwards and secured by bindings. The effect was not so much for notice and pleasurable comment by men as it was for adornment and restriction of young girls and women. They were just thought to look better that way.

If that is not enough to turn a girl from the princess notion, perhaps this will be. During the heyday of the medieval and Tudor Kings and Queens of Europe, a girl and woman with any value became the immediate property of her husband. She, in effect, became the husband's chattel of which he could do with as he pleased. She had no protection under the law whatsoever. If a King/Prince became suspicious of a Queen/Princess or just wanted her eliminated, the princess or queen could be executed rather easily by an order from the King.

A princess life was that of liberticide; that is, a destroyer of civil liberty. Without her liberty, how can any girl or any woman feel her life, feel her rapture?

Still in a Very Small Box

In 2006, more than thirty-six million girls aged eighteen and under are living in the United States. They live in a most progressive country when it comes to the rights and liberties of girls and women. Yet many girls report that what they see for themselves is often countered by oppositional views from boys, families, and the culture.

In a Harris survey of more than one thousand girls in grades three to twelve, girls were asked if they believed they had access to those rights described by Girls Incorporated. The rights are:

GIRLS' BILL OF RIGHTS
- Girls have the right to be themselves and to resist gender stereotypes.
- Girls have the right to express themselves with originality and enthusiasm.
- Girls have the right to take risks, to strive freely, and to take pride in their success.
- Girls have the right to accept and appreciate their bodies.
- Girls have the right to have confidence in themselves and to be safe in the world.
- Girls have the right to prepare for interesting work and economic independence.

Source: Girls Inc. Website

Finding Center: Strategies to Reveal Strong Girls and Women

These rights are those that most of us want for girls and young women in our lives as well. Nevertheless, the results of the Harris survey indicated that a high percentage of girls felt that they experienced barriers in achieving those rights. In fact, girls are more than twice as likely as boys to be unhappy with the barriers they face in obtaining these basic civil rights.

Sample Finding of Harris Survey of Elementary and High School Girls

Barrier When asked about this idea that some believe...	Finding This percentage of girls believed this barrier existed for them
Believe girls are only interested in romance.	52%
Girls are told not to brag about their accomplishments.	59%
Girls are expected to spend a lot of time on housework and taking care of siblings.	65%
Black girls are not good leaders.	63%
White girls are not good leaders.	48%
Girls experience stereotypes that limit their right to take risks.	49%
Girls believe that girls and boys have the same abilities and strengths.	47%
Boys believe that girls and boys have the same abilities and strengths.	29%

Summarized survey from: *http://www.girlsinclynn.org/harrissurvey*

Seventy percent of the adult women surveyed believed that life is more difficult for girls today than when they were young. However, fifty-six percent of adult men believe life for girls is harder today than in the past. It is clear that women are more likely to recognize how harmful the stereotypes of girls and women continue to be. You may be thinking that girls are impressionable at this age and perhaps their mothers are being overly protective. Perhaps men are more realistic in their increased sense of optimism regarding girls and the barriers they still encounter in their lives. I wish I could say they are correct.

In a 2005 study sponsored by the General Motors Corporation, *Women "take care," Men "take charge:" Stereotying of U.S. Business Leaders Exposed*, 296 corporate leaders were asked to rate how effective men and women were at ten essential leadership skills. Researchers have found little difference between women's and men's leadership abilities. Even though women now comprise fifty percent of the managers in business, senior managers still perceive sharp differences between women's and men's leadership capabilities.

The report reveals that senior managers appeared to accept false beliefs about women and men as leaders. Of all the leadership behaviors described as being traditionally associated with men, problem-solving capabilities were seen very differently between women and men within the organization. On the "take charge" trait, men judged men leaders as being most superior to women and women saw women leaders as far outperforming men. While men persisted in their stereotypical beliefs concerning women and men and their abilities to be leaders, women did not. The study explains that because men far outnumber women in corporate leadership positions, it is the men's belief system, grounded in bias, that predominates in the workplace.

Finally, the General Motors study highlights the power of these one-size-fits-all belief patterns of both men and women. Women and men who worked in occupations traditionally dominated by women, e.g., nursing and human resources, also rated women leaders' problem-solving effectiveness higher than that of men's. Those men and women who worked in male-dominated occupations, such as management and administration, rated women leaders lower on their problem-solving abilities. Also, those workers whose boss was a woman had more stereotypic view of women leaders than those workers who reported to a man. For both men and women, getting used to a woman as the boss or one in charge does not equate with what they were taught both in their homes and by their culture. The authors of the report conclude that:

> "The implications are clear: To help advance women leaders in masculine occupations, organization need to b especially vigilant against stereotypes. By focusing on occupations typically dominated by men, organizations can promote women being successful in positions where they have been less prevalent."

Research evidence supports both girls' and women's feelings and beliefs that they both are still treated inferiorly with respect to who they are and where they can go in life. The problem to be solved by any of us is to figure out how a girl or woman can successfully get herself out of the box so she can build a richer life for herself and enjoy a wider range of experiences during her life.

Creating a Vision

The first step in challenging the boundaries of a one-size-fits-all girl is to create a vision of what and how we want girls and women to lead their lives today. This important work begins with a girl's most important teachers: her mother and father. Adhering to a girl pattern whether it is the old pattern or a new-age pattern leads to the same mistake. One pattern is not the answer. What is more helpful is for girls to hear ongoing messages from their families that what is important is growing as strong and healthy bodies as they can, learning a variety of skills, studying a host of topics, and becoming independent. These were the common expectations teachers in one-room schoolhouses in America and other democratic lands taught both girls and boys a hundred years ago. What is different today is that girls and women have many more opportunities than girls did in 1850 or 1950.

What is also different today than in the past is that we have strong scientific information that counters old beliefs in the inferiority of the female mind and capability. Over the past twenty years, a compelling picture of the intellectual strengths of the female brain has been constructed based upon brain and gender research. Here are some attributes that are commonly listed as being stronger in girls and women than in boys and men:

STRENGTHS OF THE FEMALE BRAIN CENTER
- Strong verbal communication skills
- Superior language and fine-motor skills

- Strong intuitive sense
- Strong capacity to multitask
- Coordinates both sides of brain better for increased problem solving
- Strong memory capability
- Superior listening and communication skills
- Possess strong tactile sensitivity
- Better impulse control when in crisis situations
- Use most advanced areas of the brain, cerebral cortex
- High adaptability skills

Girls are already wired to be strong language performers, problem solvers, and multi-skilled players regardless of the game, sport, or career they tackle. They must be reminded of these strong building blocks and held responsible for taking good care of what they already have and for developing the strengths already within them.

Being reminded is most effective when girls can play at it; for example, play at being *Little Women* living in Concord, Massachusetts at a time when everyone expected a girl to act like a girl. Louisa May Alcott's book was a pivotal force within my own life. When I heard words of discouragement along my path, the image and voices of the March girls and women floated from their house to mine at times when I needed to be inspired to persevere. I literally became "Jo" for long enough to get through wanting to give up and give in.

I also used Jo's ways and Jo's voice both in raising my own daughter and now in "playing" with my two granddaughters. The video recording of the latest version of *Little Women* has been played numerous times at my house as well as at my daughter's. Regardless of the age of the "girl" watching, we all are reminded of the importance of finding the unique gifts housed within each of us and the responsibility in bringing these gifts to our families and within our own lives. An enduring truth that is transmitted in Alcott's *Little Women* that is as true today as it was when it was first published in 1869 is the essential relationship between mothers, daughters, sisters, and among all young women. It is to those women that know her very well in her family that any girl can turn and receive affirmation of her worth, her strengths, and her dreams.

A good start in creating a vision is to use strong images of girls and their families and encourage girls to play at being them. By turning off television programs that contain an overwhelming proportion of negative girl messages and opening up creative play space, girls and their parents can add necessary, positive dialogue and encouragement to the script.

The following suggestions were written for fathers but are excellent beginning points for both mothers and fathers. Post these in full view for you, your daughters, and your sons. Paste them on notes for them to read each day as you send them out the door. Most importantly, talk regularly with them about what they think the words of advice mean to them, or to you as a parent. Encourage a wide range of experiences. And above all else, tell girls about their endless possibilities.

FOR MY DAUGHTERS AS YOU START THIS NEW DAY
- Listen to girls. Focus on what is really important.
- Encourage her strength and celebrate her savvy. Help her learn to recognize, resist, and overcome barriers.
- Urge her to love her body and discourage dieting.
- Respect her uniqueness. My daughter is likely to choose a life partner who acts like me and has my values.
- Get physically active with her. Play catch, tag, and jump rope or just take a walk.
- Get involved, really involved, with her school.
- Get involved, really involved, with her activities.
- Help make the world better for girls.
- Take your daughter to work.

Drawn from "10 Tips for Dads with Daughters" by Joe Kelly, DADS Executive Director

From Finding a Prince to Being a Performer

Joseph Campbell, an accomplished author on mythology and comparative religion, gained international fame by relating myths to lessons all of us can learn in our life. I feel what he wrote is true—that what most of want in life is to feel the rapture of being alive—and that a girl will need to feel her own rapture and live her own life.

As I think back on my life as a very young child, I recall having my very first irresolvable difference with my mother when I was five years old. It was summertime. I was running around from one field to another when my mother called me in and instructed me to put on a shirt. I was running with my chest naked to the wind as was my brother, exactly one year older than I. He was not called in and given the same direction.

Limited Life Experience

Leaders **Media Players** **Career Focused** *Changers*

Girls in the Box

PLIABLE

Perfect as Picture   Caretakers, followers

Focused on Looks   Dismissed

Speak Soft

Money Managers   *Passive*   Preoccupied with clothes

Good at school

Body Conscience television addicts   For Sex   Done To

Producers   Told to   Not worth as much

Skinny, beautiful and *Pink*

Home Girls

Operators   *NICE*   **Advertisers tell me how I am**

ANXIOUS   FRAGILE

Resilient

Girls of color

Performers

Do-ers

Athletes   Knowledgeable   **Confident**

Strong   Valuable

The wind and sun on my bare chest in the spring air created a feeling of rapture in me. I was happy. When I challenged my mother by asking why I should cover my chest and not my brother, she ignored my request for an explanation and just repeated the direction. When I persisted, she gave me the explanation that untold girls before and after me have heard: "Because," she said slowly and with emphasis, "you are a girl." This was not new information to me, but hearing it used in this context was.

The following spring just before my birthday, I asked my father for a bicycle. He looked at me and said quickly and resolutely, "No." Once again, I queried for an explanation and was told the familiar reason, "Because you are a girl and girls should not be riding bicycles far from home." I saw the pattern. I learned to run with the wind, climb branches of trees stretched high into the sky, and lay in the fields at night to look at the stars, but away from easy view of the house and those adults who resided in it. I learned to ride the bikes of my friends who were boys and one girlfriend lucky to have a father who felt differently about girls and bikes. Calculated risk-taking was in my blood and I was wise enough to do other things that garnered the approval of the adults that lived with me in that big house on the hill.

My young student Jasmine had a different sort of problem. She was in the primary grades and was not getting to school on time. On some days she did not get there at all. Other days she arrived at ten or at lunchtime. The problem was that her mother was not always up in the morning to awaken Jasmine for school so she would miss the school bus and miss the breakfast served at her school before classes began. Her mother needed her more at home to look after her needs. Her tardiness and absences became a growing concern. We talked about what she could do to get herself up and on the bus. I bought her an alarm clock and taught her how to use it. She was able to get on the bus more regularly whether her mother was up or not. Her joy for school returned and her teacher's displeasure with her irregular attendance decreased. She learned to make the clock perform for her benefit. She could wait until her mother became drug free and able to more effectively parent her or she could learn to help herself, no matter how unfair her situation seemed.

A little at a time, many girls find that their natural instincts and pleasures are waylaid in order to meet the cultural and gendered stereotypical expectations of first their families and, later, their schools and communities. Parents, teachers, and mentors have a stake in developing girls who will know that life will send a number of challenges and tests their way; challenges that they will have to solve both on their own and with the significant others in their lives. Girls require those of us who love them to encourage, support, and listen to them. Girls need direction in developing visions for their own lives. Every girl needs her own plan of action by which she will build a strong body, promote self-care, feed her spirit, follow her joy, and which always includes play.

REVEALING STRONG GIRLS AND WOMEN

Feed and exercise the whole body and brain
by moving, thinking, and exploring.

Follow natural strengths and interests both inside
and outside of the home.

Foster self-care and healthy independence.

Foster a belief system that does not support
stereotypes for girls and women.

Offer girls and boys the same kinds of experiences and opportunities.

Encourage the adventure spirit in girls.

Put up a sign that says: Both Girls and Boys Play Here

Things can and will be different for your girl if you recognize and verbally affirm and reaffirm to her that you value her just as she is. Your words spoken out loud give power to both your intent and her expectation that the world will treat her fairly and with respect. Together with teachers, mentors, and other adult leaders in her life, you and she can make choices and find experiences that develop her whole person—physically, emotionally, and spiritually. Your words can be the first thing she hears as a new day dawns and the last ones she hears when her head nestles in the pillow.

Why Some Want Girls and Women in the Box

Support for the idea that girls and women be provided with the full range of opportunities provided to boys and men, and that women should have an equal role and influence in their homes and society has been growing steadily in America over the past thirty years. The National Election Studies have asked the American public for their opinion every two years since 1972 on the proper role of girls and women with this question:

> "Recently there has been a lot of talk about women's rights. Some people feel that women should have an equal role with men in running business, industry and government. (Suppose these people are at one end of a scale, at point 1.) Others feel that a woman's place is in the home. (Suppose these people are at the other end, at point 7.) And, of course, some other people have opinions somewhere in between, at points 2,3,4,5 or 6. Where would you place YOURSELF on this scale, or haven't you thought much about this?

In 1972, forty-seven percent gave a rating of 1-3, indicating that they supported gender equality. Twenty-nine percent gave a rating of 5-7, stating that they believed a woman's role was in the home. However, by 1978 fifty-six percent of Americans polled said they favored gender equality, and by 2004, eighty percent indicated that they favored gender equality. Those who still believed a woman's place was primarily in the home dropped from twenty-nine percent in 1972, to eight percent in 1998, and then further dropped to six percent in 2004.

The Gallup International Millennium Survey 2000 revealed that ninety-three percent of those surveyed rejected the idea that "education is more important for boys than for girls," seventy-six percent rejected the notion that " on the whole, men make better political leaders than women do," eighty-two percent rejected the statement that "When jobs are scarce, men should have more right to a job than women," and finally, eighty percent rejected the idea that "A woman needs to have children to be really fulfilled."

However, it is apparent that a small number of people are more comfortable with keeping girls and women in a small box that would narrow and minimize their value and experience. It is what they have come to know as normal "for girls." The thought of a society where both men and women have equal opportunities across the board, are paid the same for equal work, and are valued for their contributions both within and outside the home is very threatening to those who are clearly outside of what the majority of American citizens believe. It is as if they believe that they will have to give up a major portion of their life in order to allow girls and women equitable treatment and opportunity already provided for them under United States law. In surveying some of the arguments of those that counter gender equity, it appears that they believe that if anything results in the downgrade of the role of men as protector and leader of women also results in the undermining of the traditional family. They present arguments, such as women moving from the home to the workplace into paid employment, as the primary reason for the erosion of social connectedness or the reason behind the high divorce rate, father absenteeism, and a host of other social ills. While a small cadre of opponents to gender equity presents these arguments in a loud and authoritarian manner, there is no evidence to support their claims.

For others, it is much like the game of marbles many played as children. The idea was to get as many marbles for yourself as you could. If you can acquire more money, benefits, a home, and absolute authority over your wife, family and those assets, and if, for whatever reason, the woman and man may discontinue their marriage, the man retains the greater pile of assets. If you are single and you can insist that by virtue of your maleness and your physical strength, and because you will never be a mother (maybe a father) and miss work or take a leave from work, that all of this makes you a more valuable employee, and you may be able to get more "marbles." But if the game is won by getting more money and you can convince an employer to give you more money, then you have won. Some players are more skilled than others. Less skilled players resort to force and intimidation. It's part of the game.

Girls and women must look past the personalities within the game and use the support of both the law and the majority voice. An overwhelming majority of the citizenship base of the United States and in some other countries believes women can and will pursue a wider path in order to meet their desires and goals. But one thing is very clear: To play the game, you have to enter it. And to win the game, you have to play it. Many girls and women have not been willing to enter or play because somewhere along their childhood paths between the ages of five and fifteen, they bought into the "for girls only" rule: one-pattern-fits-all-girls.

Chapter 4
Alcohol in the Family

"Leap and the net will appear."
JULIA CAMERON

Twenty years ago, the scientific data base was small as to the nature of alcohol abuse and addiction on the part of a husband and father. Much more is now known about the effects of an alcoholic spouse and of a father's behavioral pattern on a mother and children. The initial research on alcoholism and treatment programs focused on male drinkers as they were the primary population that suffered the devastating effects of alcoholism on their bodies, relationships, and souls. Women who are non-drinkers are equally vulnerable to the detrimental effects of alcohol as it pertains to both their marital relationships and their own abilities to be effective mothers. Furthermore, sound information now exists detailing the unique effects and consequences that women experience as a result of their own alcohol abuse or addiction.

The manner in which young girls and young women are negatively impacted by parent(s) who drink is, in part, different than on boys and young men. Girls are prone to develop symptoms of passivity and depression. They are often times subjected to verbal and sexual abuse in families where chronic drinking is present. Boundaries slide or are erased. Intoxicated persons act on base impulses making girls and young women much more open to control behaviors, sexual exploitation, or the ultimate betrayal—incest. At the very least, such a home environment handicaps the healthy development of female identity and confidence.

Women who have spouses or partners who abuse alcohol develop coping symptoms which interfere with their ability to focus on their children in ways that mothers who are not in such relationships can.

Many have described their lives as living in a war zone. They use all of their energy to cope and survive from one drinking episode to the next with little energy left to focus on the healthy development of independent daughters or sons, or even their own needs. Many are not able to protect their children, especially girls, from negative communication and control patterns often common in families where alcohol abuse or addiction is present.

Sooner or later, young girls will hold their mothers responsible for at least not openly talking about this problem with them and seeking help. Instead of exhibiting those characteristics they wish their daughters would grow up to possess, mothers with partners or husbands who abuse alcohol commonly show passivity and deference and engage in endless confrontation without resolution. This fruitless problem-solving pattern becomes the primary lesson that a daughter of a codependent mother learns. It is a rare occurrence for a mother to raise an independent and emotionally present daughter when she becomes emotionally distant and dependent herself as a primary side effect of living with a partner who abuses alcohol for an extended period of time.

Girls, young and grown alike, will hold their mothers accountable for hiding from these problems and symptoms and continuing to repeat the excuses of the past; boys will be boys—it's only one drink, just don't get him upset, it will be okay tomorrow, or don't be a baby and cry about this. A daughter's most severe criticism will eventually be that her mother closed her eyes to the damage being done to herself and to the mother without getting the help that they both needed.

Boiled Frog in Alcohol

We have all been in the situation where we've seen or heard about a loved one or close personal friend giving permission for someone to treat her/him badly by staying too long. The victim simply doesn't see what we, their friend, see. In sharing my frustration at witnessing this destructive experience of an acquaintance, a female counselor I knew explained it this way. "Your friend," she said, "has stayed too long. She no longer knows that her life is not normal, and she has forgotten what it is like to live a life in joy."

A male friend of mine responded in quite another way. He said it's the boiled frog theory. He explained that if you were to drop a frog into a pot of hot water, it will instinctively jump out. It does so to protect itself and to make its own judgment as to whether it really wants to go back into the water or not. However, if you place a frog into a pot of cool water and very gradually increase the temperature, the frog will sit in the water until it dies. It somehow tolerates slow changes in its environment. But when its surroundings are dramatically changed, the frog will not tolerate it and will escape.

For many women, living with husbands who have drinking problems is like frogs being slowly boiled in a pot of alcohol. For women who marry men already in the late stage of alcoholism, they indeed have been dropped into the pot of burning alcohol and may react in more efficient survival modes: many leave fast. However, for women whose partners have grown into the diseased state of alcoholism over years, the rather slow and steady downhill slide may be so gradual that they become acclimated to the host of problems presented by active drinkers.

In this chapter I will focus on the problems women experience in their lives with partners who have severe drinking problems, or who themselves possess drinking problems. This approach seems the most beneficial since the vast majority of alcoholics are men living with partners or spouses who are either non-drinkers or are light social drinkers. In addition, alcoholic fathers far outnumber alcoholic mothers and, therefore, the majority of studies on children of alcoholic parents have focused on fathers who are problem drinkers rather than on mothers who drink excessively.

Alcoholism has been correctly described as the family disease. It affects every member of the family in unique ways in addition to the drinker. Scientific research continues to document the ways in which spouses, partners and their children are impacted by the drinking and behavior of their alcoholic partners, and parents. The news is equally bad for all.

Alcohol in the Family Survey

Here is a quiz to help you assess your current understanding of the hard evidence of both the nature of this family disease and the high cost of remaining in an alcohol-dominated family dynamic.

Directions: Read each statement. The statement is either completely true or completely false.

Family Systems

1. True False An alcoholic can totally disrupt family life and cause harmful effects that are often temporary.

2. True False Alcoholism is responsible for more family problems than any other single cause.

3. True False Parental alcoholism has severe but temporary effects on normal children of alcoholics.

4. True False Many alcoholic husbands use the threat of a potential breakup of the family as a way to keep their wife from getting help for her and her family.

5. True False Many women unknowingly have accepted the habits of the alcoholic husband in exchange for keeping the family together.

6. True False Daughters are particularly vulnerable to parental problem drinking but do not require gender-specific health and female support programs for them.

7. True False One-quarter of all emergency room admissions, one-third of all suicides, and more than half of all homicides and incidents of domestic violence are alcohol-related.

8. True False Twenty percent of all traffic fatalities are alcohol-related.

9. True False Between 48% and 64% of people who die in fires have blood alcohol levels indicating intoxication.

10. True False One in ten wives leave a husband who is a problem drinker-alcoholic.

11. True False One in ten husbands stay with a wife who is a problem drinker-alcoholic.

12. True False Early treatment and shortened exposure of parental alcoholism is essential as family members who are affected may never recover from the problems inflicted upon them.

Women

13. True False Alcoholism is not a major factor of premature widowhood.

14.	True	False	Few wives of alcoholic husbands contribute to the drinker's habit and make it worse by covering up the problem and refusing to get help.
15.	True	False	When mothers deny the obvious and refuse to look for help, their own behavior can trigger multiple emotional problems in their children.
16.	True	False	Few women unknowingly accept the habits of an alcoholic husband in exchange for keeping the family together.
17.	True	False	Women metabolize alcohol differently than men, resulting in higher blood alcohol levels.
18.	True	False	Women who drink more tend to have problems with their closest relationships, have problems with stress, and have little to no support systems in their lives.
19.	True	False	Excessive drinking in women is not highly likely when blood family members have alcohol problems or when they have a history of depression or childhood physical/sexual abuse.
20.	True	False	Women married to alcoholics are three times more likely to abuse alcohol than women not married to alcoholics.

Children

21.	True	False	Children of alcoholic parent(s) may have problems in verbal expression, cognitive performance in school, and more often repeat a grade or drop out of school.
22.	True	False	Adult children of alcoholics often relate their problems to having grown up in a family with an alcoholic parent.
23.	True	False	Adult daughters of alcoholics tend to see doctors more often, have higher rates of bulimia, and suffer from anxiety and depression.
24.	True	False	Five percent of father-daughter incest cases involve a family member who is an alcoholic.
25.	True	False	Adolescents of parents with alcohol dependence score higher on negative emotionality, alienation, aggression, poor sense of well-being, harm avoidance, and traditionalism.

26.	True	False	Children raised in homes with alcoholic parent(s) appear to not be at increased risk of exhibiting anxiety, depression, alcohol or other substance abuse or dependence and psychiatric disorders.
27.	True	False	Male children of problem-drinking parents are more likely to have symptoms of depression.
28.	True	False	Female children of problem-drinking parents are more likely to show signs of alcoholism.
29.	True	False	College students who are children of active problem drinkers are at increased risk of depression and alcohol abuse.
30.	True	False	Girls and young women get hooked faster and suffer consequences of abuse and addiction sooner than boys and young men.
31.	True	False	Teenage girls who binge drink are 15% more likely to become teen mothers and/or become victims of alcohol-related sexual assault.
32.	True	False	Children of alcoholic mothers may be more traumatized than children with alcoholic fathers due to the social stigma attached to women who drink and children's reliance on their mothers for every day life activities.

Alcohol in the Family Survey Results

Check your answers. Each item is worth one point. There are thirty-one items.

True items: 2,4,5,7,9,10,11,12,15,17,18,20,21,23,25,29,30,32
False items: 1,3,6,8,13,14,16,19,22,24,26,27,28,31

Results:
- 32–30 Excellent knowledge base. You have the awareness to act for yourself by taking any number of steps* as well as to support others.
- 29–27 Sound working knowledge. You have the awareness to act for yourself. Choose several steps* and act today.
- 26–24 You have some awareness of the scope and depth of alcohol dependency and effects. You may have some denial patterns

that need adjusting. You have enough awareness to take several small steps* today.

23–21　Your knowledge with respect to alcohol dependency and its effects is small. You may have strong denial patterns. Begin the path of self-development by taking one strong proactive step* today.

Below 21

Your knowledge base is not yet developed. You appear to have strong patterns of denial. Begin your path of self-development by taking one strong proactive step today.

*Note: See the section "How to Move On" in this chapter for guidance in choosing steps.

Corrected statements for the false items are:

1. An alcoholic can totally disrupt family life and cause harmful effects that often are *permanent.*
3. Parental alcoholism has severe and *permanent* effects on normal children of alcoholics.
6. Daughters are particularly vulnerable to parental problem drinking and *do require* gender-specific health and female support programs for them.
8. *Fifty percent* of all traffic fatalities are alcohol-related.
13. Alcoholism *is* a major factor of premature widowhood.
14. *Many* wives of alcoholic husbands contribute to the drinker's habit and make it worse by covering up the problem and refusing to get help.
16. *Many* women unknowingly accept the habits of an alcoholic husband in exchange for keeping the family together.
19. Excessive drinking in women *is* highly likely when blood family members have alcohol problems or when they have histories of depression or childhood physical or sexual abuse.
22. Adult children of alcoholics often *do not* relate their problems to having grown up in a family with an alcoholic parent.
24. Thirty percent of father-daughter incest cases involve a family member who is an alcoholic.
26. Children raised in homes with alcoholic parent(s) *are* at increased risk of exhibiting anxiety, depression, alcohol or other substance abuse or dependence and psychiatric disorders.
27. *Female* children of problem-drinking parents are more likely to have symptoms of depression.

28. *Male* children of problem-drinking parents are more likely to show signs of alcoholism.
31. Teenage girls who binge-drink are *sixty-three percent* more likely to become teen mothers and/or become victims of alcohol-related sexual assault.

A Clear Picture of the Problem

Alcoholism is responsible for more family problems than any other single cause according to the U.S Department of Health and Human Services and the National Clearinghouse for Alcohol and Drug Information. It is a widespread problem in the United States and many other countries. In America it has been identified as the nation's number one health problem. Almost fourteen million adult Americans abuse alcohol and fourteen percent of Americans will struggle with either alcohol abuse or dependency for a lifetime.

Researchers have estimated that the number of children born to alcoholic parents is about ten percent. Approximately one out of every four U.S. children under the age of eighteen years is exposed to the effects of alcohol abuse or dependence in a family member.

Alcohol impacts every member of a family from the alcoholic's spouse to the unborn child. There are serious physical and psychological problems that impact the drinker and it is commonplace for members of the family to experience serious physical, emotional, and unhealthy attitudes toward substance abuse as well.

Alcoholism places a tremendous strain on the health care system. It harms family life and threatens the general public in terms of safety, unhealthy risk-taking, and civic and family responsibility.

While traditionally alcohol abuse and dependency has been a man's problem, the gender gap with respect to drinking and abusing alcohol may be closing. About a third of all U.S. women now drink alcohol and they represent nearly one-third of all alcohol-abusing or alcohol-dependent individuals. Of those that drink, one woman in ten averages two or more drinks a day. For women, two drinks or more a day exceeds the guidelines for moderate drinking. On the whole, women who drink consume less alcohol and have fewer alcohol-related problems and dependence symptoms than men. However, that picture is tempered with the fact that among the heaviest drinkers women equal or surpass men in the number of problems.

RISKS TO WOMEN DRINKERS
✓ Heavy censorship by society towards drinking women and mothers
✓ Serious impact on children, especially daughters
✓ Higher risk for liver, brain, and heart damage
✓ Less alcohol leads to greater intoxication
✓ Higher rates of victimization and rape
✓ Less to no support by male partners
✓ High risk of pregnancy and HIV
✓ Fast downhill trajectory

Societal Consequences

The consequence of alcohol abuse and dependency is staggering. One-quarter of emergency room admissions are alcohol-related. One-third of suicides involve alcohol. More than half of homicides and incidents of domestic violence are alcohol connected and nearly half of traffic fatalities involve alcohol. Of those people who die in fires, between forty-eight and sixty-four percent have blood levels at the intoxication stage.

Walking the Alcoholic Tight Rope: Chances of Escaping Serious Injury

Number one health problem	Sons susceptible to alcohol abuse
Half of all traffic fatalities—major cause of fire fatalities	Children possess enduring negative self-image
Daughters suffer depression and host of health disorders	Children have significant negative emotions and loss of well-being that stays with them into college age and later
Serious detrimental effects on spouse	Denial by family members triggers multiple problems in children
Compromises parenting of drinking and non-drinking parent	Non-alcoholic daughters of alcoholics are more than twice as likely to marry an alcoholic
High levels of chronic stress, anxiety and depression in children and female spouse	Non–drinking family members may not ever recover from the problems inflicted upon them by an alcoholic parent

Impact on Children

Children of alcoholic parents experience a range of health challenges as a consequence of living under the roof with active alcoholics or dependent drinkers. Many children demonstrate behaviors of low self-esteem, loneliness, guilt, feelings of helplessness, fears of abandonment, and chronic depression. A very common symptom is a high level of tension and stress. Common troubling behaviors are frequent nightmares, bedwetting, crying, few friends, and fearfulness in going to school. Older children may exhibit obsessive perfectionism, hoarding, isolating, being extremely self-conscious, and may develop phobias. Children of alcoholics have many more school-related problems as well. While not necessarily intellectually inferior, many have serious problems in expressing themselves verbally and have trouble establishing close relationships with teachers. They are much more apt to receive poor grades and to drop out of school. Strong evidence supports the belief that both sons and daughters are at risk if one or both parents is an active problem drinker. Children of problem drinkers are thirty-six percent more likely to have depressive symptoms, fourteen percent more likely to abuse alcohol, and seventy-five percent more likely to be both depressed and an active alcohol abuser themselves than children of non-problem drinkers.

There is a positive relationship between crime and violence and viewing family members as possessions and objects. Because of this pattern, battery, sexual abuse and incest are common in alcoholics' families. G. Berger reports in the book *Alcoholism and the Family* (New York, Franklin Watts, 1993) that thirty percent of father-daughter incest cases involve a family member who is an alcoholic and seventy-five percent of domestic violence cases involve a family member who is an alcoholic.

Male children may manifest symptoms of alcoholism while female children are more likely to have symptoms of depression. Females may experience both depression as well as symptoms of alcohol abuse using alcohol to self-medicate their feelings of stress, anxiety and severe sadness. Daughters seem unusually vulnerable to parental problem drinking regardless of the gender of the parent. One government survey showed that thirty percent of young women who did not complete high school had grown up in families with alcoholic parent(s).

"Children of alcoholics are people who have been robbed of their childhood," writes H. Silverstein in his book, *Alcoholism* (Franklin Watts, New York, 1990), and as such will carry their problems with them into adulthood unless they receive help. Surprisingly, adult children of alcoholics often do not connect their existing problems to being raised in a family with an alcoholic parent. This is largely due to the family pattern of denial and lack of communication among family members concerning feelings and problems.

Impact on the Well-Being of a Partner

Living with a spouse who is an alcoholic or alcohol-dependent changes the course of a relationship between two adults. A woman whose partner or husband is an active alcoholic or alcohol-dependent lives in a world filled with worry, preoccupation with the drinker, and a lowered sense of self-esteem. She often has intense feelings of hatred toward both her partner for drinking and for herself. She may believe she has caused her partner to drink and that she is powerless to alter her partner's behavior. Her family's social world narrows over time due to the embarrassment, conflict, and inconsistency of the alcoholic. She can not depend on her partner to be emotionally available and in control, particularly if the social activity includes access to alcoholic drinks. The bulk of the family responsibilities fall squarely on her shoulders. While many alcoholics are able to work and earn an income at first, as the alcohol dependency takes hold, work becomes more difficult over time. The wife or female partner must then shoulder more and more of the financial responsibility and worry over how bills will be paid. She may become increasingly resentful over the amount of money spent by the drinker to fuel his habit.

For a mother who finds herself in a marriage with an alcoholic, her life becomes one of exhaustion, stress, and frustration in that she must handle the major responsibilities of parenting on her own. She takes over the role otherwise assumed by her partner and enables his drinking behavior to continue. She is not able to depend upon her partner or trust that he can provide even brief supervision as she has learned that doing so may be the same as leaving her children alone. What is an interesting paradox is that for those wives who are the most competent, working inside and outside of the home and juggling more and more on their own, their very competence could be a major contributing factor to the continuation of their husband's/partner's drinking life.

Because of the immense nature of the problem and stress, it is commonplace for a non-drinking spouse and mother to become inconsistent in her parenting. She may make inappropriate demands upon her children and neglect their emotional and physical needs. Mothers who stay in an alcoholic family dynamic spend less time enjoying their children. They are less emotionally available to them and can create attachment difficulties due to the extreme preoccupation and responsibility placed upon them to protect their children from the active drinker.

A major challenge for women in such families is to push past the defensive reaction of denying and rationalizing the serious effects occurring with the drinkers. While it is understandable that a wife will want to protect her husband, there comes a point when her denial allows the alcoholic to continue his downward path of dysfunction. Closing her eyes also feeds the mother's and/or non-drinking partner's denial pattern.

Mothers who deny the nature and extent of the problem also do their children great harm over the long term. No one would condone a mother from withholding medical services from a child who suffers from a high temperature, is constantly ill or who is experiencing any other serious mental or physical health problem. Similarly, health care and mental health professionals view a mother who seeks help for alcohol addiction as a caring and competent woman and mother. Once a mother accepts that there is a serious problem that will not go away on its own, she will be more open to look for resources and professionals to aid her and her children. It is not a requirement that her partner/husband seek help in order to get assistance for her and her children. When a non-drinking spouse, mother, or other family member

refuses to admit what is obvious and avoids help, children may suffer profound emotional consequences that may last a lifetime, even if they choose to get help once they leave the family home. As with any other health issue, prevention and early intervention is key to acquiring the most favorable and enduring results.

My Father Drinks

Just when I think that the Sunrises in the East and Sets in the West,
    I find out I'm wrong, My Father Drinks.
I like the Mariners and boy do I like my dad, My Father Drinks.
I know the kids next door, and I sure don't want them to know about
    my Father, My Father Drinks.
I get so confused when I really think about it, how can I listen and
    believe what I know is not true, My Father Drinks.
He tells me he loves me, and I feel safe, heck he even has made me
    proud, but My Father Drinks.
Sometimes I wish he would just go away, but he's my Father,
    My Father Drinks.
If I hold on to the good memories and pray, maybe God will take
    away the bad, My Father Drinks.
It has not always been so, so he says, but I'm just twelve,
    My Father Drinks.
I think I will wait and see, just what happens with him and me,
    I pray My Father won't Drink.

James Johnson, 2005
Quoted with author's permission

How to Move On

Making the decision to reach out occurs as part of the process of recognizing that all things change—for the good or for the bad. Families engulfed in the dynamics of alcoholism frequently are characterized by a sense of helplessness. Oftentimes family members feel that things will either not get any worse or they will change for the better on their own. It is clear that nothing stays the same, especially family dynamics that surround an alcoholic. They get worse with time due to the accumulative effects alcohol has on the brain and bodily functions of the drinker, and the consequences of living with an active drinker. Clearly, things do not get better with merely the passage of time.

According to the National Institute on Alcohol Abuse and Alcoholism, a convincing body of research indicates that marital and family intervention approaches are more successful than individual treatment alone. When a spouse, other family member or the drinker decides to take major steps to change, they have begun the action phase of the change process. There are different actions, plans and multiple strategies by which a family or family member can approach change. Any action step should be supported as any step forward is perceived as progress. Without support, the spouse, family member, or drinker may give up and return to his or her former state of helplessness. One principle of change is very important: Whether the person with the active alcohol disorder seeks out help or not, the family needs help. Families can and do move forward even if the alcoholics do not.

ESSENTIALS OF CHANGING THE FAMILY DYNAMICS OF ALCOHOLISM IN YOUR LIFE

1. **Excellent information is readily available.** Explore popular or professional literature, substance abuse help lines, internet websites, clergy, health care experts, and friends to gain information concerning alcohol abuse as well as getting help for yourself.
2. **A family focus is needed.** All family members need support in order to assess the impact of alcohol on their lives and to determine appropriate support action or services for each of them.
3. **Couples do more good and less harm by working together.** Successful marital and family therapy by alcoholics generally involves couples willing to work together at recovery regardless of whether they live together, are separated, or divorced.
4. **Keeping family members safe is the first priority.** Non-alcoholic partners should not make a commitment to work with the alcoholic in a treatment capacity if the alcoholic is still drinking or has acted out in a violent or life-threatening manner.
5. **Spouses and family members support process must include awareness-building.** Specifically, each family member must determine how his or her life has been made difficult by living with a partner/family person with an alcohol problem. Why are they uncertain about changing their own behaviors so as not to support the drinking behavior of spouses or family members?

6. **A serious potential barrier to effective family change with alcohol abuse is the real potential for violence in the family.** Many active male problem drinkers view any step of family members to get help as a direct, personal threat against them. The moment a women or family member experiences a first incident of verbal or physical threat against her or her family, her immediate priority becomes working out a plan to keep her and her family safe and to contain future incidents.
7. **Women in alcohol abuse relationships require treatment programs specifically designed for the unique needs of girls and women.** Current research makes strong arguments for:
   - joining female support groups,
   - utilizing female therapists,
   - helping women plan for the continuation of income and employment,
   - screening for substance-related problems in those women whose parents had substance-related issues, and
   - supporting mothers' efforts to improve mother attachment and effectiveness. Mother education should focus on childhood experiences and any substance-related problems found in their own families of origin. Mothering curriculum should not be limited to merely skill building. The most responsive approach is comprised of a major effort at listening to and providing affective support and caring to the woman, girl, and mother.

Resilience and Adaptation

Significant risks to a child's well-being exist when exposed to a parent's or family's alcohol abuse. However, it is also a fact that all children do not suffer the same level of difficulty—some are more resilient than others in coping and adapting. There are strategies that can decrease the degree of vulnerability to adverse events for children. Here are some strategies which may diminish the negative consequences and bolster child resiliency:

FACTORS THAT INCREASE CHILD RESILIENCY TO FAMILY ALCOHOL DYNAMICS

1. supportive non-alcoholic parent who is getting help for herself
2. secure mother-child attachment and the demonstration of those behaviors

3. structured family rituals and daily functioning
4. close bond with at least one person (not necessarily the father or mother) who can provide stable care, attention, and who expresses high expectations of child and helps validate the child as a worthwhile human being
5. strong message from parent or other significant adult that the child is expected to not drink and to honor school and community rules and regulations regarding the use of alcohol
6. supervised child responsibilities that communicate to the child that they are capable and can make contributions of their own
7. supervised school activities by a caring adult leader
8. appropriate resources for the child to support their decision to remain free of using alcohol themselves
9. warm, consistent discipline by parent(s) and, finally,
10. availability of a daughter's mother to listen and provide expert care to meet the emotional needs of her daughter

Several decades of excellent research on the qualities of resilient children indicate there are factors unique to some children and not to others which provide an added buffer effect to the dynamics of family alcoholism. Protective qualities born to some children include easy temperament, autonomy, positive lookout, extroverted personality, above- average intelligence, good reader and a problem-solving orientation. These attributes are essentially qualities a child is born with and strengthened in the face of adversity. For girls and daughters, as well as boys and sons, who do not possess these traits, it is particularly important that those steps and strategies described within this chapter be made available to them as they may be more vulnerable.

Finally, research now supports what has long been anecdotically reported to be true: treatment of an alcoholic or alcohol dependent parent appears to have a preventive effect on the mental health and future use of alcohol among children. It appears that a parent's willingness to treat her/himself can be a powerful modeling influence in their daughter or son.

Strategies for Coping, Healing, and Making Choices

No child of an alcoholic should grow up in isolation and without support. Furthermore, caring, thoughtful and well-educated professionals in many areas of life are present in every community to help non-drinkers living with individuals with alcohol dependency or alcoholism. In every community there are professionals and advocacy organizations which can help individuals who suffer from alcohol dependency or who are alcoholics. Don't suffer alone. Reach out and ask for help.

My Father And I

I was my father's favorite child. After all of these years, I have found the courage to admit this without a sense of guilt. He was absolutely magic to me. My earliest memory of him is when I was three years old. It was the usual cold Wisconsin spring when Easter was making its entrance. I was upstairs in my parent's bed when I heard his loud, clear announcement from downstairs, "I see him, the Easter Bunny! He is in the field that the cows graze in. I hope he knows where he is walking." My father sang "Here come Peter Cottontail" at the top of his voice and, of course, he followed that by the encouragement that my two siblings and I go to sleep or else the big bunny would by-pass our house.

My father was a proud Irish man. He often quarreled with his sisters about their genealogy, whether they were Scottish or Irish, but in his mind, he knew he was Irish. He was five-foot-ten-inches tall, with an average build, and sturdy arms and shoulders from logging pines, fly fishing, and hunting and trapping in Wisconsin's Chequemegon woods. He had steel sky blue eyes that sparkled and danced when he sang his favorite songs, told stories or engaged in arguments about politics, war, or who owned the rights to the cold, clear water in any of the lakes in our state. He had a full head of wavy brown hair that he carefully groomed and kept a close eye on.

He served in the United States Army during World War II and was part of the occupational army in Japan. He never glorified war. While a soldier, he wrote letters home, but also wrote poetry for the girl in his life, later to be my mother, and composed a Thanksgiving prayer from Japan that is still occasionally printed in his hometown area newspapers. After the war, he stayed in California where he began in earnest to write and record music with a female Japanese singer. He returned home to his beloved northern forests when his father pleaded for his help. His mother was ill and his dad, who had lost one son in the war and another in a hunting accident in the woods, needed him.

In his early thirties when he came home he married Helen Windt, my mother. He hired on with Metropolitan as an insurance agent—a perfect job for my father. He could talk, persuade, and visit prospective clients who lived in farmhouses in small unincorporated villages, or who were owners of the many pubs that peppered the highways and towns throughout the land he loved. At one of those taverns I enjoyed my first couple dance. It was a memorable evening. After reviewing a policy with the tavern owner, my dad plugged the jukebox with a few dimes and asked me to dance. He told me to stand on his shoes, look up at him, ignore my feet, and listen to the music. He would do the rest. I have been asked hundreds of times where I learned to dance as it is natural as walking for me. I can follow any male partner doing just about any step in a matter of minutes whether I know the particular dance or not.

On a sublime day I traversed the rural roads with him in his red Chevrolet sedan visiting clients. He played the buttons of the radio like he played the piano—going from one station to another to find just the right music. I sang with him when he found a suitable tune or listened as he dissected the traits of a piece he particularly liked. He never bothered talking about the music he did not like. He just pressed a button changing to another station. When the radio was turned off, he pointed out of the window of the car at the beauty of the hills and countryside and reminded me how lucky we were to have been born in the United States. He was a proud American who as a soldier knew the cost of war.

My father, like most Irishmen, was fond of brandy. He often lit up a cigarette as the bartender poured him a shot, many times accompanied by a beer chaser. Imbibing alcohol was as ordinary to him as drinking coffee with cookies was to my grandmother during her afternoon sessions of canasta playing with her lady friends. I do not remember him ever drinking at home. Drinking was a social event he did in the pub over a client's papers, his daily newspaper with a piece of pie and coffee, or a stop to catch up on the goings on around town.

He never gave up his dream to write music and poetry, but he did set it aside as his family grew to four children and as the life of a salesman on the road gobbled up his time. He and my mother agreed to buy his very large family home from his father—provided that his father remained in the home until he died. It was the spring before my fifth birthday when we moved from a small rented house to the "big white house on the hill." There was an enormous amount of space for a child to grow and play. A small orchard of apple trees, fields and fields of my grandfather's vegetable crops, and miles of forest to explore were all part of the land that surrounded the house. He assumed the responsibility as head of a household comprised of his own family, his ill father, his divorced sister, and her adolescent son.

My mother delivered her last child, a baby boy, that summer. Within a year my mother was dead, leaving my father to grieve in his own way. He drank. He moved from absolute sorrow, to fighting with God and with my struggling, sick grandfather as to how my mother should have been provided better care. Within a year, my brother and I found my grandfather dead in his own bed of his own illness, probably pushed along by a broken heart. Within the space of two years, I saw the second family member in the enigmatic house die.

My dad left in the mornings, some days never returning. The house and all of us dependent children, my adolescent male cousin, a small baby, and an ill grandfather were left to the care of my dad's sister, my Aunt Margie. Each year brought him reason to grieve again—my mother's birthday, their wedding anniversary (they were married just seven years), her death, and on each such occasion he drank as a way to get through it.

Two years later, my dad remarried in an attempt to provide a mother for his children and to move ahead. The marriage failed miserably. When I was a teenager, his second wife apologetically admitted to me that she left because my dad was consumed with my mother's death. And, she said, he drank, and drank a lot. Liquor was his reliable companion who knew his story, eased his pain and helped him forget—until the next day.

Some of the women in my family did not understand the grave pain my father suffered. After his failed marriage to his second wife, they began to take steps to rescue his children hoping to divide us up by gender—my sister and I to Milwaukee and my brother and baby brother to Chicago. They built a case in the county court rather than working in a supportive fashion to help my father out by providing for us on a temporary basis. They were successful. My father lost custody of all four of his children. Within three years, he had lost his wife, his father, and his children.

My sister and I were packed into a car with just a few of our belongings en route to Milwaukee. I thought it was just a temporary stay. As the car slowly made its way down the driveway that circled around the house and down the large hill, my father ran down the pair of landscaped, sculpted hills, down the first set of steps, then the other. He literally hung over the railing that bordered the large cement encasement which adorned the frontage to the hill as he watched his children leave. He looked to me like an animal that had been staked in the heart and left to die. I watched him as I sat in the back seat of the car—first through the side window that was closest to me and then through the back window—as he got smaller and smaller within my view. Undeniably, that was the day my father died. He was never the same.

Except for one or two visits he made to Milwaukee that first year, I did not see my father again until I graduated from college and was engaged to be married. He had made his way through the years, from one place to the next, psychologically crippled and later further challenged with lung disease acquired from smoking. He eventually returned to our home town, then in his sixties and still struggling, but not to the big house. Our first meeting was painful. He expected to see his nine-year-old daughter. I wanted my youthful father, smiling, singing and filled with hope for our future. Time had moved on, but we both were still in front of that big white house on the hill.

A little more than a decade passed. I continued my schooling far from the place where my father lived. I saw him when I could, which was not often. One spring break, I left my children with their father, pointed the car northward home, and spent a week living with my father in his small senior apartment. By the end of the week, he knew who his grown daughter was and I discovered that some of the same Irish spirit I loved as a little girl was still alive in him.

My father called me from the Veteran's Hospital during a March winter. He knew he was dying from emphysema. He wanted to go home. He feared that the hospital would put him in an iron lung or administer some other life-support mechanism which he adamantly opposed. He said they would not release him and provide transportation. I drove hundreds of miles to visit him and talked to the hospital administrator who would not release him. I returned home and brought my husband back with me (he was in the hospital business) and sat again in the administrator's office, pleading to take my father home, again with no success. He told me he had my father's clothes and without any clothes or hospital supplies, how could I possibly take my father back to his hometown to die?

I was frustrated and furious. Then the boy side of my brain kicked in. I talked to my father's doctor who had been involved in his care for some time. His doctor thought he should be released to die as he wished. I needed the consent of the administrator who was holding on. I walked into the administrator's office and told him that I was Dr. Mack, that I had a Ph. D. and knew how to think, write, and act. I reminded him that President Reagan thought that the VA hospitals were too costly, and that he was beginning to cut the funding for all VA hospitals around the country. I told him I intended on writing to the President, my Wisconsin congressmen, and anyone else who would listen, and I would describe how this hospital had interfered with the wishes of a veteran's last days.

The administrator looked at me and asked, "Isn't your father a veteran of World War II?" with a newly emerged tone of respect and negotiator spirit. "Why yes," I said, knowing he already knew that. "Well, then, we must do everything in our power to provide what he wants."

Within an hour, I had obtained my father's authorization, an order to have medical supplies delivered to his apartment, including oxygen, and, finally, his clothes, which were brought to his room. My husband drove along the familiar highway roads to my dad's hometown in northern Wisconsin. My dad's spirit and attitude changed from being highly agitated, angry, and depressed to that of calmness, appreciation, and thoughtfulness as he stretched as best as he could to see the wintry snow-covered hills and small towns he knew so well.

It was the last journey that he took up and down those rural roads of his beloved countryside. For a week I cared for him, alone, as best as I could. I did not have one hour of medical training. I sat on his bed while he struggled to stay sitting up, fighting for each breath. He said his final words as he looked straight at me with his steel blue eyes. I knew he was talking about my mother when he said that life, every second of it, is the most precious of all gifts. Life, he said, is worth fighting for.

I prayed for his death during the few minutes at night when he could sleep. And at the end of the sixth day, when he was struggling to stay sitting, I asked him if I could help him lie back a bit. He could no longer talk. But neither did he indicate his wishes one way or the other.

I knew he was aware that if he lay back, he would never rise again. I eased him back into the stacked pillows. That night was his last.

For twenty-six years, I had waited for my father to come find me and to bring me back to a life that we once had together. He never came. He was gone forever. So the next night, alone in his apartment before any help arrived, I did what I had encouraged my dad to do—to let go, to stop being so strong.

Chapter 5
Dangers of Early Dating and Mating

> *"Do you love me because I am beautiful,*
> *or am I beautiful because you love me?"*
> OSCAR HAMMERSTEIN II, CINDERELLA

Theresa, mother of a middle school son, described this scenario to me: Her twelve-year-old boy was six feet tall and involved in athletic activities. He had been singled out by male coaches and given school jobs for extra money. He was active in boy scouts and on a path to becoming an Eagle Scout. The problem is, lamented the mother, girls are calling him day and night on the phone and literally chasing him down like a dog on the scent of a rabbit. At the same time, in conversations Theresa has had with mothers at her son's school, she is acutely aware that the mothers not only think it is okay, but talk about which girls would make the perfect match and cutest couple with her son. They ask who will her son be taking to the high school homecoming (even though her son is in sixth grade) and does she think her son will be dating soon? Theresa asked me and the class, "What is going on with these mothers?"

What is going on is what has been going on for centuries. Mothers are on the lookout for good prospects for their daughters—they are matchmaking. They are acting out a ritual that is associated with the "old world" and is not generally considered to be part of western culture. They also know what research substantiates. Well over ninety percent of all adults will marry. Men with the best social and economic capital will get the most choices of marital partners and the women who are the most attractive will be picked by the most desirable men.

Enter into this mix the issue of girls' developmental differences from boys during early adolescence. On the average, girls' bodies are transformed from little girl's bodies into womanlike bodies seemingly overnight. Accompanying the physical changes, girls experience dramatic hormonal changes that stimulate the second major stage of brain growth in their lifetimes—the first stage occurring during infancy. Boys will also go through biological maturation, but for most of them this stage begins closer to the mid-high school years. It is no wonder why girls lament to their parents that boys their age are babies. Many girls become much more interested in boys older than they are. These older types are equally interested in twelve- to sixteen-year-old girls, but for different reasons.

Most women can remember as if it were just yesterday their own unique dilemmas during the preteen and early teen years. I remember mine as if they occurred just yesterday. I went from wearing no bra to a B cup overnight and wondered what other girls were talking about when they spoke of their mothers getting them training bras. By eighth grade I was the tallest person in my grade school. I was taller than my male teacher, the male principal, my male physical education teacher, and taller than all of the three male teachers in the building—all of whom I had as teachers from sixth through eighth grade. In seventh grade, my male teacher taught a number of us to play tag football during recess and the noon hour break. I was a head and a half taller than any of the boys and had very long legs. I learned to play the receiver position really well. I could outrun any boy down the field, turn and catch the football fired off by my teacher, and head down the field to score the touchdown. This went on for some weeks until the principal of the school put an end to it. Apparently, he did not appreciate my emerging boy skills. He believed I should not be competing with boys, and most of all, beating them at their own games. He said it was not going to serve me well when I went to high school as not one girls' sport existed (I missed Title IX by a few years), and that I would be punished socially since no boy wanted to date a girl who outperformed him. He explained I was going to be challenged being as tall as I was—and I was still growing. So I was returned to the girls' side of the playground and forbidden to play football. I did not give much thought to the whole situation, thinking all the fuss was pretty silly. I continued to play football with the boys on the same playground field, but only after school. I was redirected toward cheerleading and other "more appropriate" girl activities.

However, at thirteen, I was interested in the boys. While there were a few in my class that I enjoyed as close friends, I too had the feeling that I was destined for older and better choices. I felt confident that I could handle any situation I found myself in and believed that I should be able to "date" anyone I chose. I had made good choices up until that time, doing well in school and exhibiting all of the "good girl" abilities and dispositions expected of young Catholic girls. Nevertheless, I was bored with the sameness that surrounded my life, the lack of rigorous physical challenges, and the absence of avenues to develop leadership skills. These were still the days when "boys only" rules were applied to being a school crossing guard and athletics of all kinds, and there were certainly no opportunities in the Church to become an altar girl! And yes, I was beginning to experience strong sexual urges that were anything but scary. They were entirely pleasant! I was ready for adventure and new horizons.

What Girls Want—What Boys Want

Preteen girls and their mothers may have one thing in common: It is entirely likely that they possess a naïve distortion of what dating is all about in today's preteen and teen world. What it is all about is that it does not exist! The mother of a teen girl may have visions of her daughter living a dating life that she had at the same age, enjoyed, and wants for her daughter. Or she may want her daughter to have the dating life that, for whatever reason, was denied to her. As she marches her daughter towards the inevitable first date night, the mother may have a vision of the experience that sounds something like this if she were to share it with her female friends:

James came to pick up my Katie at seven o'clock. He was driving his father's car which he had begged from his father. I had spent the day shopping with Katie for just the right first-date outfit. She bought, I mean I bought for her, a short skirt, a soft sweater with a scooped neckline, and shoes with two-inch platform heels. She spent hours on her makeup and her hair. I couldn't help her with anything because my suggestions were just not cool. Can you believe those shoes are back in style again—we wore those when we were in college! They left the house and they looked so adorable. You know he comes from such a good family. His father is a lawyer and his mother is in advertising. I know that Katie is just thirteen but she is really mature for her age and James is such a nice boy. He's a bit older—sixteen and in high school. I think this will be a good first dating opportunity for Katie and she will have an advantage in getting to know what high school is all about while she is still in eighth grade. Katie said they were going to a movie and then out for a pizza. I told James that Katie needed to be home by midnight. I was nervous the whole night, hoping things were going okay. I heard her come in right around midnight—I called to her from my bedroom and asked if she had a good time and she said yes—she'd talk to me tomorrow. The next day she was up and out before I really got a chance to talk with her. When I asked her if she was going to see James again, she shrugged her shoulders and said maybe.

However, the description of how the date really went is very different. The sexual scenario described next is factually based upon "'Teen Sex That's 'No Big Deal'" published in *Lilith* magazine.

Katie and James walk from her house to the car. Once inside, James tells Katie that there has been a change in plans. They can always go the movie another time. A friend of his has invited them to a party at his parents' house. It is a small party—they will play some music videos, dance, smoke a cigarette or two. Katie is somewhat put off guard, but wants to give the impression of being mature and sophisticated about the change in plans, so she says sure when he asks her if she wants to go.

Once at the house, Katie soon discovers the other girls are somewhat older than she is. Some are coupled off, drinking beer and smoking. Katie declines the beer and cigarettes but hangs with the other girls who are not coupled with boys. As the evening progresses, one of the boys asks if they want to play "lipstick." Katie has no idea what lipstick is but, since the others do and the boys are very interested in the game, she takes the lead from the other girls. The girls dig in their purses for tubes of lipstick, looking for different colors as well as flavored lipsticks. They apply the lipstick in heavy layers to their lips. Each girl then took turns putting her mouth around the penis of each of the boys, leaving lipstick marks in a different place in order to create a rainbow effect as each girl takes her turn. Some of the boys, reluctant to play, sat back and watch. Katie was humiliated, embarrassed, and ashamed. But she goes along with the game. She feels pressured to play along. After all, she does not want to be a baby in front of these high schoolers, and what choice does she really have. She came with James in his car. Was she going to walk out when she does not even know where she is?

What girls think they want at this age are boyfriends who will talk with them on the phone, be seen with them in front of their friends, attend school activities, buy them presents, and pay attention—a lot of attention—to them. They are looking for boys to whom they can attach their feelings of love, warmth, and caring. In fact, they desire someone who will mirror those same feelings of attachment back to them.

Boys at the same age want something very different. They are far from recognizing what their emotional needs are much less integrating those feelings in a way that allows them to make careful choices with respect to relationship activities with girls. Most are dealing with the surge through adolescent development themselves. They experience strong, intense sexual urges which most boys will relieve through regular masturbation and/or physical exercise and sex talk with friends. If girls are available to them, it is friendship and/or sexual release that they seeking. Boys live in the moment and rely on their friends and the girls they are with to guide them in making appropriate choices. They take their lead from other boys when in groups with the same sex. However, when a boy is alone with a girl, he will rely on a girl to lay down a boundary. If he is sexually active with her, he will more often than not see it as a single event in time, void of meaning beyond the moment, and not in the context of relationship language that girls and women come to expect as a result of close, intimate contact. For the overwhelming number of boys and young men, it is just sex.

From Courting to Biology to Close Relationship Arrangements

Johns Hopkins University sociologist Andrew Cherlin explains courtship as having been "a process where parents and others kept watch while young people found a spouse. It had rules, steps carried out in view of everyone . . . it was an elaborate routine of going steady, getting pinned, getting engaged and then going on to marriage." He believes, as do many sociologists, that the idea of courtship is extinct. It is gone and with it couples have lost the ability to control the increasingly rapid rush to quick, casual sex.

Daniel Cere, director of the Newman Institute of Catholic Studies At McGill University, describes three primary types of bargains or ways of thinking by which a couple approaches heterosexual pairing. His essay, based on a report prepared for the Institute for American Values ("The End of Courtship," The Public Interest, No. 126, Winter 1997) says that we are not necessarily aware that we may be predisposed toward a particular belief system as attitudes have been imprinted upon us by at least our culture, families, and religious influences. The pairing bargains we buy into are the exchange theory, the sociobiology premise and the close-relationship model or a combination of the models.

The ritual of courting was originally routed in the exchange bargain. Initially, the exchange was carried out in the homes of girls and young women under the supervised watch of a girl's parents. The young girl costumed herself to attract the most desirable suitors. A girl and her parents looked for suitors who possessed qualities that led one to assume that he could take of himself and another—a good education, a job with the prospect of advancement, an income sufficient to provide a home and a lifestyle that included all of the essentials and some of the embellishments. In exchange, the girl or young woman provided evidence to her suitor that she was attractive, well-mannered, and possessed a solid background in basic literacy and the ability to manage a household. Eventually, most men knew their best bachelor days would come to an end as they felt increased pressure to make something of their life. What the culture expected of most men with any means at all was to marry, settle down, and have a family. He would become increasingly prosperity-guided and motivated by the woman he selected to be his life marriage partner.

In the 1950s, exchange-based courtship moved from the home of the girl or the young woman to the domain of the boy or young man. The vehicle for change was exactly that: the boy's or young man's vehicle. Instead of courting the girl at her home, he now picks her up in his car and conducts the exchange away from the oversight of her family and in a public setting of his preference. Whereas her family provided refreshments and entertainment in the form of card games, music, conversation and television, he now provides trips to the movies, meals at a diner or restaurant, or entertainment in any number of venues. The criteria by which she and her family judged the man changed from social and economic assets demonstrated by him at her home to how much money he spends and those assets he shows during an evening on the town. In exchange, he can accompany the most attractive girl or young woman he can attract into public adding additional capital to his status as an eligible young man. If she continues to see him, he may expect a certain amount of gratitude to be displayed his way in the form of female affection.

Many mothers and daughters in today's culture are under the assumption that what is in force with respect to the path of dating and marriage is the former rituals of courtship, routed in exchange theory, but conducted with an eye toward capitalism and consumerism. The girl provides the best eye-appealing package and commodity for him. In return, he spends his way toward her heart. Together the couple is assured that each has what the other is seeking. More importantly, each will contribute to the other the much-needed capital for a happy and successful life together.

Another type of partnering is one that is deeply embedded within evolutionary factors and the survival of the fittest genetic theory. The sociobiology partnering type is based upon the belief that women have, over time, been conditioned to value men based on their ability to provide food, protection, security and social status for themselves, and to be fathers for children they may want to birth. According to the biological theory, females are preprogrammed to seek strong, dominant males who can provide money, social position, intelligence, education, and a strong drive to achieve. Men, on the other hand, prefer sexual partners who show evidence of reproductive viability most frequently demonstrated by a bell shape figure, relative youth, physical attractiveness and overall health. Men prefer women who are less intelligent and successful than they are while women prefer men who are more intelligent and successful than they are. Given these different preferences of mate selection, it is easy to see that men will have many more women to choose from than women will have men.

Most curiously, the most intelligent, successful women will have a far smaller pool of men who will be interested in them and who will interest the females than very eligible men will have. A high-status man gets more choices than does an equally high-status woman, as she is far more selective than he is.

Some sociobiology experts believe that this matchmaking process supports monogamous marriage, one man for one woman in a com-

Dangers of Early Dating and Mating

mitted marriage. Others believe that the more high status and powerful the man (Donald Trump, Prince Charles, Ted Turner), the more likely he will have more than one mate, whether legal or not. While Western culture does not condone polygamy, many elite men live the lifestyle anyway. A woman who attaches to a man that puts her on the fringe and rotates her according to his pleasure will need to develop an extremely strong sense of self and identity. Most women who find themselves with mates who are not monogamous experience tremendous emotional and psychological pain and threats to the very core of their being. Western culture, with its progressive record on equal rights and autonomy for women, is incongruent with practices that regard women as a commodity. For most women, the price of staying in a relationship with a man who practices ritualistic infidelity is too high a price to pay. As Daniel Cere relates in his excellent summary of courtship today,

> "The illicit sexual relationships that garnish the lives of many high-status males are forms of 'functional polygamy. . . . And today, male elites command resources, technologies, and services far beyond the wildest dreams of their predecessors. They are able to sustain relationships with a variety of women, as well as make significant investments in their off spring. Indeed, we may be in the midst of a subtle and imperceptible drift toward some form of socially acceptable concubinage for dominant males."
>
> In Courtship Today: The View from Academia, 2001

All things change and change has dramatically marked the manner, rules of engagement, and acceptance with respect to dating and mating in the American culture. Due largely to the social forces surrounding the 1960s and beyond, societal dating norms have been blown apart. The emergence of the women's movement, the availability of birth control, educated working women in the labor force, and the passage of Title IX dramatically changed the very social fabric of America. Added to this phenomenal mix of social reconstruction, the social stigma attached to dating someone outside of ones cultural, racial or religious group was loosened and challenged. It is easy to see that young men and women no longer value the highly restricted rules on love, marriage, and relationships adhered to by their parents and previous generations.

Increasing numbers of well-educated and progressive adults indicate a preference to forge relationships based upon yet another kind of pair matching which sociologists have labeled: the close relationship model. This involves selecting a partner based upon a preference for certain values and traits which both partners feel are important. Values that are chosen most often include quality communication, close attachment and bonding, and compatibility in sexual expression. Close relationship pair bonds may or may not include marriage, and the continuation of the pair relationship is not centered upon the value of having children. Children may be in the plan, but the strength and viability of the relationship is what is valued most. If the relationship fades and cannot be maintained, so be it. The couple does as best as they can to care for any children, but the children are not viewed as the uppermost reason why a relationship should be preserved. Indeed, in this arrangement, children are openly recognized as a major stress on a relationship. A couple is strongly advised to put the pair bond first and make regular efforts at nurturing and maintaining the pair as their first priority where children are also present in the relationship. Research has confirmed the commonly held notion that parenthood can lower sexual compatibility, increase stressors between a pair, and present a host of threats to an otherwise secure pair bond. Thus, within the close relationship model, investment in the pair is seen as paramount to protecting the pair's children.

Close relationship pair bonds are as different as the needs of individuals. Some are based upon sexual lifestyle. Others are based upon the need for friendship and companionship over time. Still others are centered on political or social goals of which the individual or couple may have committed a large portion of their lives. Whatever is important to the couple, the foundational principle behind the success of the close relationship pair is fidelity to and nurturance of those characteristics the couple believes are central to their mutual satisfaction and happiness.

Close relationship pair matching has been criticized for its heavy focus on pleasing and meeting the needs of individuals. When the match no longer is satisfying to one or both, the pair dissolves and the former couple is freed to seek yet another match which better meets their current or changing needs. Because marriage is not necessarily significant in the coupling, formal marriages are dissolved assisted by modern marital laws such as no-fault divorce, marital property reform, and prenuptial agreements.

The first reaction one may think is that this type of relationship is rare. However, I believe the majority of heterosexual pair bonds in the United States, including marriages, are now based more or less upon the close relationship model. Hollywood actors, super star entertainers, and trust fund mega-wealthy youth and adults offer us endless examples of matches made one day and gone seemingly the next. The impact of recent television shows such as *Sex in the City* has directly impacted everyday single lifestyles. The show followed young and not so young men and women as they experienced intense, floating and fluctuating relationships, whose end was romance and not necessarily marriage or commitment over a long period of time. College-educated adults in the middle class experience more comfort with this type of relationship than the traditional standards or the biological premises to selecting a mate.

However, this cultural change in meeting and mating leads to the real possibility of miscommunication, manipulation of both boys and girls and, more seriously, victimization, especially at the expense of girls and women of all ages. Trying to protect girls by going back to the Victorian method of keeping girls and women in the house under the direct eyes of their mothers is not a workable solution. Scaring girls by portraying boys and men as more powerful, less trustworthy, and less responsible is equally dangerous to today's growth of strong girls and women, nor does it fairly represent the pressures placed upon boys and men. Girls and adult women need to examine the real dangers adolescent girls currently experience in the changing dating world.

FROM	TO
Exchange Bargain (**Formerly courting**)	**Sociobiology Bargain**
Beat of capitalism	Mate selection a matter of genetic drive
Privileges competition	Females seek dominant males; males seek physical attractiveness
Values consumption	Women marry up; men marry down
Based on rational choices	Women drive men toward competition and success in order to attractive and be of value to women
Gains from marriage outweigh benefit of remaining single	
Based upon supply, preferences and resources	Men driven to please and be of value to high status women; drive generally results in marriage
	Allows for dominant male polygamy

Close Relationship Bargain
Focus in on finding close pair bond
Features interdependence, self-disclosure, exchange, commitment
Focus is on pair bond and not on children
Recognizes openly that children may be hazardous to the relationship
Marriage is secondary consideration
Provides for the pair to determine love style which is fluid over time

From Dating to Female Relationship Abuse and Victimization

The description of the lipstick party, which we spoke of at the beginning of this chapter, is, unfortunately, not far from the reality that many girls and young women face in their dating encounters. According to a study published in the Journal of the American Medical Association, one in five high school girls have been physically or sexually abused on a date, or both. The California Attorney General and State Superintendent of Public Instruction relates a striking example:

> "On March 27, 2003 fifteen-year-old Ortralla Mosley broke up with her sixteen-year-old boyfriend Marcus McTear, both sophomores at Reagan High School in Austin, Texas. The next day, as school let out, McTear found Mosley in a hallway and stabbed her to death with a butcher knife."

Teen dating violence has become common and is now at an epidemic level. Among the facts they report these startling statistics and facts:

TEEN DATING VIOLENCE

Twenty percent of all females reported that they had been hurt physically or sexually by someone they were going out with (Harvard School of Public Health).

Ten percent of high school students stated that they had been hit, slapped, or physically hurt on purpose by their partner in the past year (Center for Disease Control).

Twenty five percent of 7th and 8th graders reported being a victim of nonsexual dating violence and eight percent reported being a victim of sexual dating violence (University of North Carolina).

Females between the ages of 16–24 are **more vulnerable** to intimate partner violence than any other age group (U.S. Bureau of Justice Statistics).

Prevention Researcher published a report on gender adolescent dating violence and found that approximately **one-third** of all students reported some experience with physical violence in a dating relationship. Violence against boys was frequently a slap, pinch, or bite as the girls fought back against boys who tried to initiate sex or were violent toward them. Girls were much more likely to be punched or forced in sexual activity against their will.

Sixty percent said they knew a teen that had been physically, sexually, or verbally abused while in a relationship. **Twelve percent** of adolescent girls said they had been physically struck, **twenty six percent** said they'd been verbally abused, and **eighteen percent** said they had been threatened with violence after trying to end the relationship (Teen Research Unlimited /Education Week, 2005).

Twenty-eight percent of young women reported unwanted sexual intercourse resulting from a man's continual arguments; **thirteen percent** by physical force.

Dating abuse occurs at the same rates with ninth-grade girls as it does with senior high school girls. This is particularly troubling as most of us would expect that eighteen-year-old young women would possess better developed decision-making capabilities than fourteen-year-old girls. Hispanic and African American girls experience twice the rate of date abuse. Girls who report either physical or sexual abuse by dating partners are more likely to have struggled with depression, eating disorders, suicide ideation, and alcohol problems. Girls who were both physically and sexually abused were ten times more likely to attempt suicide. What is both sad and troubling is that girls who experience either physical or sexual abuse are not likely to turn to their parents for help. Thus, most parents are simply not aware that their daughters have experienced such devastating assaults.

One important conclusion emerges. Many teens go to school with deep fear and anxiety about their safety, both in and outside of school. For sexually abused girls, school can be a field full of land mines. It is commonplace for abused girls to face their abusers in hallways or in the cafeteria, or worse yet, to be required to sit near abusers in their classrooms.

Physically and/or sexually abused girls and young women often feel self-conscious and are deeply afraid. They are much more likely to turn to alcohol or other drugs and to engage in eating disorder behaviors. They are very likely to socially isolate and withdraw from school academics and activities, their peers and their parents. Far too many incorrectly believe that they somehow are responsible for being physically or sexually assaulted, either once or for many, on an ongoing basis by their partners. Girls who have been abused may believe they deserve the bad treatment they receive from the very people they have chosen as dating partners. Serious depression, dangerous injury to their self-worth, distress, and untreated trauma are constant companions to girls who suffer, and suffer alone.

New Language of Love

If we do not have the rituals of courting to fall back on, how do we prepare ourselves and our daughters for the time when they will want to socialize with boys and men? What rules are in force or is it obvious that there are not any rules at all and that it is up to each girl and young woman to make up her own rules as she goes along? While in the past parents required boys and young men to pursue their daughters on her home turf, parents may feel as if their roles have been high jacked by head-spinning, unending pick-up games. In reality, there is cause to be alarmed as the "dating scene" is controlled in a large part by ill-informed boys and young men who believe that today's culture will allow them to act out every sexual fantasy that they or their boy pack can fathom.

Boys are not to blame for the current state of teen sexual affairs. Absent is a strong presence and role of fathers in the world of boy teens replaced with the steady pounding of sexually-drenched advertising and sports media. Boys and young men are trying to grow from youths to men while attaining some degree of status from their male contemporaries. Most are grossly misinformed. Boys and young men are left to figure out both their postures and obligations as they pursue their interests in meeting and interacting with girls and young women.

What is needed by girls, young women, and their parents is to recover a sense of equilibrium with respect to the teen dating game. To borrow language from the alcohol recovery movement, *we need to take a time out and attend to first things first.* The first thing is to recognize that in all forms of human behavior there are rules, and there are consequences for not attending to the rules. Mothers, fathers, and mentors of girls and young women would do girls a great service by helping them determine their own rules of safe sexual engagement. Based on the mass of quality research on the teen dating world, girls are in critical need of explicit discussions concerning the current trends and dangers of sexual practices and the harm that can be done by engaging in endless fast- cooked microwave relationships. A young girl or woman who is on an endless quest to find her prince on a galloping white horse needs to stop. The quest she should be on is not to ask if a certain boy is Mr. Right, but rather she should be thoughtfully asking the question— *what is right for me?*

Four Rules

If the dating scene is to improve, girls and women alike need to stop making boys and men the author of their playbook and write one of their own. The playbook I would suggest for girls and women would consist of four basic rules that when well-practiced would be hardwired into their cerebral network.

Rule Number One: You come into this world alone with the gift of your life; that is the way you are going to leave. Each girl and woman is responsible for making the most of her life gifts and for determining how she will negotiate life's path in order for her to develop those gifts. It is time to take the advice given by the transcendent woman scholar, Carolyn Heilbrun, in *Writing A Woman's Life:* "Let any woman imagine for a moment a biography of herself based upon those records she has left, those memories fresh in the minds of surviving friends, those letters that chanced to be kept, those impressions made, perhaps, on the biographer who was casually met in the subject's later years. What secrets, what virtues, what passions, what discipline, what quarrels would, on the subject's death, be lost forever?" To vision a biography at the end of every woman's path requires each girl and woman to have herself at the center of her life story.

Rule Number Two: There is no prince. There is you. Each girl and woman is responsible for her own life and life choices. There is no one person who will come along and rescue her from the choices she has made or the problems she has created without extracting a severe penalty which almost always cost her independence, freedom, and self-worth. No one is coming to hand over to her an easy life with permanent comfort. Many girls and women have paid the ultimate price for pursuing such a fantasy without accepting responsibility for their own lives. I strongly believe that every girl and woman must accept the responsibility to build her own body, intelligence, and spirit by bonding with her healthy family members and becoming close to teachers and adult mentors who can provide guidance.

Rule Number Three: Your spirit, your mind, and your body belong to you. You are the driver, the decision-maker, the chief-executive officer. In life, there are generally two ways to approach choices and challenges. Either a girl or woman can be in charge and direct her own choices, or she can give that power to someone else to make decisions and solve problems for her. To take charge is to reap confidence and strength, but to give it away is to become an instrument of someone else's needs and desires. This is the path of a perennial girl and, eventually, a victim.

Coercion is a common occurrence in the dating and "romance" lives of both high school and college-age girls and women. More than fifty percent of college girls reported some form of sexual victimization in one study done by Anna Smalley Flanagan, and in a similar study conducted of high school senior girls Flanagan found the same level of sexual victimization. Most of the offenders were boyfriends or lovers. Aside from the very real lifelong health hazards, hooking up, scamming for sex, and other quick sex dates are especially hurtful to girls and women who want close, respectful, and nurturing relationships. Sex is worth waiting for. If we care about our girls and young women, we will change the focus of their evolving lives from living for the attention of boys or young men to creating lives of their own by helping them to construct their own life philosophies, ground rules, and boundaries.

Rule Number Four: Find and live your quest plot. If we want girls to find and develop their interests and abilities, we must encourage them to find and live a quest plot, as we have done for boys and men for generations. We need to encourage girls and young women to find some event to transform their lives from waiting to be found to trying something unconventional, something new, whether that is building homeless shelters or bodybuilding. It is not the nature of the event but the focus on performing, doing, challenging, dreaming, or concocting the eccentric story which is important. Girls and young women should be encouraged to mold relationships with exemplary women—mothers, teachers, relatives, and role models. Friends one's own age matter, but not when it comes to influencing sexual attitudes and gender roles. Mature women can be important influences in the lives of girls, whether the girls have been abused or not. Adult women need to build female circles of influence and support in their own lives, and then systematically teach girls and young women to do the same.

Chapter 6
Models and Mentors

> *"It's like young corn in a field. If you don't water it
> and nourish it, it'll never grow into a bumper crop.
> And who would even think of planting in soil full of rocks?"*
> MYRA SADKER

Sitting in countless school gymnasiums, I have listened and watched as young women and men walked across the stage to receive honors and financial awards for college. I have heard speeches given by the valedictorians and salutatorians as well as other leaders of the graduating class. As the years have gone by, I have noticed that more young women have been receiving the highest awards and capturing their full share of college scholarships. Young women have become the overwhelming majority with respect to leadership records in their schools. I have noted one exception: presidents of the senior classes generally have been young men. Nevertheless, like others I believed I was observing the beginning of a significant trend: the propelling of young women into fast-track careers, university leadership, and futures that had been off limits to their mothers and, certainly, to their grandmothers.

Where the Smart Girls Have Gone
Terry Denny, a University of Illinois psychologist, caught most of us off guard when he reported the results of a longitudinal study on high school valedictorians. He revealed that two-thirds of high-performing high school women had begun to lower their career aspirations by their sophomore year of college. And while they still outperformed men in college, few of the young women went on to pursue doctoral degrees.

Furthermore, he reports, in the world of work, the women valedictorians performed at lower levels than the men.

Denny and his co-researcher, Karen Arnold, found the results frightening. "We're losing the talents of some of our best women," Arnold wrote, "and if this is happening to those who have everything going for them, who have every conceivable credential, one can only imagine the handicaps and barriers that women in general face." The study documented major gender differences. The females had lowered their intellectual and career goals and aspirations by the time they were sophomores in college because they were concerned about how they could manage a demanding career with motherhood, even though most did not have a boyfriend at the time. While women still excelled in college, they did not receive sufficient mentoring from faculty members with respect to career selection, life management and leadership development opportunities.

The More Things Change the More They Stay the Same

Regardless of the potential or credentials of a young woman, the opportunities dished out to girls and women are largely based upon one's gender. Being a boy or girl predisposes one to engage in behaviors that set him or her apart from the opposite sex. Culture and society still embrace the idea that men and women are different and need to act in accordance with their prescribed social roles which are often segregated by gender lines. A girl or woman who does not embrace the softer skills and behaviors of relating over asserting, cooperating rather than competing and fitting in, and being nice as opposed to stepping outside of the box and following her own path is still viewed as deviant, antisocial, and unfeminine.

Women's strengths have long been recognized to be in the communication and support areas. Women are better at sending and interpreting nonverbal messages, developing strong relationships, and using a wide array of expressive communication skills. Men's strengths are largely thought to be in controlling emotions, working independently and autonomously and focusing on discrete tasks, one at a time. Men who rise to the upper ranks in the workplace hierarchy certainly do exhibit strong abilities and balance between human relation skills on the one hand, countered by assertive, control-oriented, problem-solving capabilities on the other. Men are still seen as the hard tool while women are expected to be the warm accessory.

Prior to the 1990s, most mothers and fathers assumed that their daughters' adult lives would center on work or a career as temporary or fractional part of their lives. Most believed their daughters would work until they had a family then leave the workplace for full-time motherhood or perhaps part-time work. Some would re-enter the workplace after their children had been raised to young adulthood in order to pay for one of the major bills, provide college tuition, or to add to the family savings. Today we recognize that due to the cultural and financial shifts of American society and families, the majority of young women will work outside of the home all of their lives or a significant portion of their lives.

Need For Female Mentors

Young women transitioning from high school to post secondary education or the workforce have been exposed to the reality that the economic roles of women in families have dramatically changed. It is also true that many are poorly prepared to accept this change in female roles and to strategize for the transition to a self-sufficient member of society. Unless they can count on inheriting a sizable amount of money, girls and women today need to plan for the inevitable change that marriage, loss of a job, divorce, expense of raising a family, and the increased costs of health care brings to both women and men. Many young women after graduating high school believe that they can take care of themselves. They do not want to marry as a way to avoid finding employment or a career path of their own. Unfortunately, most high schools girls do not understand what it will require of them to carve out their own path.

Successful adult women report that they wandered or meandered one way and then another until they found paths that worked for them. Others soon learned that without financial support from their families, advanced education, and the ability to delay marriage, the pressures of everyday life led them to become enmeshed in the life of a young man and his needs and goals. Some marry much earlier than they had originally planned with varying degrees of success, both financially and emotionally.

The greater number of professional women who did forge successful business careers report that they did not receive career information or career counseling during high school or in college. This is the case whether young women were exceptionally high or average performers.

Unlike boys and men, girls and women have always had to factor in marriage when thinking about their futures. They visualize how their lives will be while trying to work and raise a family, particularly one with small children. If they have not had women role models in their families who have managed both, they are less likely to plan effectively, or they are prone to accepting other's opinions that they should not or can not do both. This is particularly the case if a husband (when a husband is in the picture) sees that he may have to make substantial accommodations in his lifestyle that he had not counted on. The extent to which a young woman or any woman can effectively compose her life depends upon her ability to see her life tributary in its various roles and responsibilities.

The influence of a girl's family on her education and job-career status is significant. When the relationship between a girl and her parents is based upon autonomy and responsive relating, girls see their future in much the same way boys do and, thus, they enter more prestigious careers. However, if a girl was successful in undermining her mother's autonomy or if her father undermined the independence of either her or her mother, she is more likely to be marginally employed and in jobs with lower prestige.

Parents who model effective communication skills and ways of attaining their own goals in life are more apt to have daughters who develop strong senses of independence and well-developed communication abilities. They are more likely to ask and receive help along the way. For parents whose interaction style is based upon dependence and control, their daughters are less likely to possess confidence and choice-making abilities and may find themselves in jobs where they have less control, rewards, and choices themselves. Many of these same girls, even if they do possess strong talents and skills, may find themselves in work situations and relationships that are not challenging or rewarding and that offer little incentive for self-improvement or advancement.

Women with aspirations for careers in science, mathematics, and technology that require graduate school are extremely likely to face barriers which can derail or disable them from completing these degrees. Among the most serious barriers are sexism in K-12 schools and graduate schools, exclusion of female professionals in the chosen areas to serve as role models, and paternalism of institutions, teacher attitudes, and extreme competitiveness. For married women, separation from their spouses in order to complete their education may also be a serious impediment. Based on the current findings of problems in young women's transitions from high school, all high school girls need serious and well-planned opportunities to connect and communicate with successful, older women. Carefully selected, experienced female mentors can provide open and trusting environments where they can engage girls in dialogues, share stories, and help these young women to grow their decision-making abilities and leadership potential.

PRIMARY ENABLING FACTORS IN GIRL'S AND YOUNG WOMEN'S FUTURE ASPIRATIONS

    Determination
    Sense of possible self in their desired role
    Strong maternal role models
    Expectation of financial responsibility
    Support of husbands
    Single-sex schools

POTENTIALLY DISABLING FACTORS IN GIRL'S AND WOMEN'S FUTURE ASPIRATIONS

    Sexist aspects of K-12 schools
    Sexist aspects of graduate schools
    Paternalism of institutions
    Teacher attitudes
    Extreme competitiveness
    Academic society gossip
    Lack of confidence in one's own abilities

Mothers as Mentors

Interviewing fifty girls who had graduated from high school that June, I asked, how would you define a female mentor? Did you have one during middle school and high school? If so, who was she? I asked these questions during individual face-to-face interviews. The results surprised me. Over half of the young women reported that they did not have female mentors of any kind from middle school through high school. The majority defined a female mentor in either very broad terms or simply gave inaccurate definitions of a mentor (e.g., my best girlfriend). Of the girls who indicated that they had mentors during these years, nearly all cited their mothers or grandmothers—a delightful surprise given the "war stories" shared among mothers about the relationship between mothers and daughters during the journey from girl to young womanhood. My research is but one part of a growing body of research done over the past twenty years which centers on girls' career development in respect to family relationship dynamics. The young women I interviewed were keenly aware of what other recent research bears out: relationship with mother is the key.

The majority of girls and young women who are best positioned to make a healthy transition from high school to pursing their own lives independently are positively attached to their mothers and have been encouraged in a healthy way to focus on themselves and to be independent. Equally important is the ability of a mother (and father) to encourage agentic, or intrinsic characteristics such as completing tasks, problem-solving, concern for self as an individual, and school performance—the very behaviors boys and men have been coached to attend to and develop. It has been shown that mothers who are career-oriented or have professional non-traditional career roles have daughters who develop the least traditional attitudes toward family and careers. They are also less anxious about growing up and becoming independent women and mothers.

Agentic Characteristics of Independent Girls-Young Women

A Quiz

Directions: Read each of the intrinsic trait characteristics. If the trait is strongly present in you, your family, daughter or the girl you are assisting, write yes. If the trait is not present at all, or is weakly present, write no.

Trait Number	Intrinsic Characteristic	Currently Strong: Yes or No
1	Healthy attachment to mother.	
2	Possesses track record of independence.	
3	Engages in problem-solving behaviors that result in problem resolution or strategizing.	

Finding Center: Strategies to Reveal Strong Girls and Women

Trait Number	Intrinsic Characteristic	Currently Strong: Yes or No
4	Family values girls as much as the boys; has same performance expectations.	
5	Mother is career-oriented.	
6	Mother is in a non-traditional job or career.	
7	Parents encourage daughter to make her own decisions.	
8	Parents express interest in issues important to daughter.	
9	Daughter and parents hold similar perceptions of the tone and relationships within the family.	
10	Parents hold high aspirations of daughter's occupational plans.	
11	By senior year of high school, daughter has definite goals in mind.	
12	Mother actively listens to daughter, encourages her to make own choices and does not talk down daughter's ambitions or choices.	
13	Father supports daughters goals, encourages her to set own post secondary plan and supports problem-solving to accomplish her own goals.	
14	Parents support daughter's need for autonomy.	
15	Daughter is emotionally independent from her father.	

Scoring Quiz

Assign points to each trait number that you marked with a yes answer. Assign one point to items: 4, 5, 6, 8, 9, and 15. Assign two points to items: 1, 2, 3, 7, 10, 11, 12, 13, and 14. There will be a total of twenty-four points.

Agentic Levels

25–23   Outstanding! Extremely independent girl/woman who enjoys harmonious home life, strong mother attachment, and has demonstrated her ability to solve her problems, set goals and obtain them in the presence of obstacles. Ignores voices that do not support her goals and focuses on strategies and support systems to accomplish her dreams. Would benefit from second to fourth stage mentor.

22–21   Excellent! Strong, independent girl/woman who enjoys strong mother attachment and has demonstrated her ability to solve her problems, set goals, and get most of them met in the face of barriers. Would benefit from second and especially third stage mentor as this will increase her odds of attaining her demonstrated potential.

20–19   Strong sense of independence with a record of being able to meet some of her goals. Strong need for first through third stage mentor.

19–18   Average independence. Girl/woman possesses some agentic characteristics but is currently comfortable in a dependent-passive mode; will require strong support to cope with realities of a female life. Strong need for first and second stage mentor immediately.

17–   At-Risk. Girl/woman does possess one or two agentic traits. However, she will require strong support to strategize small steps for her to feel comfortable leading her own life. More than likely, girl/woman has fear if not panic about taking care of herself and/or leading her own life without someone providing for or telling her what to do. Critical need for first and second stage mentor immediately.

What is the message for mothers of girls who do not currently work or who do not have careers? It is this: Mothers can build independent, confident girls and young women by engaging in positive attachment strategies. Agentic mothers encourage their daughters to take risks and to solve their own problems. They work diligently to provide a home environment that is rich in messages that are pro-girl and pro-woman rather than messages that marginalize or demean the value of girls and women. How mother thinks and coaches her daughter and the openness with which she shares her own experiences, and how she would live her own life if she were starting out today are powerful forces in a daughter's day to day life. Then such a daughter is raised in a belief system that she can "do" and can "become" and that her mother will be there to support her efforts.

Male or Female Mentor?

Should men mentor girls in middle or high school? Does gender make a difference to women in the work place? While this is a decision that must be made on a case-by-case basis, cross-gender mentoring for young girls and for women of any age presents very real limitation and/or dangers. The male mentor and girl or young woman protégé may fall into playing a number of stereotypical roles. Stereotypical roles occur when a person holds a belief that a girl or woman is more emotional under pressure and less assertive than her male counterpart. A male mentor may unconsciously or consciously fall into one of these common stereotypically roles: parent-child, chivalrous knight-helpless maiden, tough warrior-weak warrior or, a very dangerous role, the macho-seductress. The most damaging consequence is that a power relationship is implied with the girl or woman playing the part of the child or the weaker part of the pair. A power-based role prohibits her from expressing emotions and requires her to participate in game playing, flirtation, and gender stereotypes.

Intimacy and sexuality concerns are another serious limitation of cross-gender mentoring with girls and women. It is the developmental task of girls in the middle school to begin to test out their sexual communication skills through both body and verbal language. This continues throughout the maturation process into adulthood. Practicing sexual communication is both normal and healthy but not in connection with mentor relationships. A male mentor requires deep awareness of the developmental tasks girls face at this age and the ability to draw boundaries with respect to both the mentor's behavior as well as a girl's or a young woman's behavior.

It must also be said that if a male mentors a girl or young woman, both parties must be ready for the increased public scrutiny such relationships will often endure. Resentments on the part of other girls or young women or on the part of other adults in the school or work environment are common and should be expected. This additional stress may contribute to undermine or at least limit the effectiveness of the mentor relationship.

Mentoring Stages and Strategies

Mentoring is most effective when the mentor is matched to a girl's or a woman's developmental journey. Mentors are best chosen to match one of four stages. At the first mentor stage, the purpose of the mentor is to arouse interest in the girl or young woman's world and in her personal life. This initial stage involves the sharing of experiences and the development of trust and caring between the adult and the girl/young woman. The mentor makes a commitment to developing two-way, open communication. Mothers and other women in a girl's immediate family are the favorite first-level mentors. Other excellent sources of first-level mentors are women involved in church organizations or other community organizations such as Big Sister, Sister to Sister, and girl-centered support groups. The majority of mentorship provided to girls and young women currently focuses at this first stage.

While the first mentoring stage is characterized by attention to the whole girl or woman, second- through fourth-stage mentoring focuses attention on the development of skills, talents, and interest in a particular area. The second-stage mentor's purpose is to use her expertise to specifically model, teach, and guide the girl/young woman in the learning process. Examples of second-stage mentoring include an interior designer mentoring a girl in her business one day a week or a young woman working side-by-side with an adult female volunteer on a local political campaign.

Third-stage mentors are older and possess a greater degree of expertise, experience, and longevity in their respective field than do first- and second-stage mentors. The goal of a third-stage mentor relationship is to provide expanded experiences within a particular field or expertise which builds upon those activities the girl/young woman engaged in at earlier mentoring stages.

The fourth-stage mentor is a person whose expertise and status in the field is so strong that he or she can channel the girl or young woman's abilities into extraordinary accomplishment. Most girls, and indeed most adults, will not experience mentoring at such a specialized stage. This stage is most appropriate for girls and women who demonstrate unusual abilities and intellectual accomplishments or athletic capabilities, such as Olympic athletic potential or giftedness in a specialty field.

Mentor Stages and Purposes

Stage One	Stage Two	Stage Three	Stage Four
Listens not lectures	Listens	Provides experiences in public speaking, organizing, and community service	Communicates directly the talent she sees in the girl/woman and what it will take to reach the top
Provides encouragement	Connects girl to strengths-interests		
Allows girls to voice concerns	Models, teaches and guides		
Validates feeling and thinking	Is flexible as she sees girls needs	Teaches tools and skills of the trade or profession	Coaches techniques in stress management
Sensitive to girls culture	Offers choices		Teaches competitive techniques and strategies
Shares own experiences and struggles	Encourages girls to use choice-making as a tool	Provides connections with other girls/women with similar interests and goals	Provides advanced training and educational opportunities commensurate with ability of girl/woman
Shares losses and accomplishments	Provides feedback and encouragement		
Makes commitment of time and availability	Teaches girl to establish own values and goals	Provides information on earning potential of jobs-careers of interest	
Allows girls to express concerns about prejudice, discrimination etc.	Helps girls confront stereotypes on race and gender		Uses communication that focuses strictly on abilities and accomplishments and never on perceived limitations of gender
Sensitive to socioeconomic limits and background	Explores future possibilities	Connects girl/woman to workshops, formal classes and educational programs to further skill-talent development	
Explores community activities and interests	Encourages financial independence as young adult		
Models and encourages behaviors that support self-confidence and value of female achievement	Coaches basics of handling own money		

Models and Mentors

Mentorship Exemplars

Penny Townsend-Quill, chair and mentor coordinator of the *Women Helping Girls* program in Rochester, New York, says, "I have been mentoring for six years. I think my student will agree that we are lifelong friends. My job as a mentor is to help my protégé recognize her own unique and wonderful talents, strengths, and skills. Together we problem solve and talk openly and honestly about cultural norms, education, and dreams for the future." As her comments reflect, mentoring is not an activity to enter into lightly. It is essential that individuals interested in initiating mentorship experiences familiarize themselves with a variety of sound, effective programs.

Women Helping Girls targets girls in the urban area of Rochester, New York. It is affiliated with the Greater Rochester American Association of University Women. Its home base is at Wilson Magnet High School in the Rochester City School District. Created in 1992, the program has provided mentors to over 500 seventh- through twelfth-grade girls. Initially, mentors are matched with girls in seventh grade. Girls are asked to write a short essay describing how they feel they might benefit from a mentor and their willingness to commit to a mentor relationship for at least one school year. Saturday programs are organized by WHG for mentors and their students which include visits to the zoo, artist's studios, and cultural festivals, to name a few. Service projects, money management workshops, and career day luncheons have been activities offered by the WHG mentorship programs. Truc Doan, a high school girl who emigrated from Vietnam, states, "Through the program I was permitted to meet more people and interact with girls my own age. I have also been involved in more projects and groups due to the WHG program. When everyone else is disparaging about the uselessness of the teenage girl, WHG provides information and opportunity."

SciTech Clubs for Girls is a program in which girls build exhibits for visitors to use at the Science and Technology Interactive Center (SciTech) located in Aurora, Illinois. According to Bob Russell, program officer for this exemplary program, SciTech is well-known for its innovative exhibits and for its ability to tackle difficult issues and topics. "SciTech young women developed and circulated a rotating interactive weather exhibit and program throughout Illinois classrooms," says Russell. *SciTech Clubs for Girls'* goal is to increase female performance in math and science in middle school and to increase female high school enrollments in science and math courses that are highways to careers in science, math, and engineering. Russell believes girls lose interest because of societal expectations to fit into the "accessory mode" and due to girls' lack of experience in hands-on activities with science-oriented tools. *SciTech for Girls* provides girls experience with female mentors outside of school who are in careers such as construction, math, science, and engineering. By providing fun and interesting building experiences in small groups, mentors are able to ensure a close relationship as well as effective access to tool use and exhibit building experiences.

Female role models are the center point of *SciTech Clubs for Girls*. As *SciTech* is located in a research and development technology corridor, Fermi National Accelerator Laboratory donated a day per week of a female electrical engineer's time for two years. The engineer was both science and construction mentor to the groups she directed. SciTech allowed only females to work with the girls as they believe it is vital to the program's effectiveness that the girls do all the work. Russell writes that "as soon as we let a male in, he couldn't help himself from doing the work for the girls. He would say, 'let me show you how' and then he would do it for them. On the other hand, female mentors will demonstrate to the girls and the let them do it. They understand that girls have to struggle through awkwardness before they can develop skills."

SciTech Clubs for Girls, now *Science learning Inc.* documented significant impact on girls' attitudes and behaviors regarding science and construction. The program's evaluation cited its major impact as providing the girls "real work" and that the girls work would affect others.

Another excellent example of mentorship models for girls, *Eyes to the Future*, was directed by Joni Falk, Senior Investigator at TERC, a nonprofit education research and development organization based in Cambridge, Massachusetts. Over the past thirty-eight years, TERC programs and products have reached millions of students and teachers in the United States and eighty-seven countries. *Eyes to the Future*, funded by the National Science Foundation, connected middle school girls with high school role models and women scientists. High school girls provided a bridge between middle school girls and their future as high school young women. The program was based in Somerville, Massachusetts. Middle school girls of various academic and cultural backgrounds were grouped into teams of three. Each team was matched with a high school student already engaged in math, science, and technology. An adult mentor was added to the team after the high school mentor and the middle school protégé had time to establish their relationship. Adult women mentors included a pediatric gastroenterologist, ecologist, geologist, boat builder/engineer, and a veterinary technician.

November 24 at 3:16 PM
From: B B (middle school girl)
To: C++ (high school mentor)

What's up C++ me not so good because I just got my report card and it doesn't look good formeI don't want to go to school tomorrow. YoF!, if I don't write you back tomorrow I'm absent cause I have enough of this teachers.

By: C++
To B B

Hello . . . glad to hear from you again. You sound kind of depressed . . . you khnow what I do? I push myself over their (teachers) expectations. If they think lowly of me, I prove them wrong and make them feel embarrassed that they ever said those things to me. Do extra hard in math. Make him/her EAT her/his words. Go to school . . . although school may not seem fun, at least your're with your friends. That's what I want you to do. Hope to talk to you soon!

From Many Futures Mentoring Middle School Girls,
by Joni Falk and Brian Drayton
By: Linda (adult mentor)
To: Soccer (middle school)

What does building or fixing boats have to do with physics? When I started working with boats, I learned about how they move through the water, what the wave profile (waterline) looks like on a boat as it moves at different speeds through the water. That's where some of the physics comes in. Figuring out how fast something moves is a kind of physics problem that involves a distance and, some specific amount of time; and then you can determine the speed or velocity of the object. Are you still looking for a science project? What would you say if I told you I think hot water freezes faster than cold water? How would you prove me right or wrong? How can you explain your results if you test this out?

From Many Futures Mentoring Middle School Girls,
by Joni Falk and Brian Drayton
By: Soccer (middle school)
To: Linda (adult mentor)

All that stuff about how building boats is related to physics sounds really cool. I'm still stuck on my science fair project, I don't know what to choose for a topic. I don't undertand how hot water can freeze raster than cold water, I'll try to find out. But, I would guess that it probably has something to do with how the molucules in hot water move around faster than in cold water. What made you want to become a physicst? (Did I spell phycist right) Gotta Go.

We can learn from this project that distance does not have to be a barrier in creating strong, innovative, and highly meaningful mentorship programs to girls and young women. By using computer communications, high school girls provided a critical link to middle school girls who needed an older, accomplished girl that they could look up to and admire. High school girls chosen for this project were located at the high school that the middle-level girls would transition into thus providing a much needed safety net in that the high school mentor would serve as a source of welcome and inspiration to them when they arrived at the high school as freshmen. The young middle-level girls were provided with a rich opportunity to see firsthand how science, mathematics, and technology live out in the day-to-day lives of professional women in their community. Women professional mentors were able to coach work habits, attitudes, as well as teach how to handle failure and setbacks.

What is not surprising is that all the participants, high school and professional women mentors and the middle school students alike, valued their role in the team relationship. Professional women, when given the chance to share both their expertise and stories, get a second chance to evaluate their own lives in a way they do not get dealing with the busy realities of a professional life. The greatest reward for an adult woman is to coach another girl along the road she once took with the hope that by telling her own story, the next girl's road will be filled with fertile soil and fewer stones and boulders upon which she can stumble.

A Jasmine in My Path

I met Jasmine in a very difficult time in my life. It was the year my father died, the year I had earned tenure and the same year that my thirteen year marriage went under. My children were eight and eleven and still needed a lot of my attention. However, I also served on the executive board of a nationally known organization whose mission was to provide mentors for girls and boys. I was asked by the director of our agency if I would consider mentoring a girl from the hard to match list, those children who had been waiting to receive a match for more than a year. I agreed to review the girls currently on the list primarily as a courtesy. My own life was such that taking on someone else's problems seemed more than I could handle. I selected a seven year old Caucasian-Japanese girl, who had no siblings and whose Japanese father was not in her life.

I first met Jasmine at the agency office. She bounded into the room and it was as if she held the energy of the sun in her smile. She was radiant. She was petite with blond hair and Asian facial features. She had waited so long for a match and her body language communicated that she expected this first meeting to result in our both committing to the relationship with each other. Thus was the first of eleven years with Jasmine.

Jasmine was years older than her seven years. Life had been hard. Her mother struggled with alcohol and drug abuse and poor choices in men. She went from job to no job to job again. As is the case with many poor single mothers, she moved from one place to the next as the landlord pressed for back rent or as another man friend entered her life. Jasmine's language indicated that she had been exposed to conversations about men, sex, and life in general that no child should hear once much less numerous times. My objective for our time spent together was to provide child-centered activities, both alone and in the company of my own children. We played cards and board games, went to movies and lunches, read books, and talked about life. I took her trick-or-treating with my children on Halloween and we celebrated her birthdays. I encouraged her in school activities and tried to coach her with respect to getting to school on time and staying the full day.

In the beginning her school attendance was a big problem. Her attention span was very short and most of her teachers described her as being hyperactive, although I never considered her to be. Jasmine had learned to reach out to her school counselor, who arranged to have her participate in a children's support group located at the school. She once told me that no matter how hard she tried, if she was upset over something that happened at home, she first needed to meet with her group or her counselor or else she simply could not pay attention in her class. She told her teacher that until she believed her and let her see her counselor. Jasmine had an effective way of teaching the adults in her life to take care of first things first.

After a few years, Jasmine made numerous moves. The first moves were from one part of the city to another. With each additional move, Jasmine and her mother lived a number of states and then a half a country away from me. She called on the telephone and sent me short letters. In the summers she returned either with her mother or alone as she became older to visit with relatives in the area. We met and spent a day or two together or just an afternoon. I would listen. She shared what was happening in her life. I had encouraged her to set goals for herself and to stay as connected to school as possible. But mostly, I listened. I learned what it was like to grow up with a mother who, according to her daughter, left her daughter vulnerable to the behaviors of men in her house. Jasmine was very angry with her mother's choices but, on the other hand, as she shared with me when she was just ten, "My mother is all I have. It has been just me and my mother my whole life."

The first time Jasmine was told she was moving out of state she was terrified. How would she stay connected with me and would she be okay? It was then I told her that where ever she was, we would stay connected, by phone and by mail and any summer she could return home, I would arrange time for her. The following summer when we were in a shopping mall, over a soft drink, I told her that wherever—not whenever—wherever she was going to school, I would be there for her high school graduation. Each time we talked, I repeated the reminder and in subsequent meetings, she shared what was going on with her mother and how she was doing with her schooling.

From Jasmine one learns the sense of survival coupled with unabated enthusiasm that Jasmine possessed. One summer on my break I was working at home on a writing project when the phone rang. Jasmine was calling from a mental institution in the Chicago area. Her call needed to be quick, she said. Any moment she would be called to go to one of two mandatory group sessions and might have to call back. Her mother had moved to the Chicago area and was living with a man who had a drug habit. Jasmine said she confronted her mother about the problem and said she would call the police. Her mother called the authorities to have Jasmine taken away because of "crazy" behavior. After hearing both sides of the story, the police and social worker told Jasmine it would be better for her to leave and be admitted to a children's psychiatric center where she would be safe and where they could arrange for help.

She called me three times that day, in between the group and individual sessions. She said she never regretted demanding that she and her mother leave the crack house, and that all in all, she felt the authorities did the right thing by removing her.

From treatment center, to foster placement, back to mother and away again, Jasmine called, wrote, and found her way back in the summer. One summer it took her more than twenty hours on a Greyhound bus to get back home to her grandmother, her foster grandparents, and for a visit with me. Each year she grew taller, more attractive than the last year, and even more determined to stay in school, to remain drug free, to abstain from sex, and to go on to college. I received pictures of her swinging from ropes in a ropes challenge course, or a picture of her and her date for the junior prom. Her letters showed the growth she was making in her reading and writing, and she talked about the part-time job she had and of her dream of getting into college. I encouraged her to find several colleges, junior colleges, and technical education programs that she may be interested in. In my heart and based upon my experiences in higher education, I knew Jasmine might not have the academic record, test scores, or monetary means to pursue a four-year college or a program too far away. However, Jasmine said that distance was not an issue. She really did not feel that at age eighteen she would have a home place: home would be where she decided to be.

She had finally severed the cord from her mother. At the age of sixteen, Jasmine left her mother, and her mother's friend, bought a Greyhound ticket, then knocked on the door of her father living in another state. She had called him on the phone and said she needed to leave her mother and she needed a place to live and finish high school. Her dad had moved on with his life when Jasmine was a baby, and Jasmine had not seen him since she was five. He accepted her on limited terms, until she graduated and under his rules. She found a job, followed his rules, and found her way at the local high school.

Several years later, I was sitting in an outdoor athletic stadium looking up at a June Indiana sky. It had been hot and humid that day, but the breeze was cool some forty feet in the air. Alongside me sat Jasmine's father, whom I had met for the first time that day. He was thanking me for caring about his daughter and noted that I was the only one to show up for his daughter's graduation other than himself. As I waited for the high school graduation ceremony to begin, I was thinking of how far Jasmine had brought herself. She had gained admittance to a major university with money left to her by way of her grandmother's will. She said she thought the money would be enough for one year of college. She was certain that once she got to college, she could figure out how to stay. I had no doubt about that!

Her father let me know that Jasmine had to be out of his house the day after graduation. It was part of the terms for accepting her. He had a new wife and young children and needed the space. Jasmine, he said, had a job at a video rental store and would be living with two female cousins in an apartment in suburban Chicago.

As he was telling me this, I pictured Jasmine's move as a summer transition before college. As the day continued, I watched Jasmine as she walked across the stage to receive her diploma and quickly descended the stadium benches to meet her on the field below.

That night Jasmine returned home to pack up her belongings. She met me the following day in my motel room. She confirmed the story of what had happened and said she would work in the suburb for the summer and try to find a school for the fall. While she was not bitter, she was careful not to reveal to her father what money she received from me as a graduation gift. I also gave Jasmine a necklace given to me years before by a college mentor of mine.

Several years later, I heard from Jasmine again. She was nearly twenty-one and was inviting me to her wedding. I could not attend due to a conflict with a family high school graduation, but we spent some time having a good talk. She said she was taking classes at a technical college and was studying horticulture. I smiled knowing that Jasmine always had been interested in color, flowers and sketching dress designs from the time she was a very little girl. But what struck me most is that the little girl with sunlight in her smile would want to help a plant grow and bloom. And what might be said of any committed mentor relationship is that I received more from my protégé than I could ever provide for her. It is Jasmine and her light that helped me see how much I had in my own life, and how much my family and I had to share with a child in need. It is a lesson I still recall each time I am confronted with what might seem like a hopeless situation. I see Jasmine's light and her smile and I reflect on how she has overcome the past and I know things can work out—no matter how difficult circumstances seem at the time.

Chapter 7
Sensuality and Sexuality

> *"To ask women to become unnaturally thin is to ask them to relinquish their sexuality."*
> NAOMI WOLF

Emilie Coulter, in an editorial review for TOYSRUS wrote, "Guess what! Dora the Explorer has jumped on the royal bandwagon! This intrepid explorer is now a fairy-tale princess with magical hair that grows when the jewel in her crown is pressed with a wand. Dora talks and sings, too, in both English and Spanish: 'Vamanos! Let's go to fairy-tale land! Will you brush my hair?'"

Dora the Explorer, a program which premiered on Nickelodeon in 2000, lives in animation land and is an immensely successful show on Noggin. In terms of revenue, the show is much bigger than Barney ever was. She is a cartoon Latina girl who lives inside a computer and goes on adventures with her trusty monkey, Boots. She solves problems and learns something about herself in the process. Dora and her licensed products have earned an estimated one billion dollars since her debut in 2000. What needs to be altered about a mega successful stereotyping-bashing girl character with action-oriented story lines in 2005? Apparently, the answer to that question is turning Dora into a Magic Hair Fairy-tale Princess!

A reviewer of Dora following her princess transformation writes, "Rapunzel (the author reminds you that she was the girl locked up in the tower waiting to be rescued) gets a makeover with the new Dora the Explorer: Magic Hair Fairy-tale Princess Doll. The doll was very fun for my daughter to play with when she opened it on Christmas day. However, after making Dora's hair get longer, then shorter, then longer again, she got bored with it rather quickly (thank heavens for that, the author exclaims). Sure, Dora sings, compliments your child's own hair, squirts out a little Spanish, and has on a fairy hat, but in the end the doll just doesn't offer enough to hold a young mind's attention. This isn't a bad doll, just be warned that after you buy this thing, your child won't get much play out of it."

Personally, I believe that for a little girl who has come to expect adventure and action from Dora, it would be better to discard the doll rather than changing her focus to fixating on her looks, her hair, and her body as an ornament.

Sexy as a Princess

What has happened to make this country a nation of little princesses? Maria Tatar, Harvard folklorist and editor of *The Annotated Brothers Grimm,* states "most of Disney's princess tales reinforce the idea of achieving power through fabulous clothing and great wealth." The problem, she says, is that the princesses don't work for it. "These stories impress upon girls the importance of beautiful dress and gorgeous good looks, she states, "but in many of the original versions of these classic fairy tales (original Grimm's stories), the girls were feisty and cunning; they used their intelligence and worked very hard to liberate themselves." Just like Dora the Explorer before she was turned into a princess. The most dangerous notion about girls and women becoming beauty objects and not working for their success is this frequently results in their learning it is good to be subservient to another's pleasure without the responsibility or experience in taking action on their own.

Sensual and Sexual Portrayal

Once a girl or woman creates a life that centers upon taking control of her desires and dreams and putting them into action (in other words, develops that part of her that is typically referred to as male behaviors), how does she go about liberating herself sensually and sexually? Mary Pipher warned, in her best seller, *Reviving Ophelia: Saving the Selves of Adolescent Girls,* "Our culture is deeply split about sexuality. We raise our daughters to value themselves as whole people, and the media reduces them to bodies." On the topic of sexual issues, she laments that "Girls face two major sexual issues." She goes on: "One is an old issue of coming to terms with their own sexuality, defining a sexual self, making sexual choices, and learning to enjoy sex. The other issue concerns the dangers that girls face of being sexually assaulted. By late adolescence, most girls today either have been traumatized or know of girls who have."

Over a decade has passed since Pipher's book hit a cord with women readers. Today, Laurie Abraham, executive editor of *Elle* magazine, maintains that the biggest problem with print and media is "how much we lie about sex." She believes the culture, through media messages, conveys quite effectively that women's sexuality is secondary to a man's pleasure. Jean Kilbourne, a scholar and media activist, agrees with the notion that the bulk of media encourages women to "labor to be beautiful," to believe "that we are not good enough as we are, to be strong but don't speak up too much, don't be too loud. Don't."

Kilbourne captures the angst girls and women struggle with each day. She supports her argument with hundreds of current examples from the media. The advertising and media culture drum the message that women have a right to remain sexy, but only if they are thin, passive, and exposed. Women are not given the right by the current culture to choose their own sexual roles or to explore and define sensuality and sexuality for themselves. Instead, women are asked to accept the pseudo-sexuality that the media culture throws in their face each day. Pseudo-sexualizing begins with the use of sexualized girls in advertisements targeted toward the adult market as well as those ads targeted for teen girls. Kilbourne stresses that with all of the negative and unrealistic body images projected upon girls and women by the mainstream media, "how sexy can a woman be if she hates her body? She can act sexy, but can she feel sexy?"

One central challenge for a girl or a woman is that of determining a sensual and sexual life for herself. It is the right and responsibility of each girl and woman to select her own means of expressing her sensuality and sexuality. She needs to find one that is comfortable and true to whom she is rather than allowing the media or others to define them for her.

Sensuality or Sexuality?

Are sensuality and sexuality the same thing? Looking and listening to mainstream media, most girls and women would answer yes. But, in fact, there are some very distinct differences. Sexuality has to do with the feelings we have about ourselves as sexual beings. Women may express their sexuality through their dress, how they move and speak, and by intimate physical behaviors such as touching, kissing, hugging, masturbation, and sexual intercourse. Feelings about our sexual identity and how we express sexuality are very powerful and strongly influenced by at least our family, culture, and religious beliefs. The choices women make regarding sexual expression or the messages that the mainstream culture sends to girls and women, if internalized, will no doubt impact our self-esteem, our confidence, and our sense of enjoyment of sexual expression.

Sensuality is very closely linked to sexuality, but it is different in many respects. Sensuality has to do with receiving and interpreting stimulus by all of our senses such as touch, sight, smell, sound, temperature, and taste, to name a few. By using our senses, we learn to explore our world, and by trial and error, we acquire preferences for those sensual experiences that soothe us and give us pleasure and avoid those sensual experiences that are unpleasant, painful, or disturbing. Research conducted in orphanages over fifty years ago documented the disastrous effects that sensory deprivation, especially touch, has to the normal development of infants and children. Since then an increasingly dense collection of studies on child attachment and bonding has taught us that the human being requires body contact, physical stimulation, and quality verbal and nonverbal interaction for maximum brain functioning ability and a sense of overall well-being and personal attachment to significant people in one's life.

As girls reach puberty and grow into adulthood, they must assume the responsibility for choosing, developing, and balancing their sensual experiences. By exploring a variety of them, girls and women will develop sensory antennae. When honed over a period of years, women so sensitized will be in better places to negotiate the outside world and make choices that are in their best interests rather than being accessories to other people's goals and motivations.

Clarissa Pinkola Estes, in her stunning book *Women Who Run with the Wolves*, describes the problem a woman falls into when she stays too long from home, in other words, becomes disconnected from her own feelings and from her own nature. She loses her sense of how she is feeling about herself. When she ignores the feelings within her body, the image of her true nature fades, her eyes go on low dim and she begins to go blind. She becomes an anemic portion of her former self. This is not far from the way girls and women are depicted by mainstream media today. But rather seeing this portrayal as a problem, the current media culture pushes this look of women as the preferred one.

Estes tells us of a group of people who live in the wooded hills of Michigan and Indiana who originated from rural Kentucky and Tennessee many years ago. Their language is colored with "I ain't got no" and "We done this the other day." Being frequent Bible readers, their verbal expressions also includes words such as iniquities and aromatical. She tells us that these unique farm people have numerous words about women being worn out and unaware and consequently making poor choices. Among the most colorful are: "Gone too long in harness, worked her hind legs off, suckling a dead litter," meaning she is wasting her life in a futile or unrewarding marriage, job or situation. Estes says it best when she writes:

> "When a woman is too long gone from home, she is less and less able to propel herself forward in life. Instead of pulling in the harness of her choice, she's dangling from one. She's so cross-eyes with tiredness she trudges right on past the place of help and comfort. Her fuse burns shorter and shorter."
>
> Clarissa Pinkola Estes
> *Women Who Run With the Wolves*

Women do need to take back their power with respect to defining and portraying what their sensual and sexual lives are rather than allowing mainstream for-profit media inform us and others who we are. To get an indication of the scope of the challenge, I reviewed a sample of current media representations of girls and women found on *genderads.com.*, a sample from women's and men's magazines, and I examined the website Northstar's Gallery "Bomber Girls": Sensuality in Bomber Nose art. The bomber girls essay asserts that the use of a sensuous female nude image has long been associated with celebrating the female in both secular and religious settings. Since the first boats were made, sailors have adorned their boats and ships with symbols of faith to protect them from the unpredictable gods and forces of nature. The most frequent symbol selected by these rugged men was a full image of a sensuous female body. Whether the beautiful nude was a ship's figurehead or adornment on the nose of a World War II bomber plane, their sensual image conveyed a strong positive message. They offered comfort to the men who were entering unknown seas and territories of peril and they reminded them that they were not alone. As she did in classical art, the female form became the symbol of perfect beauty, genius, friendship, truth, and sacred love.

As I examined the samples of bomber art contained within the Northstar Gallery, I was thunderstruck on how great a step backwards the portrayal of women has taken since the 1940s. When I viewed "Helen in Briefing Time," my first impression was one of strength. She is well-proportioned, with ample-size thighs, hips, and a bust size that is in exact proportion to the rest of her body. She sits up straight with most of her back to me, but her head is turned over her shoulders. She looks straight into my eyes. Her arms, showing obvious muscle and mass, are held up in ninety degree angles above her hips as if to say to me, "Are you coming my way?" Her legs are long, strong, and her thighs are full with obvious solid muscle structure. Overall, the impression Helen leaves me with is that she is a strong, very sensual woman who has taken good care of herself so she can meet both the pleasures and challenges in her life. She invites me to come along and do the same.

Next I reviewed current images of girls and women in print and non-print media. I was sickened at what I saw. I was drawn, in the same way your eyes are drawn to an image of a starving child in Africa, to the female image at Versace, a cutting-edge fashion designer of luxury products for both men and women. She had no name. Rather she was referred to only by her corporate owner's name. She was starvation-thin by any physician's standards. She was stooped down on her haunches wearing solid high-heeled shoes, but her ankles appeared to be entwined with leather straps which are not ordinarily part of the kind of shoe design she was wearing. She was waif-like. Her face—white, lifeless, and trance-like—stares off into the distance. She holds one arm up into the air with hand and fingers reaching up. Her fingers were spread apart with her pointer finger meeting her thumb as if barely holding onto an imaginary object. Her other arm rested limply on her stooped knees. Her fingers of the hand attached to the arm reaching up reminded me of the arms stretching up from barely alive people dumped into the ocean by the sinking Titanic. She was saying, "Please help me—I am dying!"

We know that women have made dramatic gains since the 1940s in many areas of life, especially in America with the help of laws like the marital property reform and Title IX which opened the door in all areas of academic life and helped confront sexual discrimination and harassment. However, the current dominant media portrayal of women does not accurately represent the successes of women over the last fifty years, nor does it accurately encapsulate the authentic American women as found in the current millennium. One of the reasons behind the degrading of the female body image may be due to the fact that during World War II women made powerful contributions by working in factories, health care, and numerous other jobs while still taking care of the families that soldiers were forced to leave behind. When any human being is faced with a fifty percent change of survival as many of our soldiers faced, it becomes very clear as to what is of greatest value.

Fast forward the clock to our current time and another war and to an economy and lifestyle that is dominated by corporations and businesses still largely controlled and managed by men. Most well-educated successful men are safe from involuntary subscription into military life and free to center their energies on making money and enjoying life. Today, in a more sexually permissive but still man-dominated culture, women are depicted with images that isolate their legs, mouths, and breasts and other body parts from their whole body. When they do portray the female body as a whole, it is often characterized as weak, fragmented, powerless, and dependent.

So Sensual

Sensuality is acute awareness and feeling about your own body. By learning how to be in touch with your own feelings, you are more likely to be able to read the feelings of others and to respond in a healthy way. Advocates for Youth present a candid message on the varying attributes which contribute to our sensuality. When you consider that the following ingredients lay the foundation to effective sensual development and expression, it is easy to understand how the misuse of these sensory pathways by adults or the media can cause girls and women much emotional damage.

ATTRIBUTES OF SENSUALITY

Body image

Experiencing pleasure and release from sexual tension

Satisfying skin through close physical contact

Feeling physical attraction for another person

Age-appropriate sexual intercourse

Fantasy

Based on *Life Planning Education*, a comprehensive sex education curriculum. Washington, DC: Advocates for Youth.

So Sexual

A woman's sexuality encompasses her sexual desire, arousal, and sexual activities to enhance arousal and orgasm. In most of the world, young women become sexually active during their teen years. In America, a little more than half of all teen men and women engage in sexual intercourse, and if you include those teens who engage in either oral sex or sexual intercourse, the percentage climbs significantly. Traditionally, in the U.S., a young woman's first sexual experience was with either her husband-to-be or husband. However, that has changed dramatically since the 1960s. While early marriage in the United States is less common today than it was thirty years ago, that too varies depending upon the region of the United States and whether the region is rural or urban. While cultures around the world hold different views of young people engaging in sexual activity outside of marriage, in the United States sexual activity of young men and women between the ages of sixteen and twenty is the new cultural norm.

In France, Germany, Great Britain, and the United States, more than half of all adolescents who give birth are unmarried. While sexual activity among young people is not new, what is a dramatic change is that the majority of young women and young men in the U.S. are delaying marriage well into their mid-twenties and beyond. Delaying marriage is an obvious advantage for women as they may be able to pursue educational opportunities and /or obtain valuable work experience before marriage. In the United States, teen women with less than twelve years of schooling are six times more likely to give birth by age eighteen.

Girls and women are severely admonished about the negative effects and consequences to them if they are sexually active at a young age and/or outside of marriage. Compared to Sweden and Denmark, western civilization has long held a tradition of negative attitudes pertaining to sexual activity particularly of young women. Cultural attitudes towards boy's and young men's sexual practices have been characterized by researchers as "we say don't do it but those words are accompanied with a wink and a smile." It is true that early, unprotected sexual activity is extremely risky to the physical and emotional well-being of girls and women. But the same concern about early and unprotected sexual contact applies to boys and men as well. If we are to be honest and helpful to girls and women regarding one of the most important aspects of their adult lives, we must be open and balanced with our message. While much of what we know about women's sexuality is theory-based, it is becoming apparent that there are key differences between men and women's sexual feelings and experiences.

A major difference emerging from women's sexology research is the importance of the entire sexual event and context. Unlike women, men's sexual desire appears to center on arousal, orgasm, and release. For many young single men, sex is an event; for the majority of young single women, consensual sex is the beginning of an extended emotional experience with herself and between her and her partner.

Rethinking Female Sensuality and Sexuality

The work of Dr. Shere Hite, an international expert on human sexuality, is instructional to women of all ages, but particularly for young women whose sensual-sexual lives are beginning to bloom. Hite maintains that the female sexual nature is not the mirror image of a man's. She believes that a woman's sexual nature is more sensually based than a man's (although she is quick to qualify that statement as well due to the limited research base). She believes that women prefer, and most require, a significant amount of sensual stimulation in order to become sexually aroused to experience maximum pleasure from sexual intercourse, and to forge enduring emotional bonds with her partner.

From Hite's writing, one can see that a woman's senses—such as touch, smell, and visual beauty, to name a few—are paramount in both

Finding Center: Strategies to Reveal Strong Girls and Women

"Reflection"
Illustration by Patsy Grandberg, used with permission

their love lives in general and sex lives specifically. Many women do find great sensual satisfaction in receiving red aromatic roses from someone they find attractive on two levels: the pure sensuality of experiencing the rose and the possibility of emotional arousal and attachment to the person sending them if the woman finds the man and relationship desirable. A man may not understand why receiving a fresh flower means a lot to a woman. It is costly to him and from his point of view, the flowers expire in about seven days, so how cost effective is a gift that dies in a week? But that is just the point for a woman. The gift of flowers is that much more precious as she learns to appreciate, with each sensual provocative gift, that the experience is intense, short-lived and reaches its peak and then goes away. It is precisely that it is in short supply, yet intensely sensual, that most woman love sensually oriented gifts.

Shere Hite encourages men to rethink "their idea of sex and to incorporate much more of this sensuality." And she challenges women to re-define their sexuality and make changes in how they see and practice intimate physical relations as well as how they express and share their bodies.

> "Though the choices are theirs, really theirs, it can still take some time to wake up and see that one is free, in charge of one's life, that all decisions are possible; like sleeping beauty waking up, after

> 2,000 years of misinformation women need a little time to begin thinking clearly. Unfortunately, women are currently encouraged to be 'active' in 'male copycat ways', not in their own new way."
>
> Shere Hite
> "What is a Woman's Sexual Nature?" 2005

Healthy sexual expression, as demonstrated in a growing multitude of research, impacts women's overall quality of life. Women's sexual desire may increase dramatically when they have periods of increased well-being as documented in studies. In addition, many women and men show increased personal happiness when they are sexually active. In addition to overall quality of life and happiness levels, studies conducted with women of various ages have confirmed that positive sexual expression and activity has been shown to reduce stress and lower anxiety due to the surge in oxytocin in the brain following orgasm. Positive sexual activity and orgasm can also enhance female self-esteem and promote bonding and greater relational and sexual satisfaction.

Recent studies have also demonstrated that the expression of sexual feelings in a positive manner is an important ingredient in pair-bonding and attachment and has been demonstrated to be important to a couple's bond to one another. Pre-coital sex play under the age of fifteen in the form of masturbation may be a factor in the development of long-term relationships. Not only can masturbation impact individual sexual release and satisfaction, it may also be associated with improved relationship satisfaction as well.

Finally, the majority of religious traditions include positive messages about the relationship between sexuality, sexual expression, and the potential connection to spiritual development and enlightenment. A study in which over 3,000 people participated (conducted by Gina Ogden) revealed that those who indicated that they connected their sexual experiences with their spiritual lives were more likely to engage in better relationships overall and experience more positive lives.

Positive Context for Expressing Sensual and Sexual Energy

I agree with Mary Pipher that it is the responsibility of each girl and woman to come to terms with her own sexuality and to define a sexual self. She must learn how to make sexual choices and to determine how she enjoys sex. However, in order to enjoy sex, a girl must hear sex presented in a positive context and not just exclusively as something that can cause harm, lead to bad outcomes, or something that will cause her abuse or violence. Rather than focusing on sex as the first step, I believe we should put the focus on what is essential and most natural to human survival. We need to explore our sensory system and develop it as a strong vehicle for respecting oneself and others. By doing this, we can appreciate how a fully engaged sensory system can contribute to our health and to our sense of well-being and happiness.

Sensuality involves being open to our energy force. Women who are in touch with their bodies and their life energy force understand the importance of developing and regulating touch, breathing, movement, visual sensations, and emotion such as happiness, anxiety, and emotional pain. Without effective sensory tools, a girl or woman may find that she is exposing herself to experiences and situations, if left unchecked by her, will result in emotional and physical pain and trauma. When sensual awareness and growth is inhibited or stunted in girls and women, they may grow up to lack the openness, tenderness, and love skills to maintain effective relationship and intimate bonds when they want to. Without the encouragement by parents, female mentors, and teachers to develop sensual experiences, girls and women are left on their own to cope with a negative, restricted cultural message of female sexuality. Overprotective parents and sexual demands, both in aggressive and passive forms, all contribute to the problem. It is imperative for girls and women to experience a variety of sensory life force experiences in order to develop strong, empathetic, sensory communication systems of their own.

Recall those times in life when you have felt free, happy, and perfectly in tune with your life energy force. Think back to where you were, what you were doing, and describe the setting using as many details as you possibly can. Did the experience involve the energies found in the out of doors, the wind, heat from the sun, the pounding of waves of water? Perhaps your experience required you to push the muscles in your legs in order to conquer the snow in skis. Or you may have pushed your leg muscles to stretch out over an iced lake as you alternated between riding a sleigh pulled by a team of sled dogs or walking alongside of them. These are sensual, active experiences that stimulate both the brain and the body by providing challenge, strength building and focused attention to the sensory stimulus of the setting—the descending sun over a lake replete in its dramatic display of hot colors and the warmth it causes on the observers skin, or the same sun descending this time over a frozen, barren lake. However, this time, the sunset helps the observer to push on to the journey's end despite the icy coldness of her face, hands, and feet.

Perhaps the biggest cause of the depletion and weakening of all of our sensory systems, girls and boys, men and women alike, is that we have become a world of "sitters." Many people prefer to be passively entertained in such ways that most of our sensory system is either turned entirely off or we choose to watch images of trauma, violence, or those sensory images that are dull and flat. As a result the very tools which are hardwired in our brains and extend to every cellular systems—be it muscle mass or the visual sensory system, to name just a few of hundreds we all possess—become undeveloped at the very least or damaged and destroyed if accompanied by other poor choices.

Sensory Building for Confidence and Pleasure

Two of the most powerful senses we have are that of touch and movement. When combined, as in dance, running, equestrianship, or biking, they are powerful. Touch and movement-oriented arts, sports, or hobbies provide opportunities for a girl or woman to connect the activity with her own body, thus building body awareness and personal confidence. For example, in the process of acquiring skills in the art of equestrianship, a girl must build a relationship with a horse and learn how to communicate with it in order to make progress both in the care of the animal and in riding, jumping, or competing. She learns that she can ask her body—through the manipulation of her leg muscles, the position of her body in the saddle, and the rhythm of her pelvis in her sitting position—to communicate with her horse whether she wants to run, stop, or jump. In the process, she increases her body strength and learns to communicate with herself and her body by using few if any words. Over time, she grows confident in her abilities to care for herself, her horse, and to control both herself and her horse in riding, jumping, or equestrian competitions. It takes just a few months of regular training before her body begins to look forward to the exercise and the sensual experience just for the pleasure of the physical expression in its own right. It is at this point that the experience has been integrated by her brain and its sophisticated network into her pleasure system. She bonds with her horse, her trainer, and other riders she has associated—she has grown part of her individual identity. The same analysis I have applied to equestrian training can be brought to any touch-movement activity, especially when a girl or woman participates in it over time.

The visual sensory system, when combined with the olfactory sense of smell, is also a potent duo. Activities that stimulate these senses include gardening, artistry, and outdoor adventures such as fishing, hunting, and sailing. Each of these activities requires the use and development of the eyes, visual imagery, and visual-motor skills combined with the scent of the natural world in its entire splendor. Almost nothing can be more sensual.

When one compares sensual action-oriented activities with visual choices such as watching teen images on television, paging through teen magazines, imitating the looks of teen models, fixating on being rail-thin or purging as a weight control or weight loss method, it may be seen that part of the formula for developing positive sensuality is turning off media and turning toward action-oriented alternatives. Girls and women of all ages desire experiences that offer them both pleasure and release from the daily stressors of life and/or sexual tension. They long for experiences that will satisfy skin and body touch. It is important, however, to focus on positive ones.

POSITIVE SENSUAL EXPERIENCES FOR GIRLS AND WOMEN

Take warm bubbly baths

Self-massage

Walk in the moonlight

Walk at sunrise

Dance at dawn; at sunset

Dance in long flowing clothes

Drink scented teas in lovely cups and teapots

Burn scented candles while bathing

Burn a scented candle as ritual morning greeting to self

Play Celtic music, chants or instrumentals

Give yourself a thorough foot massage and pedicure

Paint your fingernails and toenails

Force tulips and daffodils to bloom inside

Sleep outdoors under the night air

Sing and dance with your girlfriends

Spend a weekend of solitude at home in a completely silent house and state of being

Play yourself to sleep with lullaby music

Stay in bed a full day in a nest of blankets, books and music

---

Healthy Sexual Expression

An article in *The Sydney Morning Herald*, an Australian newspaper, in August 2003, described a product developed and offered by a company in the United States. The product's purpose was to help parents detect the presence of semen in their daughters' underwear. The article triggered a whirlwind of attention from national media on the topic of teenage sex. Dr. Melissa Kang, a specialist in adolescent medicine at Sydney's New Children's Hospital and a lecturer in the Faculty of Medicine at the University of Sydney, mused, "How I long for a positive, innovative and thoughtful approach to teenage sexuality. And why is it the girls who get all the airplay—so often portrayed as either a bit too promiscuous, or as victims at the mercy of amoral, insensitive teenage boys?" Dr. Kang's position is that we are all sexual beings, including adolescents and young adults. The issue is not what young people should or should not be doing but rather as a culture and caring individuals in young women's lives, we need to see them for who they are. Yes, they are young, and still maturing, Kang states, and some will have more positive experiences than others as they grow and mature. "Though if we're talking sexual trauma, it is often at the hands of adults," Dr. Kang clarifies. She advises us that focusing only on the mechanics and pitfalls of sex is telling just half of the story and omitting the lovely mystery of sex and its equally important spheres of self-esteem, love, desire, intimacy and sharing. Kang reminds us that none of us wants our daughters to experience an unwanted pregnancy, a sexually transmitted disease or to be exploited, abused, or raped. However, Kang instructs us to remember that:

> "All the research suggests that girls who delay intercourse, or have sex safely, are those who are well informed, well supported by adults, have close relationships with a parent, and can access appropriate services. So why, then, the interest in surveillance (particularly in secret!), prohibition, or simply denial of a very normal aspect of growing up? Perpetrators of sexual abuse and assault among children and young people are most often adults who are known and once-trusted—if protection from serious harm is our motivation, why isn't more of our attention turned to this?"
> Dr. Melissa Kang, The National Forum,
> e-journal ON LINE opinion

Female Initiation Ceremony

In a class I teach which focuses on girls and women in the United States, a non-traditional woman majoring in nursing shared with the class her family tradition of celebrating a young woman's coming of age. She said that it was a family tradition that the grown women in the family would plan an event to celebrate each young woman as she crossed the threshold of girlhood to young woman signaled by the beginning of her first menstrual cycle. The older women would bring both the women and girls together to celebrate, much like a birthday. They would serve food, light candles and each woman would share her own story of growing up and offer insights into her own process. She said a major purpose of the celebration was to reinforce both the circle of life and a female circle of support and community. Each girl in the family participates in an older girl's initiation ceremony and eagerly awaits her own when the onset of her monthly cycle begins, thus making the transition one to look forward to and celebrate rather anticipate with a sense of dread and embarrassment.

For those interested in designing your own coming-of-age ritual for young women in your family, The Rites of Passage Institute suggests that the ceremony focus on a holistic vision of the girl to woman growth and that it not focus entirely on menses. A female initiation ceremony becomes an event all invited members look forward to when it includes some of these spiritual and community ingredients:

ACTIVITIES TO INCLUDE FOR A GIRLS' COMING-OF-AGE RITUAL
- Contact with the natural environment—a day or more spent in nature
- Ordeal—a test of strength, self-discipline, all night vigil
- Solitude—withdrawal from the pressures of life, reflection
- Public recognition—a ceremony of female members to acknowledge transition
- Symbolic representation—an object that symbolizes the girl's new status in her female circle

Recognizing Redirecting and Releasing Sexual Energy

Female sexual energy and its corresponding drive is as much within the control of the individual as is the occurrence of a first menstrual cycle or the budding of nipples into full, soft breasts. Sexual energy and sex drive is a part of the life force exerting its dominance. It sets off an explosion of activity, feelings, and distractions. One of the best descriptions of the arrival of sexual energy is found on *clitoris.net*. This version is condensed from the full description.

> "Suddenly, their body has a mind of its own. While sitting in school, at work, and in the middle of the night while they sleep, their body may explode with desire. Their vulva and vagina suddenly come alive and make themselves known. They are full of boundless energy and excitement. Sexual thoughts and images become over powering."

Few people would be surprised if this description was about boy's sexual experience during adolescent and post adolescence. Many still find it hard to believe that girls and women experience the same intense surge of sexual energy. While it may be true that a female's sexual drive may not be as strong and continual as it is in the early adolescent male, it is real and it is powerful. Adolescent and post adolescent female energy and urges and the resulting pleasure when expressed through release and orgasm are very important in a woman's life. It is extremely important that girls and women see female energy and their need for release and orgasm as a celebratory part of female life.

For many girls and women, sexual urges are successfully managed by expressing the sensual side of themselves as previously discussed. For others, sublimating the energy into another part of their life, such as any number of performance activities, redirecting the energy to accomplish other goals, such as schooling or work and careers, are all effective. However, as is the case with boys and men, girls and women can express sexual urges and learn how their own bodies can provide sexual pleasure through practicing masturbation or self-pleasuring; that is, stimulating one's genitals, or other erogenous zones, so as to express pleasure.

Self-pleasuring is extremely common among women and most discover it on their own at very early ages. Sex researchers maintain that most women masturbate without needing to be told how and most begin before they are sexually intimate with partners. Other writers encourage self-pleasuring citing the benefits of the release of sexual tension and the release of brain endorphins which elicit a sense of well-being and relaxation. But just as important is the knowledge that the more orgasms a woman has, the more easily and frequently she will have them, and this strong response can be carried throughout her lifetime. In addition to building a strong sexual response repertoire, regular masturbation/self-pleasuring helps a woman learn what she likes, what feels good and, just as important, what she does not like or want. Many young women today still turn over the decision as to when they have sexual intercourse for the first time to boys and young men who talk them into it in order to meet their needs. A girl or woman would have much to gain by taking responsibility for exploring her own sexuality and finding ways to experience her sexuality alone, and on her own terms, rather than turning over her sexuality to another.

Chapter 8
Women as Assets

"People think at the end of the day that a man is the only answer [to fulfillment]: Actually a job is better for me."
PRINCESS DIANA

Though *Pretty Woman,* the film starring Julia Roberts, earned an R rating, many teenage girls paid full price to see the movie voluminous times. It was a new plot with the old Cinderella story line. But this time Cinderella, whose name in this movie is Vivian, is a prostitute working the streets of Los Angles when Richard Gere's character, a rich, successful corporate raider visiting the city, "rescues" her to be his paid escort. The film grossed over 178 million dollars. In the film's opening, Roberts' body is stunning but sleazily dressed. Then Gere decides to transform her into his princess. Of course, since this is cinema rather than reality, the audience is never let in on how he plans to integrate a high school dropout hooker into his upper-crust life.

In one scene embedded in my memory, Vivian is attempting to earn her keep by making sexual moves on Gere. She asks him which color and flavor condom he would like her to put on him. While the viewer does not see Vivian perform oral sex, you get the picture that the act is consummated—that she performs and he receives. After all, she is a prostitute. Since many teenagers long to (and do in some cases) attempt to emulate screen and music idols, one could ask if films like *Pretty Woman* inspire middle-level girls to engage in oral sex in their school buildings, on their school buses, and at preteen and teen parties. After all, it worked for Julia as Vivian, and didn't she look great!
Adopting this train of thought to the film's negative effects on girls, The National Coalition of Girls' School writes, "It's a standard fairy-tale

scenario: The damsel in distress is rescued by a knight in shining armor. That's fine for childhood storytelling, but in the 21st century, financial literacy is a much better means of achieving a happily-ever-after ending. If she had her own money, Cinderella wouldn't have been sweeping floors, and she would have bought her own shoes." Films such as *Pretty Woman* offer flip but ultimately poor role models for young girls.

Some young women need not work at all but can live a version of the princess lifestyle. In recalling the life of Princess Diana in his article, "Now I am convinced. The monarchy is finished. Let them all rest in peace." (*New Statesman*), Peter Wilby acknowledges he has a hard time working up much empathy for a woman born to wealth and privilege that never had to worry about how to feed her children and whose public image was way out of balance with any talent she possessed. Yet, as hard as it is for him to credit her with anything, he does admit that Diana became a force for public enlightenment and social tolerance that set new standards that were unattainable by others. "She achieved her special place in public life," he writes, "only by breaking the royal rules, by stripping away the magic and mystery." Princess Diana destroyed the royal magic and replaced it with her own sense of glamour and style while becoming an international leader for her charity work. She brought light and compassion on issues such as AIDS, land mines, and the homeless. She obtained both personal power and political influence when she traded her tiara for a protective uniform and gear used by men in removing undetonated land mines. Before World War I just 11,000 families owned three quarters of all the land in Great Britain and Ireland. For those few women who either were born or married into the landed elite of England, life was a matter of marriage-brokering and keeping powerful landed families to themselves. Female members of this privileged society played a vital role and worked hard to maintain the family's power and influence. Historian Gerda Lerner expresses herself well when she wrote that "as members of families, as daughters and wives," patrician women were often "closer to actual power than many a man" meaning, of course, the ordinary man. Titled women, whether they were a baroness, viscountess, lady, duchess, countess or marchioness, were responsible for planning the events of high society. Even though the gatherings were most definitely arranged by and with women's society in mind, high-society functions operated as political events of a kind.

Linda Colley tells the story of Elizabeth Vassall, a beautiful and intelligent woman who in 1797 deserted her first husband to marry Henry Richard Fox, Lord Holland. She was initially excluded from other wealthy female members of society because she was a divorcée. Every week until her husband's death she entertained at least fifty guests—politicians, ambassadors, and literary figures of the time. Her home became the unofficial center of intelligence and the lavish meeting place of Britain's Whig Party, which, in turn, benefited Lord Holland. Being able to advance men's careers gave elite women considerable power and influence of their own.

However, such women's usefulness was strictly determined by their husbands' needs, wishes, and often whims. They were subordinate creatures to their husbands' power and ambition. While women who played significant roles to male politicians could use their positions to obtain power and influence of their own, in the end, wealthy women and men's lives were conducted in two different spheres of influence. Men played in the corridor of politics by participation in the British House of Commons, and later in the United States House of Representatives. Women did not.

Today, while women in America, for instance, earned the right to vote in 1920, very few women own the right to take their elected seats in either of these houses of Congress as elected representatives. Women continue to live on the margin or be excluded from having their interests represented until they play their own parts in the political arena. Ultimately, this means women must learn to take risks and learn the rules of the game, both financial and political.

The American Dream for Girls and Women

Most people see the United States as a special place where there is plenty of opportunity for someone to work hard, play by the rules, and get ahead—maybe even become wealthy. Today, though, nearly one in five American households have zero net worth or actually owe more than it owns. And the odds of a son or daughter rising above their parents in such a financial predicament have shrunk." David Francis warned the public in May of 2005 in his essay for *The Christian Science Monitor* that the American dream may be more of a dream mythology than reality. When describing financial security, Francis reveals that one in four households cannot hold off a three-month earning shortage and that women's household net worth is less than forty cents to every dollar of a man's. He supports the argument that our current financial difficulties are not due to shopping sprees and irresponsible spending habits, but more often are created when families experience unexpected medical bills, household expenses, or unemployment.

During the past twenty years, American society has made substantial gains in women's participation in the workforce and in the reductions of gender stereotyping in both schooling and employment. While the pace may be more accurately described as a slow crawl, women have also made inroads into those occupations that have been the exclusive terrain of men.

While women around the world have made economic and educational strides, in many countries they have been left out or have found themselves outside of the solid economic mainstream. The loss of a job, the birth of an ill baby, or a divorce—all extremely common events in the fabric of modern life—can drop a woman from the middle rung of the middle class ladder to a free fall in terms of economics. Women, like men, have common needs and these needs cost money. The culmination of assets is the means by which both men and women meet those needs. Both males and females, independent from one another, require the growth of certain assets over their lifetimes:

ASSETS FOR FEMALE ECONOMIC WELL-BEING

- Earnings to sustain growth during a working lifetime
- Knowledge and skills to enhance those earnings
- Physical and mental health to fully use knowledge, skills, and other capacities, pensions for support in retirement
- Insurance or other protection against risks—unemployment, illness, disability
- Financial resources to complement and enhance all of the former
- Networks of personal, community, and professional connection, and
- Community-based infrastructure of resources and services

Asset Development Institute, Brandeis University

Female asset development is directly tied to living out the values of a modern democratic society. It is hard to vision a life for our daughters, granddaughters or ourselves that does not include women having the same rights as men to build strong futures for themselves, on their own. Secure women require, not "may like to if they want," the traits we will next discuss during the various stages of their lifetimes.

First they need opportunity. Every young woman has her own right to choose what the good life is for her and to construct a plan that when steadily worked over a lifetime, provides her opportunities to grow and develop. A flexible plan accompanied with genuine life skills will help her to cope with inevitable changes, to make choices, such as having a family or to sustain her during serious challenges, such as recovering from illness.

> Female "assets are what women need to make choices about their lives; what they need to succeed in the choices that they make. When we possess assets, the future holds promise; there is reason to hope and strive for a better life."
>
> The Asset Index

Secondly, attaining a female dream requires fairness. Girls and women should be pushed to take part in creating financial skills of their own and having their voices heard regarding the very issues that are critical to their well-being. This certainly includes being active players in the representative government, be it local, state, or national, where they can help shape policies that directly impact their lives.

To dream is easy. To build a secure future requires personal and social responsibility. It is not truthful to tell girls and women that they do not have to take initiative in assuring that their basic needs will be met. Each girl and woman must hold herself accountable in doing as much as she can toward creating the life that she imagines for herself on the one hand, and at least maintaining a life that includes safety, security, and a social fabric on the other. Women, who develop their capabilities to a higher level by taking more risks and making more sacrifices, should reap the financial benefits we have come to expect from men who do the same. To pay women eighty cents on the dollar is unacceptable. What can women do about current wage and institutional practices held in place by gender bias and discrimination? What would happen if every woman now earning her living, for instance, as a waitress in the food industry stopped working for thirty days? Answer: First, a lot of name calling followed by higher wages!

The Women's Report Card

She has made considerable progress . . .

- ✓ The poverty level for women fell in all but eight states.
- ✓ She received expanded parental leave insurance in twenty states.
- ✓ Her wage ratio, as compared to men's, rose in all but four states.
- ✓ She receives nearly wage equality with men in Washington, D.C.
- ✓ She has laws mandating health insurance coverage for contraception in about 20 states.

She is still failing . . .

- ✓ As a single woman, she has half the net worth of a single man.
- ✓ As a retired woman, 75% of her constituency depends on Social Security for most of their income.
- ✓ She still works in pink collar jobs that offer low wages and no/little benefits.
- ✓ She is discriminated against in pay as employer's still base wages upon their biases views of acceptable working roles for men and women.
- ✓ She still believes that her partner will support her in retirement in return for sacrifices she made in raising their children.
- ✓ She stills believes she will have a choice as to whether or not she will have to work for pay.
- ✓ She is still being told by society that she cannot have a career that holds power and influence.
- ✓ She experiences substantial earnings and wage gaps compared to men in two-thirds of the states in the U.S.

Using a more sophisticated strategy, girls and woman require increased information and encouragement to enter those careers and professions where their hard work, training, and dedication will reap substantial higher earnings than those jobs and careers where women have super-glued themselves. It is time to coach our girls and young women the same way we coach our boys and young men. One day not long ago I struck up a conversation with a young woman teller at my local bank (the only gender of teller found in the bank). She told me she would be taking classes beginning in one week at our local technical college. I said I assumed it was in the area of banking, but she corrected me and said it was in cosmetology and barbering. I responded by encouraging her to explore the financial difference in moving up the ranks in the financial industry as opposed to starting at step one in the grooming industry. She replied by stating a stereotypical female view—that she was really interested in cosmetology. I encouraged her to consider owning her own salon eventually because after ten years at work, work is still work and you really want to be earning some substantial financial rewards as well. It is surprising how a good paycheck can alter how much you like a particular career choice. She said she would consider my view, but as I walked away I knew this was doubtful. We must start to teach young women at a very young age and to continue imparting such knowledge as they conceive and educate themselves for careers to "paint a larger canvas." Otherwise, like the young woman at the bank, they will choose traditional women-geared careers and not compete or earn the rewards of big business and politics.

Building an Asset-Rich Female Kingdom

Why do so many women fight against the obvious fact that girls and women must be raised in these times to take care of themselves for their entire lives? I believe that many women find that this statement devalues females. It is necessary to question whether we are giving something up acknowledging that we no longer expect men to take care of us as they did in our mothers' and grandmothers' generations. In my case I never found the image of me having a one dimensional life that attractive—that my time would be spent playing one character in one limited role and setting all of my life. Growing up motherless and seeing my family of origin torn apart provided me with a deeply entrenched life lesson. I learned I would be responsible for my own happiness or the lack of it.

Like it or not, the first step in adequately preparing all women and men for stable yet flexible futures is to live in today not yesterday, or worse, in a day that never was. If we resist giving into disappointment and change, we can create a life that is beyond what a fantasy life could ever bring. As grown women and men, we must extend more effort at encouraging and coaching girls and women to push themselves to be their best selves as suggested in Madonna's song rather than rehearse the tired excuses used to keep women dependent and at the bottom rung of the economic ladder.

In "*Push*" by Madonna, the lyrics state:

> "You push me to go the extra mile
> You push me when it's difficult to smile
> You push me a better vision of myself
> You push me only you and no one else."

Women's Choices Matter

Depending upon the voices of her parents and her teachers, a girl will believe in herself and the endless possibilities so she can achieve or she will be plied down to accept that her purpose is to help others reach theirs.

In America, during wartime, the population needed to believe in the possibilities of women and their contributions to the economy, national leaders used government resources to get the word out that women were needed, able and ready to build planes, "man" the manufacturing plants and run hospitals. They did just that. Yet, when men returned from battle, a similar campaign was launched to dismiss the women from the workplace either politely, or not too politely if they resisted, and to tell them "thank you very much, but your talents and commitment are no longer needed." After the war women in many occupations were instructed to go home, turn over their jobs to the men, and assume their "proper" role robed in dresses and aprons. Their instrumental function at that point was producing babies and making the men in their lives happy, and if they did not have a man, then by all means they needed to get one.

While women had finally won the vote, former suffragists morphed into peace activists and antiwar demonstrators during the Korean and Vietnam conflicts. Men who were for whatever reasons having trouble finding work felt that they were more deserving of jobs than well-qualified women were, and overall, the male establishment agreed. Women in the workplace were evaluated using different standards and paid less. Most received treatment that was one part condescension, one part hostility, and a third part harassment. That is, unless they accepted their proper workplace roles: secretary, nurse, or teacher.

Sally Gregory Kohlstedt, a University of Minnesota expert on science in American culture, cautions us that while "history is not tidy, it is useful to know. Moreover, history . . . makes it clear that there is no guarantee of progress or even stability in the gains made in policy and practice" with respect to the gains of women in science careers or in the workplace for that matter. She goes on to explain that "history has taught me, at least, to modify any undue pride about my achievement and to mitigate any self-blame for failures that were structural and not personal." Yet, she insists that women must support and direct younger women if they are to sustain the gains made by the women of previous generations. The first responsibility all women and men have is to tell girls and women the truth about what the economic nature of a woman's life is today and the path to building a secure and happy life.

So let's do that: get at the truth. Truth number one: "She" has to help herself. No rescues allowed. As women and men who have stable and secure lives, we can and must help our girls and women by helping them to set goals and supporting them as they go. We can't do it for them and we can't take away meaningful life lessons by providing for her in the same way that was done when she was a child—paying her full bill while she spends her earnings on fluff.

Truth number two: Women who work full-time earn more security. They are paid more and receive full benefits. They are taken more seriously and receive more opportunities for advancement. Full-time women workers have more support services to assist them in their work and have access to free training in their fields. They are more successful in moving up the occupational ladder as they establish relationships and credibility with their supervisors. They have made the necessary sacrifices and adjustments in their personal and family lives (less social time with peers) and may be recognized for this in the workplace.

Truth number three: Women should limit their work in all women service occupations such as waitressing, retail work, and low-ladder health care. If you decide to work in these jobs, set temporary goals such as, "I will waitress only while completing my associate degree in business." Avoid the traps of staying too long in these low-paying jobs with no benefits, where everyone is your boss but you.

Truth number four: Education counts. The U.S. Department of Labor Women's Bureau's report advises that more education translates into lower unemployment. Women with less than a high school diploma have a ten percent chance of unemployment; with a high school diploma that rate drops to five percent; some college the rate drops further. The lowest unemployment rate is among those with a college education—2.7 percent.

Truth number five: Women can balance work and family life. Working will not make you a bad mother and ruin your children. To opt out of the workplace or to change goals in college (as I reported in a previous chapter) because a young woman sees working and having a family as an either/or deal is baseless thinking. Finding balance is a challenge all women face whether they work outside of the home or not. Women carry the bulk of parenting for the young and the not-so-young and perform most of the routine and constant tasks required to maintain the care of a family and a home (preparation of meals, laundry, bill payment, supervising children, playing with children to, name a few of the hundreds on this list). The problem is not whether a woman can find a balance in her already complex life as much as it is getting the other partner in the mix to assume a balanced role.

Truth number six: Girls and women are assets over lifetimes and should view their private lives as their own businesses. By learning fundamental principles, such as pay yourself first and invest in your training and education, a girl or woman can shape a sense of vision and control over her own destiny. Financial management skills should be as important to teach and integrate into girls' lives as watching baby brothers or learning how to prepare breakfast. Seeing a woman's life as growing equity over time is the first step. Young women need hands-on experiences to start and grow a business of their own. If mothers and fathers have reasonable comfort with seeing their young daughters go into other adult's homes to provide care for their children (babysitting), it should be as easy to encourage these young women to deliver services or prepare products of their own. By practicing start-up small business skills when young, girls will be increasingly comfortable in shaping future ideas for business as young adults.

Women who are either employed part-time or are full-time mothers are also prime candidates for building small home-centered businesses. I have caught myself saying and have heard countless other working women remark that what they really need is a wife. For internet savvy women, there are numerous support services such as Home Based Working Moms (*http://www.hbwm.com/*) ready to assist creative women. Full-time at-home mothers can add substantially to their families' incomes as well as acquire skills, knowledge, and experience that will translate to employment in the workplace if and when they choose to enter the business world in the traditional sense. While women recognize that staying at home with children is as much of a choice as is working outside of the home with children, so is working from a home business an increasingly wise and profitable option for many women.

Truth number seven: Sell the hard stuff. Women are great talkers and even better at analyzing the details of topics. Combined with sound interpersonal skills, it is no wonder why they are comfortable and successful in retail sales. Retail sales yield poor pay and few if any benefits, while selling automobiles, machines, health care products and home housing materials is lucrative. While the number of women selling automobiles has increased over the years, few women when compared to the total number of women who work as sales persons sell the hard stuff. Women who do sell cars do incredibly well, especially when you consider how the demand for new cars by women consumers has increased. How difficult was it for these women car sales people to learn the vocabulary of the trade or the nuances of the car business? Not difficult at all, particularly when you consider that most men do not know that much about the workings of a car nor do they do their own car repairs. The most challenging part for women selling the hard stuff is getting the notion firmly entrenched into their psyches that they should and can sell such commodities as easily as they can sell women's underwear and dresses.

Truth number eight: Negotiate and get it in writing. If a man stays at home and takes care of the children while the woman works full time for pay, how will the man's contribution be taken into account? If a couple is marrying for the first time, how will each know what the debt load is of his or her partner and what expectations each has in assuming responsibility as a married couple in paying down both individually acquired debt and couple debt? How will the costs be distributed when a husband pays for the family health premium as part of his payroll deduction while the wife does not have any such costs?

Today, if two individuals are forming a legal partnership, e.g., marriage, the details of how the marriage will play out financially should be discussed, negotiated, and spelled out in writing. Call the document what you like—a premarital agreement, a yearly marriage fiscal plan, or the goals for the financial growth of our marriage. If a woman believes that she can expect her partner to pick up all of her bills accumulated before their marriage, and expect her spouse to sign on to a "pay for her as we go" basis, that woman is looking for a partner who will keep her dependent and child-like. It is important to talk, negotiate, and write it down.

Truth number nine: Girls and women are of equal value as human capital. Traditionally, economic policies were crafted with the eye on investing and protecting working men and their families whether the policy was Social Security, the GI Bill, the Homestead Act, or employment-based health insurance and unemployment. The society that both men and women live in today is light years away from the world of their parents and grandparents. Yet much of the mindset and most of the policies have not changed to address the changing nature of the workplace, families, and all of our obligations tied to the care and nurturing of our young children and to the largest generation of aging adults in American history. Girls and women have both the right and the responsibility to develop their human capital—the cash income and benefits gained from their individual skills, knowledge, and experience. Human capital is acquired over a lifetime. Every girl and woman needs to be told a positive story about the life that waits for her by making choices that are commiserate with her potential.

Truth number ten: Activism matters. Many women have moved away from the activist roles of their mothers' and grandmothers' generation believing that most of this work has been successfully completed. Among nontraditional and traditional women alike, many shun the feminist or women's liberation connotation believing that it will hurt more than help in both the labor and love market. In truth, at the end of the twentieth century, women's value, economic, social and emotional net worth is at best eighty percent and, at worst, twenty percent of men's. Experienced professional women, be it in traditional careers such as teaching or nontraditional domains such as engineering, are still not represented proportionately at the upper ranks of their professions and are paid two-thirds of what men make. For women who work within the home and outside in occupations and jobs that are at the lower tier of the economic ladder, their fate has become much worse than women in similar lifestyles just ten years ago. For those women, the changing policies with respect to benefits, divorce, unemployment compensation, and lack of health benefits have all combined to put them and, in many cases, their children at serious risk.

GENDER DIFFERENCES IN EMPLOYMENT

1. Gender segregation has replaced gender exclusion. Women workers now land the lowest paying jobs disproportionate to their numbers in the workforce.
2. The retail sales industry is one of the lowest paying and fastest growing industries in the U.S. today. Eighty percent of cashiers are women earning an average $6.29 per hour, usually with no health insurance or pension benefits.
3. The retail industry is the largest employer of part-time work in the U.S.
4. Employers in retail prefer part-time workers because compensation is low and hours can be increased without paying overtime and benefits.
5. Women and men still tend to be concentrated in different occupations. Women are overrepresented in clerical and services. Men are disproportionately employed in craft, operator and laborer jobs.
6. Ninety three percent of registered nurses and eighty-four percent of elementary teachers employed in 1995 were women.
7. Three of every ten computer systems analysts and scientists and less than one of ten employed engineers were women. Six percent of construction inspectors were women.
8. Women accounted for one of every two sales employees. They made up eighty-three percent of apparel sales but just thirty-one percent of employees selling securities and financial services.
9. In general, the higher the level of education, the smaller the occupational difference between the sexes.
10. In 1985, forty eight percent of women were in female dominated occupations. In 1995, thirty eight percent were. Five percent of women worked in male jobs in 1985 and four percent of women worked in male occupations in 1995.

Based on *"Gender Differences in Occupational Employment,"* Monthly Labor Review

Jobs Most in Demand

US Jobs Most in Demand	Industries with Fastest Employment Growth	Fastest Growing Occupations for College Graduates
Automotive	Software Publishers	Network Systems and Data Analysts
Advanced Manufacturing	Management, Scientific, and Technical Consulting	Physician Assistants
Biotechnology	Computer Systems Design	Medical Records and Health Technicians
Construction	Employment Services	Computer Software Engineers, Applications
Energy	Rehabilitation Services	Computer Software Engineers; Systems Software
Financial Services	Ambulatory Health Care Services	Physical Therapist Assistants
Geospatial	Internet Services	Fitness Trainers
Health Care	Water, Sewage Systems	Database Administrators
Hospitality	Child Day Care Services	Veterinary Technologists-Technicians
Information Technology		
Retail		
Transportation		

Source: workforce3one.org

The Influence of a Determined Woman

Joline Godfrey believes girls can manifest their character and their dreams by being smart with money. She created Independent Means Inc., an education and training company targeted to girls. Her mission is to get parents, teachers, and adults of youth organizations to rethink the way they engage girls in looking at their own asset development. Godfrey and her 500 associates travel the world work to bring their message and training modules to girls of all ages. Beginning in 2004, The National Coalition of Girls' Schools teamed up with Godfrey and conducted a nationwide tour which brought literacy seminars for girls from Los Angeles to New York City and Hawaii and is still "growing strong asset knowledge." Godfrey has built a curriculum that is targeted to girls, parents, and teachers.

I interviewed Godfrey regarding the barriers that she believes continue to exist with respect to predisposing girls and women to believe they must take responsibility for their financial futures. I also asked about the reaction of parents with whom she has worked. Godfrey believes that girls and women still seem to be determined not to be financially responsible and that they are still looking to be rescued rather than doing the tough work of being self reliant. She feels there is still collusion between the culture of consumerism, advertising and quick satisfaction, and that of hard work and taking the long view. She admonishes parents for still not talking to girls about money and readily admits that there may be some class and cultural issues still present with respect to giving females specific skills in finances.

GODFREY AND INDEPENDENT MEANS INC. PRO-GIRL FINANCIAL CURRICULUM

Curriculum Strands for Students: Ten Money $ecrets Every Girl Needs to Know by Age 18

- How to save and keep track of money
- How to handle credit and live on a budget
- How to be an entrepreneur
- How to get paid what you're worth
- How to use money to change the world

Curriculum Strands for Parents: Raising Financially Fit Girls

- Guiding your daughter as she learns money skills
- The Seven Money Styles of Kids

- Activities and easy ways to heighten the financial conscious of your children
- How to shield kids from the credit card campaigns and retail advertising
- How to use financial literacy to instill solid values and goodness

For Teachers: Financial Literacy in the Liberal Arts Curriculum
- How to integrate financial literacy into existing curriculum
- How to develop oneself as a money mentor
- Hands-on activities to bring to the classroom
- Connections between financial literacy and mathematics, science, history, and the arts

Robert Kiyosaki, co-author of *Rich Dad Poor Dad* and author of *Cashflow 101*, has created a board game that teaches financial skills. While his materials are not directly targeted to children or women, he gives important information on what poor dads say to their sons and what message rich dads make sure their sons hear. It is insightful to relate these ideas to the messages girls and women have grown up hearing from their families, teachers and culture and how those same messages get played as internal dialogue in the minds of women for years to come.

Poor Dad vs. Rich Dad

Poor dad says:	*Rich dad says:*
My house is an asset.	My house is a liability.
I can't afford it.	How can I afford it?
The reason I'm not rich is because I have kids.	I must be rich because I have kids.
I'm not interested in money.	Money is power.
Play it safe with money.	Learn how to manage risk.
Pay myself last.	Pay myself first.

Source: *Rich Dad, Poor Dad* by Robert Kiyosaki

Dependent Girl vs. Independent Girl

Dependent girl says:	*Independent girl says:*
Girls do not need to get good at math.	Play math games.
Ask someone what to do.	What do you think is the best thing to do?
Do something that you know how to do.	Try something new; it will be fun!
Ask a boy to do that for you.	You will have to do that yourself.
Your husband will bring in most of the money.	You will need to support yourself and your family.
Your value is based upon others.	You are valuable.
If it's hard or if you don't like it, quit!	New things take time to learn and to like. Try again tomorrow.
Nice.	Thanks for carrying those groceries in the house for me. I needed the help today.

Rich Dad and Independent Girl scripts are far more constructive and positive than are Poor Dad and Dependent Girl. While it is obvious that providing girls and women with accurate financial messages and skills by which to guide their lives is essential, those with the most financial assets may have more to lose if all women engaged in financial restraint and conservatism. Those at the top tier of the money chain have also found Godfrey and her curriculum to be valuable tools.

With increasing resources for parents such *as Jump Start Financial Smarts for Kids* (jumpstart.org/search.cfm), and a host of other programs offered by public television and local financial institutions all over the country, making both girls and boys money-smart is an attainable goal. The question that begs asking is: Why are schools lagging behind in offering serious and usable skills and information to all children concerning money as a life tool and the management of earnings and finances over a lifetime? Not long ago I asked this very question to a state department of education representative in my state. The answer was intriguing. School boards who control "controversial" curriculum may find that it is not in every business person's best interest to provide an equal playing field when it comes to securing the best credit loan rate, in paying wages that reflect equity, or any host of other issues that may lead to more progressive business and employment practices.

Godfrey maintains that schools have been preoccupied with the standards-driven curriculum dictated by the state and federal government, and that teachers are simply overwhelmed with all the expectations placed upon them while their schools face cuts to fund innovation. Furthermore, she believes that there is also the matter of financial literacy for teachers. Many teachers lack basic confidence, skills, and abilities in this area as well. However, by providing the same financial knowledge playground to all students regardless of whether they are male or female may alter those student's decisions as consumers.

Chapter 9
New Age Schooling
with Katherine Bowman

> *"What we know about the future means that women must be prepared to become marathon runners. Life in the twenty-first century will not be simpler or less taxing. The course will be set whether a woman chooses it or not. We've got to be sure that girls are prepared for the marathon and that those who drop back to the sidelines can gather the resources to re-enter the race."*
>
> SARAH HARDER

Today there are serious challenges in creating innovative schooling for girls. In order to offer every girl and young woman a strong chance to complete the marathon race of life with choices, security, and balance, parents and teachers alike must forge more responsive schools and school curriculum.

The experience of Katie Bowman, a senior at a Midwestern college, is all too typical of young female students growing up within the American public school system. Katie is a high honors student who has received academic awards for both her writing and academic abilities. Yet, Katie maintains that her high school teachers and peers reaffirmed the sexist status quo regarding gender roles and female place. In her essay, she says,

> "I could act either as "one of the boys" or "one of the boys' girlfriends." For girls, this dangerous duality offers very little moderate gray area for self-improvement, growth motivation, and achievement. As a female student, the best and sometimes only way to achieve high levels of scholarship and personal growth in

> the current system is to subscribe to masculine and patriarchal standards—specifically, standards based on "objectivity" (if that is, indeed, definable or applicable); individual achievement; hierarchies based on student-teacher relationships, classmate relationships, and gender relationships; elitism, ego, and patriarchy (i.e. the school is a man's world). The only credible and respectable ladder to achievement for girls is one that has been constructed by a sexist, male favoring—and, therefore, a female ignoring—society. This is not to say that schools are the only sector of American society that have fallen victim to sexist, dualistic standards; indeed, schools are like other institutions—they are deeply embedded in patriarchal ideology and are merely the facilitators of a larger social illness of sexism."

Mothers' Voices

While there is no magic wand or formula to construct new age schools for girls, a strong start entails eliminating those barriers which stand in the way. In my mind, the first barrier to address is the diminished voice and influence of mothers in the formal schooling process. While I deeply believe that today's teachers are the best-prepared, most ambitious generation of teachers we have ever had, they still lack understanding of what mothers know and what mothers do in the development and day to day raising of their children.

For those of us who have been both mothers and teachers, we know the overlap that occurs between the dual roles of mothering and teaching. While we too had a wrenching feeling in our guts and tears in our eyes as we delivered our children to the schools as the law requires, we were in a better position to prepare a bridge between home and school for our children. We knew our own children the best; what drives them, what makes them insecure, and what lights up their faces. And because we are teachers, we know what questions to ask of the schools and how to connect with our children's teachers in the few moments of precious contact as we scurry them in and out of our cars, school buses, and classrooms. Whether teachers or not, as mothers, no one had to tell us that there are differences between girls and boys and how they develop and learn.

Yet, as mothers, we learned a harsh reality. We give teachers the most valuable asset we will ever have in our lives. Teachers provide very little opportunities for mothers to work side by side with them for the mutual benefit of our children.

Research conducted by Martha Whitaker and others recently described how schools still engage in the dynamics of silencing mothers. Yet it is exactly what mothers know that teachers need to hear in order to address the individual needs of girls as well as boys. We can and should encourage mothers and teachers to engage in meaningful dialogues pertaining to the realities of parenting, the realities of the classroom, and the realities of the world into which we will send both our boys and girls. There is no systematic method for teachers to hear the voices of the mothers of those children they teach. The challenge then is to include mothers as active and equal partners in the education of their children, especially girls. Working together, mothers and teachers can focus on the realities of daily life, both in the home, in school, and in the world that both mothers and teachers are preparing their children to enter.

What do mothers know that teachers need to know? In a study I conducted on teachers at one-room schools during 1880-1950, I was struck by how immensely successfully they were. The literacy and education levels of an entire American society were literally lifted by the hands of thousands of young, single women. They were high school graduates with little more than six months to a few years of training as teachers in teacher institutes located close to their hometowns. Most of these young women lived at home with their families prior to assuming their roles in their own rural one-room schools. Yet, the results they achieved were no less than miraculous. They took a mix of students from homes where most parents had little to no formal education at all and where students were as diverse as many of those we teach now. They single-handedly, one female teacher at a time, taught a generation of children to read, write, and compute at rates that some teachers today could only envy. What made them so effective? In part, it was the strong connection they still had with the realities of the home and the knowledge that the persons they were really working for were the children's mothers. In many cases, they were the eldest girl in large families themselves and knew from first- hand experience what the demands of mothering entailed as they were often their own mothers' substitutes. While they engaged in the teaching methods they were taught by the teacher institutes, they modeled and imitated those characteristics of effective mothering. They reached out to mothers by visiting homes (those were the days of no phone service) and making connections with the mothers of individual children. Those conversations were the fundamental way in which rural teachers constructed a communication bridge between the goals and activities of the school and the child's home.

What did a rural teacher at a one-room school know that teachers today need to know? She knew the developmental milestones and how to tie those to learning. She knew that teaching children face to face, one to one, and in small groups the majority of time enabled her to make connections to the world of the child. She expected the children, much as in the home, to help and to teach each other in a loosely structured fashion. She allowed older children to teach and assist younger children in the way the more mature child thought the younger child would respond best. She recognized the power and value of child intuition because she had developed it herself in her own home under the wing of her mother. This allowed the one-room schoolteacher time to work with other children individually and in small groups. The chief explanation behind her success in that rural and lonely schoolhouse was she instinctively knew and valued the importance of the mother bond and she imitated it.

Seeing Female Leaders

As important as hearing the voice of mothers is the presence of female leaders in our girls' schools. According to the 2005 report, *Profile of Teachers in the U.S.*, conducted by the National Center for Education Information, and a 2004 report, *The Careers of Public School Administrators*, prepared by the Rand Corporation, "the gender gap is alive and well." While the public school teaching force in the United States is even more female and experienced than a decade ago, with eighty-two percent of the total teaching force being women, women are still significantly under-represented among school principals, superintendents, and other administrative positions.

The Rand Corporation report results indicated that the greatest barrier presented to a woman who decides she may want to become an administrator is at the point when she lets it be known she is interested. Men are two to three times more likely than women to leave teaching and become administrators. While the Rand Company report indicated surprise with the finding that the gender gap for female administrators is larger in primary schools than for high schools, most women are not at all surprised. While women constitute an overwhelming majority of elementary teachers across the nation, they still comprise less than half of all elementary principals.

Hiring practices in both private and public schools are managed and controlled by those persons already settled into administrative positions. It is common cultural practice for principals to identify candidates they already know—either younger prospects already working in their building, coaches within their districts, or friends and colleagues who may be assistant administrators of one kind or another. In other words, men choose people with whom they have a high comfort level, share the same cultural roles, and see as natural team buddies. It is no surprise that they choose men.

It is important that the education administrative workforce responsible for our children's schooling be balanced in proportion to the number of women teachers. When young girls see a majority of men as leaders over female teachers, girls learn by what they see—that a woman may not have the capability to lead others. They may grow up to draw the same conclusions about their own roles despite evidence to the contrary.

Just as important, female and male teachers alike may find that their suggestions to decrease gender bias in the curriculum may not be listened to by a school leadership team that does not see the problem. It would not be unusual for a substantial majority of males in charge of the decision-making process to view this message as a direct threat. This may be one of the most profound reasons why gender bias and the gender ceiling are alive and well in all of our children's schools. The governance principle women should be fighting against is the same one that was fought in the early days of the United States struggle to gain independence from the domination of England over the colonies. That is, taxation without representation. Currently, women make significant contributions to both the tax base of our state and federal government as well as the daily labor of work both inside and outside of their homes. In 2006, girls and women comprise more than half of all students being schooled, constitute ninety percent of all elementary school teachers, and make up eight-four percent of all K-12 teachers in the field. It is time that school leadership teams reflect the demographics of those students and professionals currently in the system.

The Hidden Agenda

Still another barrier to forging schools that will prepare girls and young women for the life they will face in the twenty-first century is the hidden agenda. School curriculum in America, for instance, was originally determined by the sex of the child: A girl was put on one path to prepare her exclusively for the role of mate, mother, and unpaid worker both in the home and in the culture. The role of the boy child and the path he was set upon required him to think from a very young age of becoming the head of the family, a leader in the community, a wage earner, and the person in charge. Girls' and boys' education has long been centered in a teaching of difference in order to prepare both boys and girls for the different roles their futures would entail. Thus, teachers and the curriculum they taught stressed how boys and girls and, eventually men and women, were radically different, rather than identifying how they as people are similar. This thinking that girls and boys are radically different and that the future holds radically different challenges is the basis for the hidden agenda and gender bias. It undermines the education of both girls and boys.

It is also evident that for most educators, the adherence to the curriculum of difference is unintentional due to a lack of awareness and education in gender equity. And for others, an adherence to the past mode of thinking still remains their predominate view of the appropriate roles of girls and women and boys and men in the schools and, indeed, later in life. This adherence may be due to religious beliefs or self-interest to maintain power and control both at the school level as well as at the family, work, and cultural level.

Just when many believed the issue of gender equity and the hidden agenda was delegated to the burial ground, Lawrence Summers, President of Harvard University at the time, brought the hidden agenda out into full view. In January of 2005 at a speech in Cambridge, Massachusetts, for the National Bureau for Economic Research, the conference agenda was grappling with the low numbers of women in the science and engineering workforce. In his speech, Summers hypothesized that the paucity of professional women, especially in science, math and technology, but generally in all arenas of professional life, is due to women's inability to meet the demands of a "high-powered" job, to "their inability to hit at least three and a half, maybe four standard deviations above the mean" in aptitude (apparently where all of those male scientists, engineers, physicists, and chemists live), and finally to what he calls their "different socialization and patterns of discrimination" in the job search process.

Summers stated that there may be some discrimination in hiring practices and personnel actions which professional men use to keep women from joining their ranks. Later in the speech he talked about those "marginal hires" and suggested that this is an issue that needs ferreting out. For every woman whose record indeed had to be 200 percent higher than a male applicant, ten stories of men hired with marginal records and promoted with lackluster performances have been written about and documented as professional women finally took their argument to state and federal courts and won systematic redress for proven discrimination in hiring, promotion and tenure practices at universities (including my state), not to mention the hundreds of legal actions won documenting similar problems in private business.

His speech is now accessible at *www.president.harvard.edu/speeches/2005/nber*. It is tempting to slice through Summer's position, but many qualified men and women science professionals immediately put wiser words on the record, analyzing both the weakness of his arguments and the lack of his own gender equity education. Harvard's record of promoting female professors to full professors has been lackluster. Summers reinforced a stereotypical and blatantly false message that all too many men and women still buy—that women do not possess the genetic brain capacity to study, earn proficiency and apply math and science, that women cannot and will not work as hard as men do on the job (as they have domestic responsibilities to juggle and distract them from their profession), and that maybe cultural roles, past legal civil restrictions of women, and hiring practices may have some bearing, but not to the extent intellectual capacity and a willingness to work does.

Everyone familiar with current social trends knows that in America, for instance, girls and women have had specific gender roles, educational niches, and occupations that are different from men's. For example, females have been associated with language arts, social sciences, liberal arts, and nursing, while males have been tied to science (biology, physics, chemistry, etc), mathematics, medicine, and athletics. Futuristic and well-informed mothers and fathers of female children contend that girls are pushed into specific fields and boys into others due to subtexts of stereotyping and sexism, *not* due to a lack of talent or understanding in traditional "boy-related" areas. Teachers, parents, peers, and mentors often push girls and boys into liberal arts and science, respectively, due to their own sexist presumptions regarding gender roles and academic aptitude. Some people assume that boys and men are capable of doing anything—literature, science, the arts, nursing, medicine or mathematics, for example—but prefer to pursue more prestigious, high-profit-yielding fields related to science, medicine, and mathematics (rather than literature or the arts). Meanwhile, girls are thought to have a more limited base of interest and knowledge that revolves only around literature, social sciences, and liberal arts. Incidentally, "feminine" career fields that are focused around literature, social sciences, and liberal arts are less prestigious and less profitable than "masculine" occupations. This is largely due to the unfortunate fact that our male-dictated society places less value on female-oriented activities, occupations, and behaviors than masculine ones. Even more unfortunate is the fact that schools follow in the same sexist footsteps as the larger society by placing more value on traditional male-oriented fields of study than the typical female academic areas.

The hidden agenda promotes dualism; that is, two sets of values which oppose one another. In our society, dualities are usually placed within an oppositional value system, where one is better/good and the other is worse/bad. Some common dualities would include: man/woman, blue/pink, dominant/passive, masculine/feminine, and leader/follower, intelligent/simple, and rational/emotional. In all of the above dualities, the first word in the xxx/nnn grouping is considered "better than" and is also indicative of common masculine associations. Men are considered dominant, predatory, leadership-oriented, of the mind, intelligent, scientific and rational, while women are associated with being passive, prey-like, follower-oriented, of the body, simple, social and emotional. These dualities are quite dangerous for both sexes because they are stereotypical and limiting. They dictate very narrow gender roles and educational requirements for both females and males.

Today's schools help to reinforce sexist dualistic stereotypes by valuing science, mathematics, technology, and medicine over language, literature, liberal arts, social sciences, and fine arts. Additionally, schools fail to meet students' needs by not integrating important values learned from all the disciplines into their teaching methods. Teachers who instruct classes in science and math generally use lecture, forced note-taking, brief question-answer forums, and Scantron test taking. Teachers involved with language, literature, and liberal arts employ class discussion, small group activities and conversations, multimedia (film, art, etc), in-class writing assignments, journal writing, and essay tests. A more progressive teaching approach would be one that integrates strengths from both teaching orientations into one more useful, gender-inclusive practice. Since it is generally agreed that girls are more social and linguistically inclined than boys, perhaps girls are not as involved in the sciences, mathematics, and technology due to the lack of group learning, class discussion, and journal writing. It would make sense, then, for *all* classrooms in languages, science, and mathematics alike to take on this progressive atmosphere of open communication between students and teachers. This would inevitably encourage more girls to become involved in the sciences, math, and technology, and more boys to become better oriented toward social learning and communication. Thus, the sexist stereotypical barriers would be broken for both genders. Schools free of teaching-related stereotypes would promote open-mindedness, communication, critical thinking, and deeper levels of achievement for *both* sexes.

Sexist Traits of Men and Women Teachers

Teaching in today's classrooms is very hard work. Little time is left at the end of the day for teachers to reflect or plan teaching approaches that may better meet the needs of today's children. I have spent thousands of hours visiting classrooms as part of my professional role as a university educator—supervising student teachers and working with classroom teachers in a variety of ways. As classrooms once again increase in pupil size due to the decreased funding to school budgets, teachers are more apt to focus on keeping students in line and delivering the basics. Teachers, like the rest of us, do not naturally ask the question "What kind of world will I be sending my students into and how can I change what I do here to better meet their needs when they leave the doors of this school house?"

Perhaps the biggest changes for every twenty-first century boy and girl is the need to be prepared to take care of themselves, to work, and to provide for their own financial security over a lifetime. Yet, what has emerged time and time again from studies of watching how and what teachers teach is that the majority of teachers—men and women alike—engage in stereotypical sexist behaviors in the classroom.

The bulk of the responsibility for sexist traits can be put on the shoulders of women teachers, as they hold the compelling majority of all teaching positions from kindergarten through eighth grade. Teachers are not sexist because they are bad people; they are sexist because their teacher education programs and in-service programs do not include substantial and meaningful content and strategies on creating a non-sexist classroom environment. Women remain sexist because they are reluctant to fight to become school principals and superintendents who are in the position to advance both curriculum change and alternative teaching strategies in the schools they lead.

What I often observe as I enter a classroom, generally coed, is students sitting in desks lined up in rows facing the teacher who stands in front of them. Boys are more often seated in the front and the girls are seated toward the outer semicircle of the lined desks and in the back. I usually quickly count the number of students and, in general, I am looking at a class size between twenty-two and thirty students. Next, I scan the classroom environment. I am looking for evidence of interesting photos and visuals that would draw a girl or boy into the classroom community. More often than not, I see one or the combination of the these items: posters of male professional athletic teams, e.g., Green Bay Packers, posters of animals, picturesque landscapes or motivational phrases, such as remember to plan ahead, or make the most of each and every day, etc. And very often, I see posters that reflect a particular school's mission statement or the school code of conduct. Also popular with teachers is a poster that reminds students of the classroom rules.

Then I focus my attention on the lesson or unit for the current day of study. I pick up the lesson plan, already reviewed and approved by the supervising cooperating teacher. I am looking for instructional methodology, regardless of what the lesson objective is, where the teacher opens the lesson and connects the content to events in the life of a student today and does that by way of asking a variety of students to offer their insights. Afterwards, I look for teaching methods that break down the large group into either student pairs or very small groups for the purpose of exploring, studying, problem solving or researching. Next, I pay attention to how instructional technology will be used by both the teacher and students. Finally, I am interested in seeing that the students are held responsible for summing up in their own voices, writing, or laboratory exercises, what it is they learned, where they would like to go next, and how do they think they should go about getting there. I feel enthused when the teacher's voice is last and he/she can incorporate the student's reflections of the lesson and provide a road map of the next day's activities.

I am particularly keen on hearing the voices of both girls and boys. I am observing how the teacher coaches individual children during work periods. I want to see them encourage their students to be active and a partner in their learning, even if the particular topic is not inherently interesting to them. And I am listening for the kinds of motivation the teacher will use to encourage girls to pursue with passion the study of bugs and to the boys the study of healthy bodies.

I have visited approximately 1,500 student teachers, cooperating teachers, and 1,000 classrooms within the last twenty years. What I typically observe is:

- Posters of male professional sports teams boldly displayed on wall
- Teacher led instruction where students remain in their desks in lined up rows
- An instructional period where the teacher talks most of the time and students answer basic factual questions
- Very little instructional technology on the part of the teacher
- Use of small instructional groups to complete worksheets tied to the lesson
- Student use of computers in a whole class setting doing research and completing timelines, power point summaries of information
- Students copying word for word from computer documents
- Individual student presentations in front of the entire class, which takes several weeks of class time to give everyone a turn
- Little or no introductions by teachers who ask and reinforce why the particular content is important to them now and in their future
- Little inspiration offered by a teacher for all students to work outside of their comfort zones, for example, for the boys to actively listen to girls with respect, and for girls not to be so bothered by boy movement in instructional groups

So much of what is currently being advocated concerning the teaching of boys and girls can be categorized into two basic approaches: neutralizing gender in the classroom or separating students by gender in classroom or schools to better address the unique ways of learning by girls and boys. Based upon my twenty seven years as a professor in teacher education, and raising both a boy and a girl and now serving in the glorious role of grandmother of two girls and one boy, I believe that either separating out the sexes in public schools or teaching in a gender blind manner is shortsighted and naïve. They simply fail to address the enormous amount of literature on the differences in boy-girl development.

Gender-Inclusive Sex Education

Another facet of learning that is currently lacking in depth and girl-centeredness is sex education. Currently, programs are all over the board in their goals, teaching methods, and curriculums. Katie Bowman has had experiences with sex education that seem to mirror many other young women's feelings:

> "When I was in fifth grade, our class—like so many others—was divided into two halves for sex education: girls and boys. My experience with sex ed at that point was limited to what the female instructor told us (the girls). The entire conversation was based on 'feminine hygiene,' as she called it, menstruation, sexual disease, sexual abuse/molestation, and 'how to say no' to squirrelly, sex-crazed boys. Menstruation was taught as some kind of undesirable, dirty monthly vice that we all had to unfortunately endure because we were girls. The whole thing was awkward and uncomfortable. My teacher seemed to be promoting Puritanical self-denial, purity, abstinence, and fear of sex, menstruation, and masturbation. Similarly, middle school and high school largely focused on the 'bad' parts of sex—sexually transmitted diseases, HIV/AIDS, abstinence, a little bit on safer sex, and mostly, again, on self-denial. My questions were: isn't sexuality a normal part of everyone's lives? Am I weird for having sexual feelings? I really had no example of what healthy sexuality looked like for girls like me. I wanted to find out more, but I felt 'dirty' for wanting to know."

Like so many girls, Bowman's curiosities and sexual feelings were not very clearly or thoroughly addressed by her teachers. Whereas boys' sexual urges are seen by society, teachers, and parents as inevitable, girls' sexual urges are viewed as dirty and forbidden. Therefore, as Susan Shurberg Klein suggests in her article, "Sex Education and Gender Equity," girls are supposed to become "more responsible for safeguarding morals and health" than boys. Klein asserts that most sexual issues affect both genders in and outside of school—for example, sexual attraction, physical attractiveness of self, desire to masturbate, sexual orientation, sexual harassment, physiological changes, parenthood, and STDs, but most teachers treat the genders very differently. Teachers, parents, and students' peers, for instance, normalize boys' desires to masturbate through discussions of "wet dreams" and "natural urges," but rarely acknowledge masturbation as a safe, natural sexual release for girls. A more open discussion of masturbation would benefit both boys *and* girls in late elementary school, middle school, and high school.

Other important issues worthy of discussion in sex education programs and more frequently in girls' homes is that of physical appearance. Girls are often so worried about their appearance, sexual appeal, ability to attract boys, and, consequently, their ability to "show up" and compete with other girls in school that they often lose sight of their academic goals and career hopes. Girls are inundated with oversexed, half-nude, plastic-sugared and dangerously thin images of women. Boys do not have similar, invasive images in the media to reconcile, so the body image preoccupation for girls is more real and pervasive than it is for boys. Teachers and parents need to work together to show their girls that they are beautiful *regardless* of how they look on the outside. Lots of girls hear from their parents and teachers that "you're beautiful on the inside no matter what," which is a wonderful start, but they need a more tangible realization of this assurance. For instance, parents and teachers can do informal exercises with girls to show how images of women in the media are unhealthy and unattainable. Parents and teachers should also remember that girls should receive compliments based on their humor, intellect, athleticism, academics, musicality, and other abilities rather than on their appearance. Parents and teachers have the power to change girls' conceptions about themselves and the media. Adults should help girls develop a critical eye regarding institutions like the media. Girls should be encouraged to question, criticize, and analyze rather than simply to conform to female images distributed by the media.

Further, parents and teachers can help girls better realize their goals by channeling all the energy girls exert on applying makeup, fixing their hair, shopping for clothes, getting dressed (and redressed, and redressed), fighting over boys, going to the mall, etc, into positive and productive sexual facets, like pursuing athletics, hugging, writing sensual poetry, masturbation, and *talking* to family and other girls about sexuality rather than *fighting* with them over boys and trivial things. Teachers must realize that girls are sexual beings just as boys are, and girls must not be discouraged from achieving sexual release and experiencing sexual feelings and behavior. In other words, the sexist double standard that is manifested in sex education programs must be recognized and refuted by teachers in order to open a healthy sexual world for female (and male) students. Students who express their sensual and sexual side in a positive and appropriate fashion are more likely to achieve academically, socially, and, eventually, occupationally.

Creating New Age Schools for Girls and Young Women

While the nature of work has changed dramatically in all areas outside of the schoolroom, more than one writer has observed that schools have remained insulated from implementing practices encouraged by human resource professionals in other professional careers. State-of-the-art schools are easy to identify if one looks for certain categories: leadership, open and inclusive communication, respect for students, interior design of environment, building identity, confidence and instructional design.

Leadership

The new age school district would possess a balance of both female and male leaders. Women and men have different concerns and methods of communication. The overwhelming majority of professional teachers are women. A progressive school system will have women visible as curriculum specialists, school principalships, vice-principals, personnel management, and school superintendents.

Inclusive Positive Communication

The second most important feature of a state-of-the-art school is the quality and degree of a system of communication that is open, non-threatening, and oriented towards problem solving. Prospective parents and students should be able to view published curriculum units at the elementary level and syllabi at the middle and high school level via the internet posted on school web pages. Within each school, curriculum should be infused either in Language Arts or Social Studies beginning in upper elementary and continuing through the high school with content that develops effective communication skills and skills in resolving conflicts.

Sexual harassment in schools continues to have a paralyzing effect on girls and young woman as well as on boys and young men. It remains a problem of epidemic proportion in schools. Parents and teachers must acknowledge sexual harassment as a major obstacle for positive girl growth and learning. If girls are preoccupied with inappropriate, unwanted sexual innuendo in their school's hallways, gyms, and classrooms, their development and abilities to successfully learn and achieve are hindered.

Cost of Sexual Harassment to Girls and Boys

Experienced some form of sexual harassment	80 percent
Experienced sexual harassment in school	
Girls	85 percent
Boys	76 percent
Feel less confident in school as result of sexual harassment	
Girls	43 percent
Boys	14 percent
Girls who avoid school, participation in class because of sexual harassment	33 percent

Source: American Association of University Women (AAUW) study, "Hostile Hallways: Sexual Harassment in America's Schools."

Teachers need to learn strategies to monitor the amount of unwanted sexual commentary and behavior that happens in schools. Sexual harassment is not only detrimental to girls' and boy's development, it is illegal. It then becomes the social *and* legal responsibility of teachers to ensure a safe, healthy, happy environment for students.

So far as female students, one key way in which teachers can do this is simply to *trust girls*. Our society is very reluctant to recognize female testimony (juvenile or adult), especially regarding sexual harassment, rape, sexual assault, and battering, as legitimate, serious, and valid. Teachers must work against this sexist status quo. Officials must allow girls to feel comfortable to use their voices, and they must validate girls' testimony by taking them seriously. Second, in-service programs should be employed to educate all students—girls and boys alike—on the impact of sexual harassment. Many students feel the impact of sexual harassment without even knowing it. For example, a girl might be repeatedly called a "sexy mama" or a "slut" without recognizing these remarks as sexual harassment. She must be educated to identify it as such, be encouraged to disclose such remarks to a trusted authority figure (this is where the role of teachers becomes crucial as mentor and confidant), and realize the social and legal implications of such commentary. Schools need to define "sexual harassment" for their students by offering many different examples of what it might entail for individuals. Video, Power Point, open discussion forums, skits, question-answer panel presentations, small group discussions, and other interactive learning styles should be employed to help make the school environment free from sexual harassment a tangible reality for all students.

Respect for Students and Their Future

Many textbooks which students in teacher education use express this principle: "Students should be treated with respect in all aspects of the education process, so that their dignity and opportunities for educational development are enhanced" (The Joint Committee on Standards for Educational Evaluation).

One way schools can become more progressive and conducive for respectful student growth and development is through the implementation of widespread women's studies programs that specifically address gender issues, women's history, and female sexuality. Such programs currently exist only at the college level on a limited basis. Women's studies programs would help to provide a place for girls to commune and discover realms of their lives that they have in common. Women's studies programs would give students a context and a safe place where they could explore their insecurities, talents, interests, and abilities free of patriarchal judgment and female rivalry.

With our society's increasing responsibilities for women—often balancing full-time, professional jobs with children, organizations, partners, and house chores—girls need to learn at early ages how to assert themselves, prioritize, and realize that their role is not to please everyone but focus on themselves. Girls must come to understand that they are intelligent, talented, free to make their own decisions, and worthy of recognition for their accomplishments.

During adolescence, female competition and peer-related ridicule/cruelty becomes more of a problem. Similarly, women's studies programs would offer a safe place for boys to try living outside of the patriarchal status quo. For example, boys would be encouraged to explore the negative implications of strict masculinity. They would be encouraged to step outside of the stoic, domineering, insensitive, oftentimes violent social position that is pushed on them in traditional masculine terms and instead to embrace cooperative, non-hierarchical, respectful, empathetic values. Boys would be able to benefit from these qualities as men. Their relationships—particularly with women—would be more respectful, compromising, and less oriented towards aggressiveness or violence. Boys would become better adults, better fathers, and better partners. When both genders start embracing feminist-inspired qualities, boy-girl relationships, as well as girl-girl and boy-boy relationships, would become more respectful and genuine. These qualities would help both sexes develop more healthy self-images and more complete views of the world. Thus, both genders would have a better chance at healthy growth, establishing successful relationships, and experiencing higher, deeper levels of academic and occupational achievement.

Women's studies address sexism and social change while they employing teaching practices such as social/group-oriented learning, discussion-based teaching, progressive classroom settings, cooperative relationships, active/participatory learning, and teaching the ability to challenge and question institutions and ideas.

Finding Center: Strategies to Reveal Strong Girls and Women

Better yet, a comprehensive program specifically designed to address women's issues—female sexuality, body image, women's history, interconnections of female identity (gender, race, ethnicity, class, age, etc), women's politics, feminist analysis of issues and texts, and the possibility for positive feminist social change—would certainly help girls and young women to critically examine their so-called "place" as females in society and to find a more progressive, comfortable position for themselves.

FEATURES OF VIBRANT WOMEN'S STUDIES CURRICULUM
- Rich in women's history
- Includes stories of historical women leaders
- Features women's writing and literature
- Addresses female political issues
- Challenges portrayal of girls and women in the media

Teachers should be free to integrate women's studies curriculum in their K-12 classrooms. For upper elementary and middle school girls and boys, the issue of body image is especially important. In this new focus, teachers should encourage individual self-expression, building relationships with other students, challenging pop culture's skinny-minnie unachievable images of girls and women, and connecting with older role models and mentors who have already been through the often strenuous trials of teen expression. Teachers should use innovative, interactive ways to help girls identify ways of achieving positive body images. One example might be to make a slide show of magazine advertisements that depict women in negative ways and to have the class divide into small groups to discuss and write down their feelings about the ads. Perhaps the class could reconvene to analyze *why* they are having these feelings and *why* women are depicted in certain ways. As a follow-up, a teacher might ask students as a homework assignment to go find some positive alternatives to these negative ads and hand in a write-up about their findings. Additionally, teachers might choose to show a film, like *Reviving Ophelia*, which focuses on struggling to achieve healthy female body image in adolescence and afterwards have a discussion. Parents would be encouraged to take on similar teaching responsibilities at home by frequently bringing up gender role issues, discussing body image (especially with teen daughters), and reinforcing worth for their children, and teaching their children to challenge the status quo.

Because female-related materials have largely been ignored and neglected in our schools, students know little about the issues. Therefore, teachers may face some apprehension from both students and parents. It is important, then, for teachers to maintain cooperative, healthy, positive, and strong relationships with both their students and the students' parents. Cooperation is not only crucial to achieving a better understanding and point of view on these issues, but it is also a key factor in satisfying the second major task of establishing a successful women's studies program: creating a progressive classroom in which feminist issues are brought forth.

Two-way communication-rich teaching requires teachers to challenge the status quo of schooling; that is, they should refrain from acting as the disseminator of information and, instead, take on an interactive, mutual-learning relationship with their students. Teachers can skillfully examine abstract ideas like feminism, but they should also focus on tangible, applicable ideas their students can relate to, such as popular culture, careers, personal relationships, and personal experiences and stories. If a teacher shows the students that it is possible to challenge the status quo of schooling, students should be less hesitant to challenge the status quo of gender. Once again, boys and girls who are unafraid to challenge gender role stereotypes will be more likely to understand the world from a more complete, gender-inclusive perspective and, thus, be able to achieve deeper satisfaction in their schooling, relationships and jobs, and more fulfilling lives.

Choosing Gender Responsive and Dynamic Schools

Girls and young women deserve schools that are gender responsive and dynamic to the world in which they will live and work. Status quo schools and curriculum which shortchange females in terms of not building positive self images and instilling higher goals are simply not good enough. Parents and students now have more choices in determining where their children attend school due to public school open enrollment programs, the ability to combine public high school attendance with part-time college enrollment, and home schooling. More parents are beginning their children's formal schooling by selecting and enrolling them into private preschool programs that provide the curriculum and experiences which they value. While some parents can afford to send their children to private elementary and secondary schools where they have more direct influence in negotiating the curriculum, most school age children continue to receive their education within the public school system.

How Gender Flexible Schools Feel

Respectful language that excludes sexual harassment and innuendo makes girls feel safe

Stories of girls and women who have triumphed create feelings of inclusion and confidence

Discussions of what the pleasures and successes are from creating meaningful life work makes girls feel inspired

Teaching strategies and curriculum that includes the same goals and objectives for both genders makes girls feel included and confident

Teachers who encourage and support girls that question and speak out create less fearful females

Classroom settings and discussions that highlight women's accomplishments makes girls feel proud, included, and inspired to pursue their own talents

Teachers skilled in the different ways boys and girls communicate both verbally and in conflict resolution makes girls and boys feel safe, respected and confident

How Gender Flexible Schools Look

Pictures of girls and boys engaged in learning on classroom walls

Inclusion of women's history visible in the curriculum

All content offered to all students in mixed groups

Personal financial skills and career information included in the curriculum. All students receive rigorous and accurate information

Middle and high school teachers collaborate with mothers, fathers and business leaders in order to connect school curriculum to the needs and trends of the current employment market

Print materials, computer software and other instructional materials show dynamic inclusion of girls and women, both Caucasian and of color

Parents, when united and informed, are the most important players in creating curriculum and policy change within local schools. Children are the most precious part of our lives. Assuming that their child's school is progressive and gender-responsive is not the direction that most mothers, and indeed, fathers want to pursue. Parents need to check things out and invest their time and effort in establishing a dialogue with school administrators before their child enrolls in a particular school. Considerable time and energy must be expended in connecting, negotiating, advocating and supporting those who will make those dynamic changes in a girl's school curriculum.

To assist in sizing up a school a girl is already attending or in reviewing schools as part of a selection process, look at the checklist provided. It incorporates those attributes of a gender-flexible and dynamic school. In addition, view the outline of the progress that can be made when mothers are lead teachers with their girl's teachers, when teachers become gender-savvy, when school barriers are reduced, and what changes will occur as these "new age" girls grow up. Progressive school administrators and teachers expect and welcome parents to visit their schools and discuss their curriculum and school practices. Too many parents simply enroll their daughter or son, attend welcome meetings, and then drop their child at the school door each day. Schooling must first and foremost be a two-way dialogue and relationship between parents and teachers. Negotiate hard and expect change. If you are not happy with the results, look for other schools within your area, including enrolling your child in another public school that may meet the needs of your daughter.

Girls Only

Driven by organizations such as the National Association for Single-Sex Public Education (NASSPE) and research that documents both the challenges girls have in coed schools and the slow pace at which coed schools adopt effective gender teaching strategies, a groundswell of new interest in girls- and boys-only schools and schooling practices has emerged.

Before jumping on an educational bandwagon that may unravel the tools women have in place, such as Title IX, a cautious examination of the issue is required. First, in the United States, the preponderance of girls-only schools is private and costly. More than ninety percent of all school-aged students now attend public schools in this country.

Second, given current public education and civil rights law, single-sex public school classes, whether for girls or boys, must meet the needs of a particular school district as its primary function. Third, the government's notice to the public in the spring of 2002 to amend Title IX in order to facilitate an easier path in putting up single-sex elementary and secondary classes should be viewed with a suspicious eye. After decades of fighting for equal resources for both educational and extracurricular programs for girls and women, Title IX provides the fundamental protection of this civil right. In a brief prepared by the AAUW in March of 2004, their sentiment is that "it is unclear why now, after twenty-seven years of public education under Title IX single-sex regulations, the Department of Education has determined to amend such regulations." For a detailed examination of their position, see *www.aauw.org/issue_advocacy/actionpages/positionpapers/PDFs/SingleSexEducation*.

Choice in educational schooling is an important overriding concept for all girls and women. A small percentage of parents will choose private schools for their daughters based upon religious objectives; other parents have the means to align their daughters' abilities and talents to the best match available in an all-girls school wherever it is located. Since the vast majority of girls-only schools are located in the eastern or western corridors of the Unites States, a challenge for parents is locating a quality school within commuting distance or making the decision to board away from home for the academic year. In most cases, the cost of an all-girls school is equal to a full year of college tuition and fees.

For the purpose of reaching the goals which are presented in this book, the avenue of first choice is to provide an appropriate education to the ninety percent of girls who attend the public schools. Changing teaching and curriculum practices that impact all but ten percent of American school-aged children is the most efficacious route in delivering a gender-savvy inclusive education. The phrase "new-age school," as used in this book, is code for employing those strategies documented by research and which are integrated in the best of girls-only private schools.

Finally, let the buyer beware: An all-girls or all-boys classroom or school label does not guarantee the delivery of state-of-the-art curriculum or a teacher who is skilled in gender-specific strategies, nor does such a label assure that the teaching staff possesses that art of interpersonal sensitivities needed to inspire and mentor students.

My Child's School and Teacher

Moving Toward New Age Schools: How is your School Doing?

Directions:

A. Arrange for a visit at your child's school. Observe as you walk through and sit in on a least two classes (not necessarily your child's).

B. Meet with several other parents of children at your school. Choose a variety of people who have different experiences. Talk about the items and complete the ratings.

Interior Design of Environment

My child's school/teacher incorporates the following:

1. Yes No   Real pictures of all students at the school
2. Yes No   Visuals in hallways that reflect students at their school engaged in a wide range learning activities (clubs, sports, art displays, leadership)
3. Yes No   Visuals depicting girls and boys of variety of cultures
4. Yes No   Theme centers in school/rooms that reflect technology, careers, leadership and families
5. Yes No   Refrains from displaying images primarily related to teacher's interests (pro sport teams, music posters, etc.)
6. Yes No   Visuals pertaining to families of students at the school not exclusively of parents in in-school activities (at home, work, community, and school)

Give yourself one point for each statement you answered yes to.

Score _____

Open and Inclusive Communication

My child's school/teacher . . .

1. Yes No   Knows my name

2.	Yes	No	Uses relationship building strategies
3.	Yes	No	Bans all labels of children-youth
4.	Yes	No	Brings successful men and women to classes to show how to lead to be successful
5.	Yes	No	Displays enthusiasm
6.	Yes	No	Uses well designed small work groups in order for all to work together
7.	Yes	No	Encourages, encourages, encourages
8.	Yes	No	Conducts discussions about role of women in society and culture
9.	Yes	No	Talks person to person-not always teacher to student
10.	Yes	No	Tells personal stories; real life disclosures

Give yourself one point for each statement you answered yes to.

Score _____

Respect for students

My child's school/teacher . . .

1.	Yes	No	Focuses on positive attitudes and counter negative messages with actions strategies
2.	Yes	No	Holds professional staff accountable for overt messages and behaviors that cross the line
3.	Yes	No	Includes in curriculum that include fifty Percent stories of girls/women; include fifty percent that include children/adults of color
4.	Yes	No	Provides peer workshops to discuss troubles, accomplishments, current issues lead by skilled teachers
5.	Yes	No	Builds identity and confidence
6.	Yes	No	Include mothers as speakers and action players in the school and classroom
7.	Yes	No	Brings in female role models and sophisticated mentor programs

8.	Yes	No	Connects with community to support activities that build girl and boy competence
9.	Yes	No	Provides opportunity and exploration in new areas
10.	Yes	No	Takes a strong, visible stand by using posters, displays and teacher follow-through

Give yourself one point for each statement you answered yes to.

Score _____

Instructional Design

My child's school and teacher . . .

1.	Yes	No	Uses predominantly well-designed small groups and individualized learning approaches
2.	Yes	No	Limits whole class-teacher controlled teaching
3.	Yes	No	Incorporates a full spectrum of men and women and persons of color in readings, study of approaches in readings, study and teaching approaches
4.	Yes	No	Offers multiple learning opportunities for student success
5.	Yes	No	Offers career units with equal balance of full range of occupations, both traditional and non-traditional for boys and girls/men and women
6.	Yes	No	Offers instructional units pertaining to minority women and men
7.	Yes	No	Offers women's studies as curriculum option for middle school and high school study
8.	Yes	No	Provides free study opportunities for students to explore topic, issue, and problem
9.	Yes	No	Publishes curriculum units and syllabi (middle school—high school) on school web page

> 10.　Yes　No　Uses a variety of electronic communication systems targeted to parents and families—including grade books
>
> Give yourself one point for each statement you answered yes to.
>
> Score _____
>
> **How to Use the Rating**
>
> 1. Add up your score. Find the level of "New Age" your school is currently at.
> 2. Share your results with your child's teacher, administrator and Parent-Teacher Organization at your school. With a variety of school professionals, work together for a follow-up meeting to discuss findings, prioritize strategies to enhance school climate and overall communication, and plan for the future.
>
> **Results**
>
> 36–32　Super Model of a New Age School!
>
> 31–28　Good progress in implementing many sound practices of New Age Schools; but more work is needed to bury those old belief systems.
>
> 27–25　W—e—l-l; we are basically good parents and teachers. We love our children and/or teaching. But are we up to this New Age Schooling shift—I mean this is a lot of work, isn't it? Let's get going!
>
> Below 24　Emergency room candidate! Ask for help.

Lorraine Finishes School

Lorraine, a Caucasian woman raised in the Midwest, completed high school in the late 1960s with an excellent academic record. What sets her high school record apart is that she completed four years of high school mathematics. She went to college, completed her freshman year, and did not go back. She was engaged to be married and she said she did not want to be a teacher or a nurse, so why continue?

Marry she did, but to someone other than the first fiancé. At twenty, Lorraine began working for an insurance company in an urban city as a receptionist-secretary. After a few years, the boss in the office encouraged her to attend night school and get a license to sell insurance. She never took him up on the suggestion. She did not see herself in a man's role nor did she have aspirations to do what her male boss did.

Lorraine relocated to the east coast with her husband as he sought work with a brother in a small business. She worked part time as a cocktail waitress in an upscale restaurant-bar frequented by politicians and the occasional film-television celebrity. When she was twenty-seven, she had the first of three children. She and her husband moved back to the Midwest where she settled in as a full-time mother with the usual chores and responsibilities. She had a middle-class family lifestyle, managing the money and paying the bills of a family of five on a modest working class income.

Entering midlife Lorraine examined her life. She made the decision to return to college and complete a degree. She missed the stimulation of a classroom but was not at all confident she would succeed. After all, she observed, she did not have any skills in the real world after not being employed for more than twenty years.

Lorraine was worried about paying tuition as she did not have any money "of her own." She did have half of the combined assets from her marriage including a paid home and excellent credit rating in her husband's name primarily due to her abilities in financial management. She received little if any real support from her husband. He really did not want to second mortgage the house to pay for what he thought was a frivolous and unneeded expense. After all, men with college degrees and management experience were being laid off from work.

Mustering up her courage, Lorraine walked into a college class during a summer session. Within just a few weeks, she cemented her decision to stay and pursue a degree in business. Because of an excellent freshman college record, all of her credits transferred and she was admitted as a "continuing" student, though she had left college thirty years prior. This time, due to hours of work and pure dogged persistence, she graduated from college with highest honors.

Her business "advisor," a young man with a Ph.D., in an apparent attempt to steel her against what he expected to be disappointment, told her it was unlikely she would get a job since she did not have any real work experience and, also, because she was in her early forties. He encouraged her to lie about her age on job applications, appalling advice from anyone, but doubly so as Lorraine's major was in the field of human resources. She felt hugely disappointed in the advisor's tone, demeanor, and utter lack of respect for her academic record and her fortitude.

Lorraine disregarded his advice and sought and obtained her first professional job in her field. After two years of doing stellar work, she asked for a raise. Her boss countered with the offer of a bigger office. She began the search for a different job.

She was offered a position with a large corporate business. She had applied and interviewed as a good experience not really thinking she would get an offer. She worked hard and took on challenges in her new position. Over the next ten years, she received substantial raises in her salary as well as the eventual promotion to director of the entire service area, earning her a six-figure salary with fringe benefits.

She was asked by the university recruitment office at the school she had graduated from if she would have any interest in conducting a session targeted to women entering the university and especially returning adult women. As she told me this story, she smiled as she said, "I told them I would be most happy to assist them in their efforts."

WHEN MOTHERS ARE THE LEAD TEACHERS

- They negotiate curriculum with their daughter's teachers
- They verbalize expectations to their daughters
- They share with daughters their stories, strengths, and wishes
- They retain their authority and do not release it to teachers, other adults and parents or to their daughters and children
- They explore their world together with their daughters
- They seek a balance between educating girls based upon their innate strengths and challenging girls to acquire boy skills and behaviors as well
- They stress the interconnectedness between girls and boys and women and men as reflected in the dynamics of modern families

This leads to . . . **strong mother-daughter relationship**

New Age Schooling

WHEN TEACHERS BECOME GENDER SAVVY

- Families hear the importance of educating girls in different ways than in the past
- They employ gender-flexible curriculum strategies
- Girls hear that they have choices as to their roles in society
- Girls develop interest and competence in areas not traditionally experienced by girls and women
- Girls and women assume greater responsibility for their own growth and development over their lifetime
- Girls and women demonstrate confidence in their ability to change roles over their lifetime
- See women as leaders

This leads to . . . **confident girls with concerns**

WHEN BARRIERS ARE REDUCED

- Mothers and teachers work begins the school year with dialogues and mutual goal setting
- Teachers get intimate view of each child as unique individual
- Teachers connect to mothers and families directly and frequently
- Women serve as principals, superintendents and members of school boards in equal numbers to men
- Women are in various roles of educational leadership and are visible to girls and to the girl's parents
- Girls learn how to compete, manage stress, focus on their strengths while developing competence in areas formerly reserved to boys and men

This leads to . . . **visible women leaders and mentors**

Finding Center: Strategies to Reveal Strong Girls and Women

WHEN NEW AGE GIRLS GROW UP

- They have skills and abilities to earn a living
- They are more likely to enroll in post-secondary training and education
- They gain economic status and employ financial skills for themselves and for their families
- They delay marriage
- They live independently before marriage
- They have fewer children and have higher aspirations for those children they do have
- They work in a range of jobs and careers and demonstrate increased sophistication in seeking employment and moving up a job and career trajectory
- They become confident, knowledgeable mothers who work well with others to advance common maternal and educational interests for themselves and their children

This leads to . . . self-actualized girls and women

Chapter 10
Teens Off Track

> "Confidence is the sexiest thing a woman can have.
> It's much sexier than any body part."
> AIMEE MULLINS

At eighteen years old, Jessie set off to college with the goal of becoming a medical doctor. She carried excellent academic credentials: high school honors, formidable College Board scores, experience as an athlete, and an assertive personality profile. She was not one of those needy high school girls who followed her boyfriend to the college of his choice. In fact, she was not attached to any boyfriend. She was well financed by parents who lived in separate houses and ran separate post-divorce lives. No college loans, no need to work to support living expenses and no need to give up accessories that she considered essential: cell phone, a wireless, pastel-colored laptop computer and a car of her own with a gas credit card billed to her parents.

In her second year of college, Jessie found the premed science curriculum tougher than she had expected. Away from home for the first time, she met a boy and began a serious relationship. By the end of the year, the young man moved on without warning. Life was harder than she expected. To ease her pain, she abandoned her goal of medical school in favor of another major in which she could more easily maintain a high grade point average.

I shared this dilemma of teen girls and their struggle to focus with Lynda, mother of a teenaged girl. She revealed she was dealing with the beginning of the boy-crazed world of her thirteen-year-old daughter, Carrie, and her friends. She described her daughter's emotional torrents when Lynda refused to allow her to dress like Paris Hilton or when Lynda calls a boy's parents to inform them of the sexually explicit emails he sent Carrie. Yet Lynda said that her daughter was extremely candid when she described the sex acts girls her age engage in with boys they know. Without blinking her eyelashes she said, "Mother, everybody does it. It's no big deal." Much to Lynda's horror, her daughter confided that kissing boys seductively is as ordinary as passing notes to friends. Pulling guys into bathrooms to engage in every kind of kissing, including oral sex, is what some of the more popular, pretty and aggressive girls do—it's a kind of game. When I suggested that it would probably be best to have her daughter's friends over at her house so the bathrooms and bedrooms could be monitored, Lynda looked straight into my eyes to correct what she perceived to be my naive misunderstanding and exclaimed, "The kissing bathroom game goes on at her school! Some of the girls pull guys into the bathroom during school hours to a minute or so in between classes and before and after school. No one monitors the bathrooms!"

How do we get young girls off this track in their formative psychosexual years and establish core identities that neutralize this obsession with boys and eventually men? That seems to be at the root of the struggle. Once girls begin practicing the habit of looking for boys (and later for men) to use as their cornerstones to identity and well being, it becomes an automatic response that appears to be hardwired as they proceed through life.

Why make boys and men the crux of the problem? They clearly are not. But it is the way in which girls and women use boys and men to juxtapose their lives that is the problem. According to many females, boys and men are the reason why girls and women do not provide better security for themselves and for their children. And when girls and women are left alone, pushed aside and traded in, boys and men become the prime focus—first to blame and then to replace! When boys and men lay down threats like "If you don't like my drinking, leave" or "You can't use my money to buy the kind of attorney I can so you had better just go along with what I say," far too many girls and women believe the boy's strong words rather than turning to themselves for the strength to make sacrifices and strike out on their own.

When a daughter experiences a father's cowardly act of walking away from her life with little or no notice, it can be devastating. One day he comes home from work, perhaps grabs a meal with the family, and the next day he just leaves with a note or a short announcement, never to return again. This kind of abandonment can leave a teenager emotionally reeling and bleeding in full view of those closest to her. When her father leaves her mother in this manner, it creates an emotionally intense scene of devastation that a daughter is unlikely to forget. She learns quickly that she never wants her boyfriend to leave her because, unlike or perhaps like her mother, she may not survive. Early in the girl-boy game, many teenage girls become convinced they *need* boys.

Tell the Truth

To do better at helping our daughters keep on the right track, grown women and mothers need to begin with themselves. When a mother is left in unresolved emotional pain, she may feel forced to move ahead in silence and simply endure. If she speaks of her pain, it is still raw. If she heals, she may remain silent, perhaps feeling shamed. She moves forward while raising her family, perhaps hoping another mate may still be in her future. Some women invest enormous energy in finding another boyfriend or man friend immediately; others activate their replacement action plan before the current significant other is out of their life.

If a woman shares with her daughters and sons how the experience of latching on to someone else feels, how it costs her and what she learned, she would speak out to what her inner voice already knows. For others to gain from her experience and for her to not recycle nonproductive behaviors and choices, a woman simply must do the brave thing: take responsibility for her role in the situation. By speaking and making real her emotional pain, she is more likely to identify with how things really are and how not to repeat the same behavior with another man.

How that changes a girl's dynamic home life is that she will hear open, honest conversations centered about relationships. The daughter will be more likely to emulate an internal focus by doing the same. Her center will grow depth, weight and muscle. It will grow a thick shell to protect her. She will grow intellectual capital with which she can maneuver herself forward and achieve those things in her life that reflect her values and talents.

Equally important is what she learns *not* to do. A teenaged girl learns that a boy is someone exactly like she is. They are both in the stage of late childhood, struggling with integrating their own personal and family issues within their own conscientiousness and acquiring patterns of behaviors by which they both will conduct their life. Much of this learning is done through trial and error. A teen to early twenty-year-old boy is not able to be much help to his boy buddy when it comes to social-emotional matters. Nor is he developmentally ready to step into the role as a sensitive and responsible love interest to a young girl. He will, however, take what opportunities are presented to him to gain experience. Many boys and young men are too shy and easily embarrassed to receive sexual banter and favors from the opposite sex. Many are enticed when in the company of other boys, which raises the danger level for both boys and girls.

Teenaged girls in their pseudo-belief that they are too mature for boys their own age sometimes turn to young men out of high school and beyond. While more experienced sexually, young men four years or more the girls' senior present real balance-of-power issues. Some girls looking for more mature partners will turn to married men or, more accurately, married men will turn to them and exploit their vulnerabilities to meet their own sexual desires and fantasies. The media is filled with such stories of the rich and famous. But the truth is that this scenario is commonplace and played out in the ordinary lives of the not so rich and famous as well. Sadly, the older man and the teen girl cat-and-mouse games generally have a very predictable ending.

The experience of sixteen-year-old Annie is a variation on this theme. A twenty- three-year-old college woman in my education of girls and women class told this story to us. It was an incident that she had observed while attending a club in a metropolitan city on a weekend evening. She indicated that she did not know the girls all that well but had witnessed the event. However, from the look in her eyes when she connected with me (she was seated next to me in a discussion circle), I am not at all convinced that she did not know the girl.

Annie was a dark-haired beauty who dressed part fashion model and part little girl. Bored with both her high school studies and friends, she frequented places where she could come in contact with older and more experienced men. She soon met twenty-one-year-old Luke, fell madly in love and quickly began scripting the details of her wedding day. Pulled into his crowd and away from her high school friends, she believed she was hipper and soon became disconnected from her own girl pack. While young and impressionable, Annie was basically a morally grounded girl. She wanted to make Luke the center of her life, get married and have a family just as her mother had done.

One evening Luke took her to a club in a city not far from where she lived. Excited about the new opportunity and wanting to appear older, she dressed in a miniskirt with bare legs and high-heeled shoes. It was spring and the club would be packed and hot. As the night went on, with alcohol flowing and music pounding, patrons turned to sexual exploration on the dance floor. Couples acted out intercourse via dance bumps and grinds, pulling down clothes and lifting skirts in dirty dancing style. While Luke was dancing with another girl, Annie's dance partner, a stranger, shoved her up against a wall on the edge of the dance floor. Before she knew what was happening and dizzy from too much alcohol, she was quickly pressed against the stranger's body as he lifted her skirt then roughly penetrated her vagina. Annie doubled over in pain when he released her from the wall. She was a virgin and had just been raped by what looked like consensual sex.

In a subsequent session, I used the experience of Annie and built upon her experiences. I told the class that I was going to continue Annie's history and what I wanted from them was their impressions. I told the rest of Annie's story, which went like this:

Annie crumbles down the wall of the dance floor as the stranger walks away. Crying and dazed, Annie finds her way into a bathroom where she throws up in a stall and remains sitting there on the floor for what seems like hours. Eventually she returns to the dance floor and finds Luke, who harshly asks where she has been. She says nothing to Luke; she is in shock and embarrassed. Annie fakes sleeping during the car ride home with Luke, and when he drops her off at home she stumbles into her bedroom without waking her parents.

The next day, Annie initially believes the rape had been a nightmare. However, within moments, nausea hits violently and she realizes what really did happen. Annie hides the events first to herself and then to others. At school Annie steps through her day, feeling extremely alone and alienated. She has, after all, distanced herself from her friends with the exception of Jan. She hesitates confiding to Jan as she has spent little time with her these past few weeks.

Days and weeks go by and Annie holds the experience and the pain inside. Her relationship with Luke falters. She does not want to continue to go out with his crowd. She prefers to stay at home or do things as a couple near her home. Luke does not understand Annie's dramatic withdrawal from his friends, but continues to hang out with his own crowd. Annoyed, Luke stops initiating calls to Annie. Eventually he stops returning her increasingly needy calls.

Now piled on top of the undisclosed rape pain is Annie's additional loss of this young man whom she believed would be in her life forever. She reacts to her mother's caring questions about Luke's absence with indifference at first. As the days go by and her emotional state is observable to her parents, she lashes out in rage when her mother tries to get at what is happening with her daughter. Jan, noticing the changes in her friend, begins to connect with Annie again quietly, waiting for her to reveal what is going on. But Annie continues to live the rape nightmare alone. It is a month later and what weighs on her every moment, every time she uses a bathroom, is the possibility of being pregnant.

I stopped the story at this point and looked at my senior class of women and two men. Initially silent, they begin to confirm my gut feeling that Annie's story may not be unique. Several young women agreed that the story is extremely credible and that either they or someone they knew had experienced near rape episodes, especially in clubs, vacation spots and at private parties. One young woman opened up and told the class about her experience of being raped by her older boyfriend. She said her boyfriend never considered it rape as they were a couple. No longer with the boyfriend, the young woman said she eventually did reveal the episode to her mother only because her mother exerted pressure upon her to return to the "nice boy."

Time to Re-Center

When I first listened to Lynda's description and the intense emotions that her teenage daughter stirred up and displaced at her mother's feet, I could feel myself wince.

When the girl is a teenager, female emotions and their force can often throw her far to the right or perhaps to the left. Sometimes they knock her completely off her feet. For many teen girls, the storms swell, burst open and recede in alarming frequency.

When a girl is in the midst of such an emotional surge and pain, she can react. She can lash out, hide in her room, push close girlfriends away or wage war against a wiser mother. She also reacts defensively by grasping on to what she thinks she cannot live without. Some cut themselves off from girlfriends when they are in the midst of the emotional attachment phase with their boyfriends only to need them more than ever once an inevitable breakup or relationship storm hits. Others trade girlfriends who are without boyfriends for girls who are entrenched with the boyfriend game. Still others maintain their girlfriend base but wear out their female support base by focusing exclusively on the details of their boy attachment. Such behavioral patterns are symptoms of the need to realign the female center whether they occur in the teen years or midlife.

Girls need to learn re-centering by engaging in small steps with experienced mothers working as a team. Even with the unbelievable complexities in the life of today's families, the answer to riding out a storm, calming down and having a plan is not new. It means finding the time to do for ourselves and for our daughters what we are in the best position to do best.

First, stop, observe and listen. Second, drop activities and events or delegate to others in order to direct prime time toward your daughter's needs. Unplug the television then sit and eat dinner together without having to say much. Just be together and try to relax. Listen more and talk much less. Don't ask too many questions. Wait the storm out. It will pass and she will begin to share.

If you are a teen girl or are raising a teen, you need a support team. Direct your time and energy to the creation of a teen-mother discussion group. Use the skills you have honed from playgroups, girl scouts and dance clubs. Keep each team reasonably small but diverse. Rotate the teams and host each meeting around a specific issue or theme timely to the needs of the girls and mothers in your group. Provide resources. Have one mother and daughter lead the group for each session. Provide separate talk times for teens and mothers, and bring mothers and teens together to share. Include key community links such as teachers and female coaches. Effective support teams readily use the skills of members who engage in similar activities professionally or in their leadership roles in community organizations.

Finding Center: Strategies to Reveal Strong Girls and Women

Within the safety of a female pack, our teen girls and women of all ages can feed, nurture and help build strong emotional bases. Together, that base can bring visible women's faces accompanied with proactive messages into the schools where our daughters attend, into the homes of friends that they visit, and to the fathers and boys important in their lives. The message is simple: This girl is not alone; she is on one voracious, tightly bonded team. We stand behind her, ready to guide her and redirect her back on the track to a promising future.

Chapter 11
Choosing Her

> "The problem is not merely one of Woman and Career,
> Woman and the Home, Woman and Independence. It is more basically:
> how to remain whole in the midst of the distractions of life; how to
> remain balanced, no matter what centrifugal forces tend to pull one off
> center; how to remain strong, no matter what shocks come in at the
> periphery and tend to crack the hub of the wheel."
> ANNE MORROW LINDBERGH

Dora, Jessie's mother, whom we spoke of in the previous chapter, had orchestrated a tumultuous life change of her own at the age of forty-nine. She cast out her husband of twenty some years by filing divorce papers while he was away working during the week as he had done all the years of their marriage. Dora planned to marry her current lover as soon as the papers were filed and the customary waiting period was over. Her married lover had promised to leave his wife in a simultaneously staged plan. In an overly generous (if not poorly thought through) strategy, Dora also brought her married lover into her business practice as an equal partner, financial and otherwise. As Dora exited her husband out of the back door of their domicile, she opened the front door to her lover. He immediately occupied her husband's favorite living room chair with the air of a newly crowned king taking his throne. Did the conquering king take Dora as his newly found queen? Well, let's just say this royal couple was not meant to last.

Jessie's decision to change her life's goal from medicine to an easier profession was roughed out years ago by Dora. Choosing herself first was not a lesson she had learned from her mother. At the risk of blaming women and especially mothers for all the wrongs in a marriage,

Dora's story needs to be examined by applying the standards of justice, equity and conflict resolution.

Dora was twenty-eight and a well educated, employed nurse when she married Chuck. Chuck was thirty-five, high school educated and worked in the construction industry earning more money than she. Both were employed in gender-stereotypical jobs. He had lived a carefree bachelor life consisting of construction work on the road during the weekdays and baseball and pick-ups on the weekends. Along the way he became engaged twice but abruptly broke off both.

When Chuck hit his mid-thirties, he looked into the mirror and decided if he was going to have a family, he should change some of his ways. He found Dora attractive and professionally employed (that was important to him), so he married her. His life changed very little. He worked weekdays on the road, banked his entire salary, and autonomously decided that he and Dora, and later children, would live on Dora's earnings. As two babies came along three years apart, she continued to work but eventually reduced her work week to part time. Her life resembled a single mother's in most respects with the exception that she had a husband that came home on weekends. He readily admits that he did not feel she needed much money during the week. He believed that her salary provided enough for the basics.

Alone with children all week and working both inside and out of the home, Dora was ready to engage in an adult life by the weekend. On the road all week living in motels and campers, Chuck came home for the weekend to glue himself to the house, the couch, and to short spurts of playing with his children. He had unknowingly designed a marital arrangement that closely resembled the one his dad had lived.

With her husband gone more than home, Dora basically became a poorly paid housekeeper, full-time mother, part-time paid professional and very part-time wife with all the responsibility of orchestrating the logistics for her and her children inside and outside of the home. While Chuck said she could do anything she wanted to do with the money she had left from her salary minus the cost of keeping a family (which included him), he was not a partner, companion or problem solver. He recreated his father's life, but with an educated woman who brought both intellectual and financial capital into the home. Under such strain, resentment, and significantly unmet adult needs, Dora began to seek attention from other men while her husband was away. It started bit by bit and became a well-practiced strategy.

The true story of Dora and Chuck is similar to thousands of others. What is most notable is the complete absence of communication, conflict resolution and justice. From the beginning of their relationship, Chuck believed his wife was unlikely to go far on her own and that he was better off not naming the problems as that would require solutions and a change in his status quo. The very last thing he wanted to do was come home and participate in what he regarded as the woman's role. After all, as head of the household, didn't he deserve time off to rest and play? Dora's approach in addressing her loneliness and absence of a connected husband by focusing on other unavailable men as a quick fix was equally childlike and destructive.

Dora's mistake was waiting until after the wedding to brainstorm with Chuck about how they would go about creating a married life that would go beyond male dominance to a relationship of mutual respect. However, it is very likely that if she had pressed him to communicate and negotiate with her before their marriage, she would have been dealt with the same way as Chuck's two previous fiancées. Like the majority of marriages that end in divorce, and for perhaps the majority of existing marriages, women survive within or exit from their marriages with less skill on how to construct intrapersonal justice and autonomy than when they entered them. Truly sad is that regardless of their age, most women choose to recreate or maintain ineffective interaction patterns in their current relationships even as they approach the half time or final quarter of their life.

Just Fooling Herself

As a young girl I occasionally helped my Aunt Margie with the endless daily tasks of keeping a large house for three adults (one of them ill) plus a teenager, three young school age children, and a baby. While we made my father's bed (I still make hospital corners on beds as she taught me), she said, "maybe tomorrow we will come up here and your father will have made his own bed." She would then chuckle, smile at me and say, "we're just fooling ourselves, aren't we?" It was a phrase I heard repeated often as I moved through adulthood. A woman learns early on that her work multiplies inside the domestic life because the other adults and older children often delegate their chores and responsibilities to her. She may believe that things will change somehow for the better the next day, the next year or when the children go to school. More often than not, she knows that she is just fooling herself.

Living conscientiously feels differently than assuming that today's circumstances will eventually feel better. Girls and women have acquiesced to male preference based upon how things feel for boys and men. For example, it may feel stressful for a man to combine domestic tasks with his job or career and he may tell his wife or partner that he simply cannot do both without feeling tired, out of control or loss of leisure time. If he is able to state his feelings, he does so in a matter-of-fact way and then proceeds to the next thing on his list. He considered it, he reacted or responded, and then he put it away.

However, many women feel differently given the same set of circumstances. When discussing her need to get more help from her partner with the domestic work, a woman may articulate exactly what the problem is, but may hesitate at describing her true feelings concerning her partner's unwillingness to make changes that would provide some of the choices he currently enjoys. She will continue to think about it as well as generate feelings each time she goes over the unresolved problem in her head. To her, the problem "feels" more serious than to him. She perceives that she has little power in solving the problem so that her needs are met. Physically, she needs less work in the home so that she can do more somewhere else (outside work, rest, hobbies). Emotionally, she feels that her partner does not care to grant her the adult needs he gives to himself. Thus, she feels taken advantage of, disrespected and subordinated to the role of domestic worker/sometimes lover rather than an equal adult partner.

The man in her life does not understand she cannot move on to the next thing on her list or in her day. In this area of emotion, he wants her to be like him. He wants her to feel less, get over it, do as he says, and accept that he will make little if any changes.

She does not move on so easily because her brain is wired differently than his. Current scientific research substantiates that women process their emotions in the thinking, cerebral cortex portion of the brain whose primary function is language, analysis and memory. Men, on the other hand, store their feelings and emotional responses primarily in the lower, more primitive part of the brain located further away from the cognitive thinking center. One can hypothesize why female and male brain wiring for emotions and thinking are quite different, but there remains little doubt that how the brain circuits emotion and problems is different for men than it is for women. Going back to the example of the increasing burden of domestic work, a woman is unlikely to easily forget and move on as he wants her to do. She feels the injustice of the problem too intensely. Her negative visceral emotional state will endure because an important issue in her life has remained ignored by her partner. She feels unvalued by her adult partner.

A girl learns early from her family, her culture and from the boys and men in her life that she is not to think but to do as she is told. This is not unusual as the majority of women have heard that their feelings "were wrong" and that their mothers or fathers knew what was best for them. Most females have experienced such a scenario at some time in their life. With enough repetition, intense negative emotion hardwires these cultural lessons, making one person's preference a truth that replays repeatedly in the female brain. A young girl may indeed believe her feelings are wrong and that her thinking is wrong. Worse, she may conclude that she is an inferior person who should not trust herself to make her own decisions.

All of that can change when girls and women realize and accept that their feelings are there for a reason: to put them on notice that they have an unmet need. They have both the intellectual and emotional capability as well as civil, legal and cultural tools to negotiate solutions that fit with their level of development and maturity. However, many girls and women respond to their emotional alarm system in fear and self-doubt. Rather than use this highly evolved system to serve their best interests, some women will overanalyze and under-respond, creating increased doubt, fear and self-condemnation. By burying themselves in negative energy, they fail to generate proactive steps to create a happier path for themselves.

The brain develops complex neurological pathways that can build productive problem-solving skill sets or ineffective passive-aggressive behaviors and denial reactions. Either way, the female brain is growing pathways. Some actions lead to effective brainstorming and problem-solving skills as well as a sense of emotional well-being, competence and esteem. Other choices kick a female brain into prolonged avoidance and self-defense behaviors which, when overused, cause the production of brain chemicals that urge her to run or fight, which is the modern day equivalent of solving a problem. Fooling herself by doing nothing is an action rippled with prolonged negative consequences to her well-being.

Building a Strong Core

Sarah, a woman I knew, once asked me what needs to be done to change the trajectory of women who say they will look out for their interests, but when put to the test, they do not. They instead crumble to the old seduction arguments that factoring in their interests will somehow cause harm to new romances, couples, the family, the workplace and, most important, to them. The best time to shore up a house is probably not during a tornado; it is also true that a more effective approach to building a strong sense of self is for girls and women to work on it daily.

As a way to introduce the strategies of building a strong female core, I have developed the following quiz. Once you complete it, think about the questions posed for reflection at the end.

Qualities of a Just Life for Women

Directions: How skillful have you been or are you now in constructing a female life that is based upon dignity, self-reliance and justice? Often girls and women can articulate precisely how they want to conduct their lives but then either fall silent when problems arise or fall prey to sabotage and either/or demands. Read each item and assign yourself a rating from 0 (did not do at all) to 5 (did at very high level) on each of the traits.

High School Age & Twenties

_____ 1. I took/will take math, science, foreign language and technology classes each of my four years of high school.

_____ 2. I enrolled/plan to enroll in math, science, technology and other specialized courses offered by technical colleges, colleges or on-line options and had them applied/will apply toward my high school program.

_____ 3. I participated/currently participate in summer courses that developed/develop my competence with business tools, financial skills or career focused capabilities.

_____ 4. I worked/currently work on my high school goals and did/do not change or waiver in them in order to align my interests, time and plans with a boy/young man.

_____ 5. I limited/currently limit my part-time work during the school year in order to study, enjoy hobbies and be physically active.

_____ 6. I delayed/intend to delay marriage and child bearing until I have well developed personal and skill assets in several categories.

_____ 7. I obtained/am obtaining specific financial skills and financial experiences which provided/provide me competence and confidence in earning, saving, paying my own bills, understanding credit and investments.

_____ 8. I chose/choose my closest friends of both gender that displayed/display similar ambitions, values, wellness and beliefs in equal opportunity and justice for individuals.

_____ 9. I held/hold myself accountable and engage in regular activities that lead to a balanced emotional-social-intellectual state of my being.

_____ 10. I analyzed/analyze the women in my family/life with an objective, detached eye not to judge but "see" the relationship between their choices and the quality of their own lives in order to plan alternatives and make wise choices.

_____ 11. I learned/learn from the actions and behaviors of family members, friends and boy/male friends that a pattern of living and behaving is real and that I must accept evaluate and make independent choices of my own even if it means dropping a boyfriend, losing a friend or distancing myself from the message and/or a family member.

_____ 12. I engaged/engage in self-reflection and make new goals in order to hold myself accountable for my own choices, happiness and outcomes.

High School Age & Twenties Section Total: Scored _____/60; _____%

Thirties & Motherhood

_____ 13. I knew/know what my individual needs are as well as the needs that are common to my family, friends and/or intimate partners.

_____ 14. I chose/am choosing close friends and/or a life partner that displays similar values, education, spiritual beliefs and goals as me.

_____ 15. I constructed/construct my close relationships by asking for those things that are important to me while helping others to get what they need.

_____ 16. I engage in behaviors that demonstrate what I am committed to in my life, e.g., I believe children/my partner should learn to be responsible thus I do not do for them what they can do for themselves on a routine basis such as picking up clothes or taking turns preparing evening meals.

_____ 17. I do not give up my work, projects, or fulfilling commitments or activities because my partner/family finds their work, projects, and activities are more important than mine.

_____ 18. I implement strategies at work and in my home to get things done that are not along gender lines or sexual roles and work both in the home and outside of the home.

_____ 19. I do not fall prey to a partner's/close friends reasoning that it is too hard to communicate and work out a flexible plan so I need to give up my position and right to have my needs met when it is important to me.

_____ 20. I can honestly say that I operate my relationships based on an exchange principle: I try to do the things that are valued for the significant people in my life and I expect that they will try to do things that are valued to me in some sense of balance or proportion.

Thirties &/or Motherhood Section Total: _____/40 Possible Points; _____%

Midlife through Wisdom Stage

_____ 21. I discussed/discuss openly and construct a plan with my partner/family about alternatives to providing home care for elderly adults and for the coverage of children/grandchildren other than assuming I am the only plan.

_____ 22. I learned and used/learn and use a variety of conflict resolution strategies in order to balance work within and outside of the home with my partner/family without becoming the primary person who does most of the unpaid domestic work.

_____ 23. I raised/raise my children teaching them how to make contributions to our households (making beds, folding laundry, making a meal once a week).

_____ 24. I made/make sure that my children learn how to do work at home/outside of the home that crosses traditional gender categories.

_____ 25. I hold and use a view of religious beliefs and role of men and women in a spirit of fairness, justice and moral living as opposed to rigid black and while thinking regarding roles of girls/boys and women/men.

_____ 26. I constructed/construct my own life and financial plan independently and perhaps in cooperation with a life partner (if I have one) as far as premarital planning, will, end of life planning, and health care directives.

_____ 27. I live a portion of my life autonomously from a partner or my family providing me time to vacation alone, connect with my own friends, conduct my work, profession or hobbies throughout my life for the value and fulfillment they provide to me.

Mid Life through Wisdom Stage Section Total: _____/35 Possible Points; _____%

Scoring & Reflection

Add up your score by totaling the numbers you awarded each item. Calculate percent scores for each section and an overall percent score. Reflect upon the following:

➤ Which stage did you score highest; lowest?

➤ Did you progress, regress or remain at the same level throughout the stages you were able to score given your current age and stage of life?

➤ How would you label/categorize those areas you perceive to be strengths; how would you label/categorize those areas you perceive to be weaknesses?

➤ What three items (behavioral patterns) to you want to improve or change?

Once you have reflected upon your current problem-solving patterns and the extent to which you possess a justice-oriented life, the tools and strategies described below, if systematically practiced, will increase your abilities to live a balanced life.

RAISE THE BAR. A fundamental concept to put in place is to believe that girls and women have extraordinary potential. Without going over concepts covered earlier in this book, a fundamental strategy is to raise the bar for what girls and women can and will contribute by maximizing their own talents, skills and abilities. If a girl becomes practiced in setting her own goals and then endures setbacks without giving up, she learns that in all things there is joy, failure, unanticipated barriers and hardships. To reach her goal she knows she cannot lower the bar or reduce expectations of herself if she is to jump that horse, make the soccer team or graduate from medical school.

A fundamental concept is if a girl or woman is going to error, then error up. By striving to make the Olympic Swim Team, a female swimmer will experience state-of-the-art training, coaching and physical development; if she does not make the team, she will be able to transfer her physical and intellectual capabilities easier to an opportunity that requires those same traits. By completing four years of math, a high school girl will increase her confidence in relating to the world mathematically in addition to many more opportunities upon high school graduation.

EDUCATE UP. A fundamental problem that I addressed in a previous chapter on schooling is that girls and women have not been rigorously educated and developed. Educating up begins with parents when their daughters are babies. It requires a mindset that escapes the false safety of a pink and blue world. Once girls participate in schooling, their curriculum simply must include math, science, financial savvy and technology beginning in the early grades and mandated in their curriculum for each of the four years of high school. Opting out of the "hard curriculum" is a strategy for remaining dependent and in the lower rung of the economic ladder.

CREATE INTRAPERSONAL FAIRNESS AND JUSTICE. It is "just" for women to expect that they can construct lives that include love, affection and intimacy as well as work and raising children while still enjoying the full range of civil and legal rights—just as it is fair for men to expect the same. In her article on love, marriage and the question of justice, author Pauline Kleingeld, professor of philosophy, states that the first step is for women to become more aware of how justice plays out in their day-to-day lives. If girls and women do not recognize that many of their day-to-day battles have to do with a justice-based life, how can they engage in strategies to correct the injustice? It is not just for a girl or woman to force herself from a schooling path that she really wants due to self-doubt and fear. Nor is it just for a woman to be forced to do the majority of the domestic tasks, child-rearing, cooking and cleaning in a workday that has no limits, compensation or flexibility.

In the past, girls and women were forced to remain within narrow gender-defined roles and responsibilities. If roles in their personal lives are to reflect the additional responsibilities, rights and obligations women now possess in their public and legal lives, they must ask for them. And as Kleingeld discloses, in some cases, they will have to fight for them. Ask or fight, women will certainly need to acquire strong skills in communication, negotiation and conflict resolution and be able to use them for their own benefit without apology. Men ask for what they need because they are taught to do so. Women hope that men and important others in their life will "just know" what it is they need and consequently will engage in fair action.

CREATE GOAL-ORIENTED PATHWAYS. A very effective strategy in carving out a balanced life is to construct a circle of influence. Here is how to construct yours. Begin by drawing a large circle in the middle of a piece of paper. Draw a small circle in the center and write your name on it. Now draw any number of other circles representing the various persons that are important in your life: family, spouse, intimate friends, children, co-workers, high school friends, etc. Write their names in the middle of the circles you have drawn for them. Position them somewhere near to your own circle or toward the circumference of the large circle.

Once your influence circle is completed, examine the circles of names. These represent your current circle of influence. Which people that you included have you seen most often? Who would you like to see more? Who would you like to take out of your current circle of influence because their influence is negative? Whom have you forgotten to add and would like to include? Who would you like to spend more time with? Are there people of mixed ages and from different occupations? Are all of the circles limited to family? Is there someone you have lost touch with over the years that you would like to reconnect with? Have you included people who are there to meet a need just for you such as a therapist, your medical doctor or a professional colleague that you have built a close relationship with over the years? Finally, ask yourself how your current circle of influence reflects and assists you in attaining a balanced just life.

Revise your circle by deleting names, adding names and repositioning specific people either closer to your own circle or further away. Don't hesitate to move someone further from your center or to eliminate someone altogether. This exercise will help you to visualize your life and needs as they currently exist.

Using your newly constructed circle of influence, write down goals that will assist you in focusing on a balanced secure life. Write at least one goal for of the following categories: safety and security, financial, health and well being, family, friendships, and spiritual. You may want to create additional categories or create more than one goal. Be careful to limit the number of goals you construct for each category to no more than five. Now review your circle of influence and reflect how the people in your circle can be connected to your goals. Really think this part of the process through and try to visualize very specific strategies and activities. For example, if you do not have anyone in your circle of influence who is either good at financial planning or is a financial planner that you can work with, you will want to add someone if your financial planning category really needs work. Under each goal, list specific tasks that will lead to the accomplishment of or progress in that goal. Last, prioritize your list of tasks ranking the most important task with a number one, second most important as two and so on.

Keep your goals in a place where you will see them on a regular basis. Tuck them into your monthly bill folder or put the list into your electronic calendar on a daily task menu so it pops up on each day's calendar. Clip it to your wall calendar if you routinely look at it each night or morning. You will want to make it visually present to you as you go about your everyday life. Once you experience modest success in meeting your goals, it is contagious. Look for books, on-line articles and one-day workshops to sharpen your skills at setting and meeting success in the goals you set.

ACQUIRE NEGOTIATION, CONFLICT RESOLUTION AND PROBLEM-SOLVING SAVVY. In order to know where you want to go it is important to set and maintain life goals. To accomplish your goals, you need to hone your skills in conflict resolution and negotiation. Women are substantially less skilled than men in acknowledging conflict as a necessary and unavoidable part of daily life. Many women avoid any kind of conflict as they have been taught it is wrong and that they should rely on and please others by giving in or giving up their wishes and goals. An excellent resource I have used for at least ten years in a graduate class is David Johnson's book, *Reaching Out: Interpersonal Effectiveness and Self-Actualization*. While it is a superb resource to read alone, its impact is far greater when read and discussed with a group of others in a class or book group setting.

Equally valuable is the input provided by Dave Hancock, a national business owner, entrepreneur and resident of the Chippewa Valley in Wisconsin. "The Hancock Principles: Negotiating, Relationship-Building and Living" reflects the messages of the seminars he has conducted for me in my graduate class for more than a decade. His message empowers men and women to increase their effectiveness in negotiation and conflict resolution while maintaining relationships both in their personal and professional lives. I have summarized Hancock's work here into "The Hancock Principles" as they furnish proactive, time-tested strategies.

THE HANCOCK PRINCIPLES*
Negotiating, Relationship-Building & Living

1. You can be a soft speaker when your actions speak loudly.
2. A non-threatening approach is the most effective.
3. Listening is key.
4. Put your priorities and your responsibilities to yourself and to others at the forefront.
5. Take informed, calculated, and well-timed risks.
6. Avoid drawing lines in the sand.
7. Use the Golden Rule for golden people; but use the iron rule for iron-hearted people.
8. Refuse to waste time being a victim.
9. An ego-less approach makes others feel important.

10. Allow people you work with or are in "partnership" with to feel equal by including them in decision-making.
11. Take the time necessary to communicate to the speaker exactly what they need to hear.
12. Do the unpleasant thing to promote growth in the organization (or in you); make the tough decision.
13. Don't spend a lot of time analyzing yourself.
14. Be authentic; live a life that reflects your beliefs.
15. To build success, to be a success, you can't go it alone.
16. There is no substitution for experience.
17. Live an authentic life by owning your statements, your philosophies and holding yourself accountable. You represent the whole of your life.

*Dave Hancock is a national business owner, entrepreneur and resident of the Chippewa Valley in Wisconsin.

The center of the Hancock Principles is putting your priorities and your responsibilities to yourself at the forefront. The challenge for a girl or woman is to formulate a vision of how she will use her life to grow, acquire love and connectedness as well as financial security. Establishing priorities and identifying personal responsibilities are fundamental steps and, according to Hancock, an effective person, girl or woman cannot delegate this responsibility to another. No one knows better than she what will make her happy, secure and fulfilled as she transitions through the stages of her life.

Many of the Hancock Principles address the importance of communication strategies. Remaining cool and articulating wants and desires with details plus establishing an action plan is extremely effective when coupled with a style that is respectful and non-threatening. Sharing problems and asking for what you want is best done by controlling your ego and not playing the victim game. A key relationship-building skill is to take time to communicate to the speaker exactly what they need and what the listener needs to hear as well. When used, this ability taps into a woman's most natural abilities. In negotiating new domestic arrangements, a male partner may wrongly infer that his partner wants out of the relationship. The more important the topic (certainly changing the domestic work load ritual is) and the more important the person is to her, the more time and care she will need to communicate and work out a plan that suits both persons.

Hancock stresses that perhaps it is equally important to focus on what *not* to do: Don't threaten. Don't make decisions on your own that affect significant others. Don't settle upon a plan without gathering advice from people with more experience than you have. And unless it relates to basic ethical or morality issues, avoid drawing lines in the sand by insisting on your way or no way. Hancock warns that such a negotiating style customarily leads to failure and produces a threat to relationships.

Historically, women have not had the benefits derived from working on teams. Thus, they have not acquired a mixture of approaches learned from members more experienced than they. Experienced and adept team players avoid compulsive reactions in favor of consulting with wiser friends, appropriate professionals and resources before taking a significant action which affects them and others. Women of any age can enforce personal boundaries when iron-hearted people force their will upon them. However, there is no fast and easy way to acquire the set of skills contained in the Hancock Principles. A woman must discipline herself to do the hard thing to promote growth within rather than spend too much time analyzing herself or playing the role of a victim. Overall, the Hancock Principles provide a strong platform by which women can advance their goals through artful negotiation and conflict resolution.

LEAVE BOYS AND MEN ALONE FOR AWHILE. Have you ever had a habit of eating chocolate bars every day that you didn't need or using your cell phone during peak periods and going over your minutes? You may have tried cutting back to one chocolate bar every other day or one a week or limiting those cell calls to ten minutes during weekdays and making as many calls on the free minutes on weekends. For many, success is short lived. Once the feeling of failure hits, we resume eating a chocolate bar a day or reluctantly paying the higher cell bill.

For reasons discussed earlier, girls and women are accustomed to relying on boys and men to meet too many of their emotional and recreational needs and decision-making responsibilities. For many, it is like the chocolate bar: an all or nothing proposition. A common psychological principle of change asks that for any behavior you are dropping or reducing, you should substitute another behavior in its place.

Like giving up eating chocolate every day, it may be easier to leave it alone altogether for three weeks and then reintroduce it a little bit on the weekends, in smaller quantities and of better quality. Leaving boys and men alone for awhile is the same idea. Because the culture has so entrenched girls and women into believing they cannot get along without the opposite sex, one way to open up space for girls and women is to leave the boys and men alone for awhile. If you are used to not thinking about your weekends because they are consumed first with domestic work and then by the boy/man in your life, find one weekend a month that you will go it alone—no boys—no men—just you.

By going it alone a woman will have to deal with the feelings that will follow. Can she go to a movie alone and what will people think? Answer: that she is at the movies. How will she feel about going to the local bookstore alone? Answer: Happy because she can stay as long as she wants as she will not have to hear that he has hunted down his book, paid for it and is now racing out to the car. Can she really go out to lunch by herself and what will people think if they see her sitting alone? Answer: That will depend if she is sitting there crying or trying to cover up her face in a book or if she is enjoying her lunch, eating slowly and reflecting upon something she enjoyed earlier that morning. I challenge you: can you leave him/them alone for one entire week?

Rhona Mahony has written a masterful book called *Kidding Ourselves: Breadwinning, Babies and Bargaining Power* in which she suggests that one possible strategy in equalizing child care among parents is that mothers simply need to leave men alone with the children. Let men do child care the way they want to do it without insisting that men supervise, entertain children and complete tasks the same way that the mothers and women do. When women give critical feedback to fathers that they really cannot take care of a baby or child as well as the mother can, they simply reinforce the notion held by the majority of boys and men that childcare is a role they neither aspire to nor are equipped to do competently. A male's predictable response to a woman's negative feedback is to inform his partner, or the mother of the child, that she had better do it herself. I recall learning to change a baby's diaper when I was eight years old. I did little right except somehow get most of the baby's bottom covered with a cloth diaper and sometimes I stuck the child with the diaper pin! How can a man acquire experience and competence in caring for children and completing household tasks that a woman needs help with if he is not allowed a learning curve which includes trail and error?

In her article titled "Sex and not the city? The aspirations of the thirty-something working woman," Joanna Brewis describes men caught in the lagged adaptation stage of childcare and household work. She develops the point that while a job or career is still at the center of who a man is, keeping a home and raising children is still regarded as the rightful role and sole territory of a woman. Even if she does work outside of the home, this commitment is regarded as being less than a man's due to the unspoken recognition of the reality of the second shift. For a woman who chooses not to work or who cannot work outside of the home while raising her children, her workday and workload is assumed to be without limits, assistance or compensation of any kind. But is that a just and fair position to assume? Because valuable work is not exchanged for money, does that mean we can throw an unlimited amount on a woman and offer her no help or relief?

If he will not negotiate and problem solve, leave him alone in whatever way that may work for you. There is always a cost to be paid for changing the status quo.

When the Center Cracks

Emotional pain and self doubt are not unique to girls and women. Boys and men too experience intense feelings and questions. Girls and women are much more likely to work over their thinking and analytical processes far longer than most boys and men. Males appear to compartmentalize their day as well as their feelings more so than females. With the female brain wired as it is, girls and women are more likely to keep themselves in the heat of the pain—reliving rescripting and catastrophizing an event or loss.

What can girls and women do when intense emotional pain, loss and doubt hit? First, I can not overemphasize the importance of women listening and affirming that the pain each of us feels is real but that it will, like most physical pain, lessen and go away with time and care. It is not all that unusual for a girl or woman reeling from a personal life event to be told stories of how another's situation is/was far worse or to minimize the significance of her pain. Another unfruitful reaction is to focus on the male endlessly and extend the dialogue to any number of other stories of the opposite sex. A limited amount of reflection is appropriate but only to the extent that it is centered on the girl and woman and her response to her feelings and what positive actions she can take. Things will not just automatically get better with time. She can make her life worse if the wrong choices are made.

Building and using a "girl pack" is a strategy I have advocated for many years. I first applied this strategy when I found myself catapulted into a serious situational depression. I wrote the names of ten people on a small index card including phone numbers and carried it with me at all times. The names included five women who could provide support and one hour of their time coaching: three women at a confidential women's crisis center, my therapist and my physician. By the time I had talked through some difficult moments or hours or days, I either felt better and/or had let out both the toxic adrenaline and other by-products of depression. On the nights that I could not sleep, I called the women's crisis telephone support centers and found a caring voice at the other end to listen and provide encouragement, assisting me in putting a plan together for the following morning to confront the feelings that I could not release.

Girls and women should set limits on the amount of emotional aftershock they expose themselves to as a consequence of reliving and retelling the events of their trauma or loss. The knowledge base on the effects of prolonged negative emotions on both the brain and the physical body are well documented. In another situation that I was dealing with that caused emotional pain, I told a close female friend that I was going to limit my grief and analysis of the situation to three days. We were sitting at an outdoor café just feet from the shores of Lake Superior at the time. On day four when I began to rehearse old territory, my friend reminded me of my intent to limit the upsetting event and if I did not focus on my current life's activities, she would drag me to the water's edge and hold my head under the cold waters of Lake Superior to wake me up! We laughed, but I have to say that it was a profoundly effective strategy. Setting limits of rehearsing sad events also aligns with other Hancock Principles of not going it all, refusing to play a victim role, and not dwelling upon the past by over analyzing beyond what is necessary to learn a lesson and move forward.

When moving through significant loss and emotional pain, girls and women need to remind themselves that the path to healing is really hard work. Having given birth to two children, I can honestly say that the energy and work I needed to do to recover from a profound situational depression was more intense, more painful and certainly more emotionally retching than the labor and delivery of either of my children. But as was the gift of the lives of my two children, it is true that learning lessons from my loss and emotional pain provided the strength I needed to compose a new life for myself.

Choosing Together

The university that I work at possesses a formidable reputation in men's basketball primarily earned by a nationally recognized male coach. When I arrived years ago as a new assistant professor, I became quickly addicted to following the team. My son and I, then just a small boy, went to home games and traveled to away games including national tournaments in Kansas City. I knew the team members' statistical averages and their strengths and weaknesses in the positions they played. I had some of them in class. Two of the young players worked with my son both as a basketball coach and mentor outlining the lessons he could learn from being an athlete. However, it was no secret that the women's basketball team and female coach were living in substandard practice and playing quarters. The team received little assistance from the men's star coach in providing an equal playing field.

A young savvy female coach joined the women's team and together with highly effective advocacy from female professors in the athletic department, the women's team eventually earned both an equal playing field and a national reputation of their own. As my office is housed in the same building where both the men's and women's team now practice and play, I often saunter pass them, stop and watch and reflect on far we have come working together for the benefit of both the young men and women at my institution without doing harm to either in the process.

The summer I worked on this final chapter, Lauren, age nine, and Hannah, age six, participated in the university women's basketball camp coached by the female head coach, her staff, members of the university women's team and female varsity high school players from the area. At the end of session, the girls walked into my office accompanied by a female athletic trainer. She was there to let me know that Hannah had been hit in the head several times and that she might experience a headache or get a bump on her head. The trainer assured me and the girls that she did not think it was anything to be overly concerned about. She looked at Hannah and then at me and said that Hannah was learning the important lesson of keeping her hands up to protect her head and face and that by tomorrow she would be deflecting those balls before they made physical contact with her.

The next morning after watching eighty school-aged girls go through drills with at least ten female coaches, I asked the assistant coach of the university women's teams if they were able to lower the baskets from the standard height they were set for the adult men. She replied that for whatever reason the baskets could not be lowered for the girls who ranged from five to thirteen years old. She quickly added that it was not a problem. The girls would learn what was most important so that over time they could hit those baskets. I nodded in complete agreement.

I walked away from what was once the men's-only basketball arena to my office and thought to myself that the young woman basketball coach had it in exactly the right order. You have to get the girl on the basketball court first, then build the girl, not lower the hoop. But a girl on a court alone is not enough. Skilled, experienced women coaches of different ages and experiences can transform a girl's thinking about herself and teach her that she needs a girl pack as well. An experienced woman, one who has traveled her own journey from girlhood to success, will inspire a novice girl. In due time and under her own power, that same girl will put her ball in flight with net swishing and swaying as her ball hits its mark.

Chapter 12
A Beautiful Girl— A Beautiful Woman

"Beauty is not in the face; beauty is a light in the heart."
KAHLIL GIBRAN

Today, in most societies, little girls and then grown women measure themselves against the beauty standard. Roget's New Millennium Thesaurus defines beautiful people as the "aristocracy, beau mode, café society, famous people, glamorous people, jet set, privileged class, the well-to-do, upper crust." Such a definition smacks of exclusion. It implies if you are not aristocratic, famous or jet set, then you cannot be beautiful. Then, you must be un-beautiful, ordinary, and not highly valued.

Yet it is equally true that psychologists and anthropologists have supported the notion that as babies, children, and grown adults, we will spend more time gazing at both members of the opposite sex whose facial features are symmetrically aligned and composed of particular attributes that, over time, human beings have labeled beautiful. Those characteristics include widely-spaced large eyes, high cheek bones, full lips and perfectly matched sides of the face. For women, additional standards of a bell curve figure, larger breasts, and feminine, baby-like faces have been judged to be visually preferred by men.

The core principal of beauty is that inner beauty lasts and physical beauty diminishes as we age. Although to be truthful, beautiful women I know who are in their seventies and eighties and who have retained their spark still maintain an edge over their peer group. However, beauty that lasts does not live on the outside. Acquiring and keeping a spark is what the life force is essentially about and then, of course, passing it on.

A beautiful woman acknowledges how those who came before her have changed her life.

I often repeat to females of all ages that we came into this world alone and that is how we are going to leave. By these words, I try to remind myself and others that we have been given our own gift of life and it is not attached to someone else's life force. The more I live in that understanding the more I am grateful to those women who came before me whose lives were filled with limitations, hardships, and early, enduring losses. In spite of those challenges, some women in our families and others dedicated their lives to intellectual development and to the care of their minds, bodies, and spirits. They were healers, teachers, nurses, physicians, and philosophers in their own right. They inspired, suffered, and provided those women of later generations with a model of what the female life can bring to others. I believe we must keep their stories alive within our family circles.

My granddaughters, age six and nine, asked me if I was ever going to die. I could see by hearing their concern and looking into their eyes that they wanted me to tell them that I would live forever. I knew this was an important moment for us and I was being called upon to tell the truth. Perhaps it is because I lost my own mother at a tender age when I needed her very much that I recognized the importance of their question. Thus, I told my granddaughters that someday I would die. I went on to explain that everything that has life eventually will die while quickly affirming that I intended to live for a very long time. I stressed to them that when I am gone, I know they will miss me. But I wanted them to remember all of the good times we have had together, the songs we sang and the music to which we danced. I want them to remember me, smile, and be happy that we shared so much love together. They listen intently and I noticed a tear or two slip down their cheeks which still burns inside of me. The youngest still asks, as if fact checking, if it is true that someday I will die and she blurts out that she does not want that to ever happen. Growing up happens in infinitely tiny steps over a long journey and I cannot deprive her of opportunities to grow strong by comforting her with falsehoods. I also am aware that I too have grown stronger and am able to talk of those things to come because I have uncovered the story of strong and courageous women in my own family.

Just as it is important to acknowledge those women in our families that have impacted our lives, it is essential that we credit the Susan B. Anthony's whether they were scientists, politicians, or social workers. The legal and civil rights won by them and the barriers they helped to rip down have resulted in improving the quality of a woman's life that is unequaled in no other country in the world. Their work laid the road for all of us as we continue to press those issues important to us both as individuals and to women as a whole. Continued dedication and hard work is a must as nothing remains static: all reform improves or unravels.

A beautiful woman knows her gifts and limitations and accepts them with grace.

Sometimes when you give a grown woman a compliment, she will argue with you, inform you that you are wrong or, worse yet, tell you of her faults or weaknesses. Is it because as women we are raised with the expectation that we need to do many things at the same time and to do them without error? We all have read that boys are given more constructive feedback and rewards than girls, which may be why so many girls seek out feedback that they are accepted and loved.

Bury forever the lie that girls and women must be good at everything. It is not required of any woman to be perfect or perfectly good. That is what saying no and taking calculated risks is all about. Life is a limited resource and eventually that resource will run out. If we determine what our interests are and what our innate gifts are, we can be more efficient about creating a life work that is fulfilling, interesting, and that sustains growth over time. We will all need to work harder in areas we find less interesting. We must stay the course and discipline ourselves to grow skills in areas we find less appealing but nevertheless are essential (financial skills). The point is that we do not have to do everything, nor do we have to do everything with the same zeal and energy. We certainly do not have to do most things perfectly.

A beautiful woman's life echoes a liberating simplicity.

Simplicity used to describe a woman's life may seem counter intuitive. Yet, the happiest women I know simplify by focusing on those activities that are at the center of their hearts. To do that requires us to name our values and to say the names of those who are in our center of caring or influence. Once we can do that, we can limit our goals in order to build a life that is rich, centered, and thus simple. When we engage deeply in those activities and work that define who we are, we are more likely to produce positive energy and joy and less likely to be bogged down with anxiety, stress, and resentment.

A beautiful woman can portray strength, leadership, and maternal caring.

Whether you are a man or a woman, life has a way of sending you as many trials and tribulations as it does joys and celebrations. We don't question the good stuff, but we can be crushed with little setbacks and not prepare ourselves to ride out the storms if we don't acquire a personal reservoir of strength, leadership, and caring. Too many women were raised in a culture that expects girls and women to be one dimensional; that is, soft, deferential and passive. While it is true that we expect men to be direct, assertive, and in-charge, expecting a person to lead and be assertive generally produces a person that is receptive to assuming more responsibility and that behavior, in turn, results in more opportunities. The lioness and female bear are instructive to girls and women in that they are tender and maternal yet they are also powerful hunters and protectors.

A beautiful woman is authentic.

We are our passion. Without passion driving us, we are driven by others' passions. If we are not careful, we use up all of our own energy while reserving little for our own dreams. It is no wonder we see so many women exhausted, anxious, and depressed with all they are required to do. They continue a cycle which reserves too little time for their own rest, relaxation, meditation, and work. It is easy to become resentful of our partner's or co-workers' successes when we feel as though it comes at our own expense. Years ago I visited my physician complaining of stomach pains and exhaustion. As he was examining me, he asked me a simple question that made me cry. He asked, "When was the last time you laughed and experienced joy?" I realized I could not remember. I had made my life unnecessarily complicated by trying to meet too many other people's preferences and expectations. As women, we must become more focused on what is at the center of our value system, our net worth as a human being, as a mother, a partner, and as an individual. The more we center on that which is our passion, the more positive energy will drive our bodies and our souls.

Authenticity requires reflection, timing, and perseverance. That which is our passion can be resurrected from our girlhood. What we loved then is likely to inspire and bring us joy as adults. I have learned from many people that we do not change the core of our beings that much from childhood. We have a lifetime to grow and nurture our dreams and depending upon the choices we make, the timeline is different for each of us. Some women will have children early on, others later in life, and still others will choose to have no children at all. Comparing our life with others and imitating someone else's life as the only right path will surely lead to anxiety, frustration, and a sense of inadequacy.

I believe the most important trait for all women may be perseverance, the willingness to continue working on your dream, your work, and your art even if only for your own enjoyment and comfort. Perseverance also entails not giving into despair, losing hope, and relinquishing your life force to darkness. Hopefully we have learned from those who have been unjustly imprisoned and tortured, and from those that have been enslaved by depression. Life matters. Thus, at all cost, women must see the importance of keeping hope and, like the lioness, guarding their strength.

A beautiful woman is a mystery that is housed in the interior.

Many mornings, I light a candle in my kitchen or burn incense that reminds me of the Chequamegon woods of my birth. Some mornings I turn on light classical instrumental music. In winter, my favorite days are cold, sunny, and snow covered. I am pulled north if I can leave and, if not, I turn toward the out of doors and imagine that I am in the woods of Lake Superior. In the winter woods, you can hear yourself breathe. There are few if any human voices. Within minutes, my mind is cleared and restored and I begin to hear the songs of birds that have stayed the winter. I can trace the path of the rabbits, moles, and squirrels in the snow. I can clearly see where the deer have bedded down in late afternoon or evening.

When I was a young child of eight, I loved to go out on the coldest of winter days for as many hours as my face and hands would tolerate. I could not go far from home so I trudged toward the outer boundaries of the forest and played under the arms of the towering pines. They offered protection from the wind and the cold, and if you went far enough under them, there was no snow at all. It was a perfect place to play, to imagine, to just "be" as a young girl. I claimed it as my secret winter domain. It was mystical and magical, but as a child I had no words to explain its power. I could only feel it.

The following year I moved to an urban city to live with my aunt. There were no trees, no hills, and no Chequamegon lands. I walked down newly paved sidewalks lined with trees smaller than I was in a newborn suburb. I desperately looked for green seclusion in the form of wooded trees, but found none. I was soul sick, depressed, and sensory deprived. I coped and adapted for the next nine years, but the concrete city would never be home. Today I have words for what I experienced as a child: I had been removed from my interior life and it was thirty years before I would reclaim it.

What I have learned I now share with you. The interior life is attained by communing with our senses and our intuitive spirit. It is a place that triggers our senses and where our emotions flow with ease. The inner core of a girl and woman's being will speak the truth to her if she learns how to tune out the world and hear its message. She has been given a life that is like no other. She is obligated to challenge herself, to lead, and finally, to leave her story to the next generation of girls to follow. By tapping into the life force, she will find her own path and live in splendor and grace.

General References

Babcock, Linda and Sara Laschever (2003). Women Don't Ask: Negotiation and the Gender Divide. Princeton: Princeton University Press.

Douglas, Susan J (1995). Where the Girls Are: Growing Up Female with the Mass Media. New York: Times Books.

Forsyth, Sondra and Ms. Foundation for Women (1998). Girls Seen and Heard: 52 Life Lessons for Our Daughters. New York: Tarcher/Putnam Books.

Gurian, Michael (2001). Boys and Girls Learn Differently! A Guide for Teachers and Parents. San Francisco: Jossey-Bass.

Kohn, Alfie (2000). The Schools Our Children Deserve: Moving Beyond Traditional Classrooms and "Tougher Standards." New York: Houghton Mifflin.

Orenstein, Peggy in association with American Assocaition of University Women (1994). School Girls: Young Women, Self-Esteem, and the Confidence Gap. New York: Anchor Books.

Rholes, W. Steven and Jeffry A. Simpson (2004). Adult Attachment. New York: The Guilford Press.

Sax, Leonard (2005). Why Gender Matters: What Parents and Teachers Need to Know about the Emerging Science of Sex Differences. New York: Doubleday.

Schuman, David (2004). American Schools, American Teachers: Issues and Perspectives. Boston: Pearson Education, Inc.

Washburne Rensenbrink, Carla (2001). All in Our Places: Feminist Challenges in Elementary School Classrooms. Lanham: Rowman & Littlefield Publishers, Inc.

CHAPTER 1: FORGING A PATH

American Association of University Women (1991). *Shortchanging Girls, Shortchanging America: A Call to Action.* American Association of University Women: Washington, DC.

Anyon, Jean (1981). Social class and school knowledge. *Curriculum Inquiry*, 11:1, 3–42.

Barbieri, M. (1995). *Sounds from the heart: Learning to listen to girls.* Heinemann: Portsmouth, N.H.

Brown, L. M. (1991). Telling a girl's life: Self-authorization as a form of resistance. *Woman and Therapy, 11*, 71–86.

Chase, S. (1995). *Ambiguous Empowerment: The Work Narratives of Women School Superintendents.* University of Massachusetts Press: Amherst.

Darder, A. (1994). How does the culture of the teacher shape the classroom experience of Latino students? The unexamined question in critical pedagogy. In Stanley William Rothstein (ed.), *Handbook of Schooling in Urban America* (pp. 195–221). Greenwood Press: Westport, CT.

Delpit, L. D. (1993). The silenced dialogue: Power and pedagogy in education other people's children. In Lois Weis & Michelle Fine (eds.), *Beyond Silenced Voices: Class, Race, and Gender in United States Schools* (pp. 119–129). State University of New York Press: New York.

Fordham, S. (1993). "Those loud black girls": (Black) women, silence, and gender "passing" in the academy. *Anthropology and Education Quarterly*, 24, 3–32.

Goertz, M, Ekstrom, R., & Rock, D. (1991). High school dropouts: Issues of race and sex. In R Lerner, A. Petersen, & J. Brooks-Gunn (eds.), *The Encyclopedia of Adolescence* (pp. 250–253). Garland Publishing: New York.

Grant, L. (1994). Helpers, enforcers, and go-betweens: Black females in elementary school classrooms. In M.B. Zinn & B. Thornton Dill (eds.), *Women of Color in U.S. Society*. Temple University Press: Philadelphia, PA.

Hooks, B. (1993). Keeping close to home: Class and education. In M. Tokarczyk & E. Fay (eds.), *Working Class Women in the Academy: Laborers in the Knowledge Factory* (pp.99–111). University of Massachusetts Press: Amherst.

Kaplan, E.B. (1997). Women's perceptions of the adolescents experience. *Adolescence, 32*, 715–734.

Koch, Patricia, Barthalow (2002). *Women's sexuality as they age: The more things change, the more they stay the same.* Sex Information and Education Council of the U.S.

Kozol, J. (1991). *Savage Inequalities: Children in America's Schools.* Crown Publishers: New York.

Luttrell, W. (1993). "The teachers, they all had their pets": Concepts of gender, knowledge, and power. *Signs, 18,* 505–547.

Luttrell, W. (1997). *School-Smart and Mother-wise: Working Class Women's Identity and Schooling.* Routledge: New York.

Mack, Maureen, D.(2005). "A Better Ending". *Open Minds Quarterly,* Summer Edition.

Mack, Maureen, D. (1998). "The Psychosocial Features of Effective Mentors for Girls and Young Women." *WAMLE Journal.*

Mack, Maureen, D. (1992). "Changing Families-Changing Middle Schools." *National Middle School Journal.*

National Council for Research on Women (2003). *Girls Report.* www.ncrw.org/research/exec_sum.htm

Orenstein, P. (1994). *Schoolgirls.* Anchor books: New York.

Planned Parenthood Federation of America (2003). *The health benefits of sexual expression.* Katherine Dexter McCormick Library, www.plannedparenthood.org

Rogers, A., Brown, L, & Tappan, M. (1994). Interpreting lass in ego development in girls: Regression or resistance? In A. Lieblich & R. Jesselson (eds.), *The Narrative Study of Lives (vol.2).* Sage Publications: Newbury Park, CA.

Sadker, M. & Sadker, D. (1994). *Failing at Fairness: How America's Schools Cheat Girls.* Charles Scribner's Sons: New York.

Stevenson, R.B. & Ellsworth, J. (1993). Dropouts and the silencing of critical voices. In L. Weis & M. Fine (eds.), *Beyond Silenced Voices: Class, Race, and Gender in United States Schools* (pp.259–271). State University of New York Press: Albany, NY.

Taylor, J. & Ward, J. (1991). Culture, sexuality, and school: Perspectives from focus groups in six cultural communities. *Women's Studies Quarterly, 19,* 11–137.

The Alan Guttmacher Institute (2004). *Into a new world: Young women's sexual and reproductive lives.*

Thorne, B. (1993). *Gender Play: Girls and Boys in School*. Rutgers University Press: New Brunswick, NJ.

Valdivieso, R. & Siobhan, N. (1994). "Look me in the eye": A Hispanic cultural perspective on school reform. In R. Rossi (ed.), *Schools and Students at Risk*. Teachers College Press: New York.

Wellesley College Center for Research on Women (1992) *How Schools Shortchange Girls: A Study of Major Findings on Girls and Education*. American Association of University Women: Washington, D.C.

Wheelock, A. (1992). *Crossing the Tracks: How "Untracking" Can Save America's Schools*. New Press: New York.

Women's Bureau. *Women Workers: Outlook to 2005*. Washington, DC: Women's Bureau, U.S. Department of Labor, 1992. (ED 356 171) <www.all-biz.com/outlook.html>

CHAPTER 2: MOTHER AND DAUGHTER ATTACHMENT

Attachment Styles: An Evolving Taxonomy of Evolutionarily Adaptive and Maladaptive Affectional Bonds. Retrieved October 13, 2005, from http://www.peroanlity research.org/attachment.html

Bhanot, Ruchi and Jasna Jovanovic (2005). Do Parents' Academic Gender Stereotypes Influence Whether They Intrude of their Childrens' Homework? *Sex Roles*, 52:9/10, 597–607.

Catalono, Richard F, Kevin P. Haggerty, Sabrina Oesterle, Chales B. Fleming, and J. David Hawkins (2004, September). The Importance of Bonding to School for Healthy Development: Findings from the Social Development Research Group. *Journal of School Health*, 74:7, 252–261.

Christine-Mizell, Andre (2003). Bullying: The Consequences of Interparental Discord and Child's Self Concept. *Family Process*, 42:2, 237–239.

Crittenden, Patricia M. Transformations in Attachment Relationships in Adolescence: Adaptation Versus Need for Psychotherapy. Retrieved October 12, 2005, from http://www.soton.ac.uk/~fri/pats3.html

Crittenden, P.M. (1997). Patterns of attachment and sexuality: Risk of dysfunction versus opportunity for creative integration.

Attachment and psychopathology, 45–93. New York: Guilford Press.

Crittenden, P.M., A. Landini, and A.H. Claussen. (2001). A Dynamic-Maturational approach to treatment of maltreated children. Handbook of Psychological Services for Children and Adolescents, 373–398. New York: Oxford University Press.

Cooper, M.L. and P.R. Shaver and N.L. Collins (1998). Attachment Styles, emotion reg. and adjustment in adolescence. *Journal of Personality and Social Psychology,* 1380–1397.

Cummings, Mark and Marcie C. Goeke-Morey and Lauren M. Papp (2003, November/December). Children's Responses to Everyday Marital Conflict Tactics in the Home. *Child Development,* 74:6, 1918–1929.

Gauze, C. and W. M. Bukowski and J. Aquan-Assee and L. K. Sippola (1996). Interactions between family environment and friendship and associations with self-perceived well-being during adolescence. *Child Development,* 67, 2201–2216.

Laible, D.J. and G. Carlo, and M. Raffaelli (2000). The differential relations of parent and peer attachment to adolescent adjustment. *Journal of Youth and Adolescence,* 29, 45–59.

Manning, Tracey T. (2003). Leadership across cultures: Attachment style influences. *Journal of Leadership & Organizational Studies,* 9:3. Retrieved October 8, 2005, from ProQuest.

O'Brien, K.M., S.M. Friedman, L.C. Tipton, and S.G. Linn (2000). Attachment, separation, and women's vocational development: A longitudinal analysis. *Journal of Counseling Psychology,* 47, 301–315.

Pendry, Patricia (1998, August). Ethological Attachment Theory: A Great Idea in Personality? Retrieved October 12, 2005, from http://www.personity research.org/papers/pendry.html

Rubin, Kenneth H., Kathleen M. Dwyer, Cathryn Booth-LaForce, Angel H. Kim, Kim B. Burgess, and Linda Jasmine-Krasnor (2004). Attachment, Friendship and Psychosocial Functioning in Early Adolescence. *Journal of Early Adolescence,* 42:4, 326–356.

Viehouser, Melissa. Finding Your Own Happy Ending. Retrieved October 12, 2005, from http://www.teenvoices.com/issue_current./tvspecial_princess.html

Whiffen, Valaire E. and Matthew A. Kerr and Veronica Kallos-Lilly (2005). Maternal Depression, Adult Attachment, and Children's Emotional Distress. *Family Process*, 44:1, 93–103.

Wolfe, Jessica B. and Nancy E. Betz (2004, January). The Relationship of Attachment Variables to Career Decision-Making Self-Efficacy and Fear of Commitment. *The Career Development Quarterly*, 52, 363–369.

CHAPTER 3: LIMITED LIFE EXPERIENCE

Alcohol: A Women's Health Issue (2003, August). *Athealth*. Retrieved August 5, 2005, from http://www.athealth.com/Consumer.disorders.womenalcohol.html

Brown, H. Dair (2000, March). Girls' Bill of Rights. New York: Girls Incorporated.

Conley, Caroline (2005, June). Re-reading Ourselves Through Little Women: Four Young Readers' Story of Feminine and Feminist Mentoring Through the Voice of Jo March. *Women Writers*. Retrieved October 24, 2005, from http://www.womenwrtiers.net/summer05/scholarly/conley.htm.

Deak, JoAnn and Teresa Barker (2002, August). Girls Will be Girls: Raising Confident and Courageous Daughters (exert). *Girls Incorporated*. Retrieved October 31,2005, from http://www.feminist.com/resources.artspeech/girls/girls.html

Edros, Stacia (2003, November). Study Reveals What Scares Girls the Most: Answers may Surprise Parents. *WPXI*. Retrieved August 5, 2005, from http://www.wpxi.com/family.2633722/detail.html

Gender Gap Enters a New Millennium: New Harris Poll Documents Girls' Desire to Break Down Stereotypes (2000, March). *Girls Incorporated*. Retrieved November 1, 2005, from http://www.girlsinclynn.org/harrissurvey.htm

Girls and Sports (2002). New York: Girls Incorporated.

Jenson, Jennifer and Suzanne DeCastell and Mary Bryson (2003). "Girls Talk," Gender, Equity, and Identity Discourses in a School-Based Computer Culture. *Women's Studies International Forum*, 26:6.

Parent Resource Center: Research About Parental Influence. *Phillip Morris USA*. Retrieved August 5, 2005, from http://www.philipmorrisusa.com/en/prc/ facts.research.asp?printer_freindly=Yes

Potier, Beth. Researcher Mia Org: Physics 'glass ceiling' intact. *Harvard University Gazette*. Retrieved October 28, 2005, from http://www.new.harvard.edu/gazette /2004/01.01/03-miaong.html

Resources For Adults to Help Girls Become Strong, Smart, and Bold (1999, January). New York: Girls Incorporated.

Strong, Smart, Bold: Ways to help girls become strong, smart and bold (1995). *Girls Incorporated*. Retrieved October 31,2005, from http://www.feminist.com /resources.artspeech/girls/tips.htm

Today's Girls . . . Tomorrow's Leaders. *United Way*. Retrieved October 28, 2005, from http://www.uwmb.org/ourwokrk/tgtl.htm

Weir, Allison (1992). The Six Wives of Henry VIII. New York: Ballantine Books.

Women "Take Care", Men "Take Charge" (2005). New York: Catalyst. Retrieved November 1, 2005, from http://72.14.203.104/ search?q=cache:CCaBIILKbjoJ:www.catalystwomen.org/files/full/w. . . .

CHAPTER 4: ALCOHOL IN THE FAMILY

Agnew, Eleanor and Sharon Robideaux. What happens to a family when Mom is an alcoholic and Dad leaves? *Commitment*. Retrieved November 8, 2005, from http://www.commitment.com/agnew1.html

Alcohol: A Women's Health Issue (2003, August). *athealth*. Retrieved November 4, 2005, from http://www.athealth.com/Consumer/disorders.womenalcohol.htm

Alcoholism and Drug Dependence-America's Number One Health Problem (2005, August). *Greater Dallas Council on Alcohol & Drug Abuse*. Retrieved November 4, 2005, from http://www.gdcada.org/stories/alcprob.htm

Billingsley, Janice (2002, September). Wives of Alcoholics Also Tend to Drink a Lot. *Health on the Net Foundation*. Retrieved November 8, 2005, from http://www .hon.ch/News/HSN/50987.htm

Chen, Ying-Yen and Elissa R. Weitzman (2005, January). Depressive Symptoms, DSM-IV Alcohol Abuse and Their Comorbidity among Children of Problem Drinkers in a National Survey: Effects of Parents and Child Gender and Parent Recovery Status. *Journal Studies Alcohol*, 66:1.

Children of Alcoholics. *U.S. Department of Heath and Human Services*. Retrieved November 7, 2005, from http://www.health.org/non-govpubs/coafacts/

Children of Alcoholics: Are They Different? (1990, July). *National Institute on Alcohol Abuse and Alcoholism*. Retrieved November 7, 2005, from http://pubs. niaaa.nih.gov /publications/aa09.htm

Elkins, Irene J., Matt McGue, Steve Malone, and William G. Iacono (2004, April). The Effect of Parental Alcohol and Drug Disorders of Adolescent Personality. *The American Journal of Psychiatry*, 161:4. Retrieved November 7, 2005, from ProQuest.

El-Sheikh, Mona and Elizabeth Flanagan (2001, October). Parental Problem Drinking and Children's Adjustment: Family Conflict and Parental Depression as Mediators and Moderators of Risk. *Journal of Abnormal Child Psychology*, 29:5. Retrieved November 7, 2005, from http://www.springlink.com

Fact Sheet: Children of problem drinking parents. London: Alcohol Concern, 32–36.

Fact Sheet: The Relationship Between Parental Alcohol or Other Drug Problems and Child Maltreatment. Chicago.

Fact Sheet: Women and Alcohol (2000, September). Retrieved November 7, 2005, from http://www.acbr.com/fas.womalc.htm

For Professionals: working with affected families. Retrieved November 17, 2005, from http://www.coaf.org/professional/emotcons.htm

Girls More Prone to Alcohol, Drug Abuse (2005, August). *Greater Dallas Council on Alcohol Abuse*. Retrieved November 4, 2005, from http://www.gdcada.org/stories.girls.htm

Johnson, James (2005). My Father Drinks.

Locke, T.F. and M.D. Newcomb (2004). Child maltreatment, parent alcohol- and drug-related problems, polydrug problems, and parenting practices: A test of gender differences and four theoretical perspectives. *Journal of Family Psychology*, 18:1, 120–134.

General References

Module 10J: Alcohol and the Family (2005, March). *National Institute on Alcohol Abuse and Alcoholism*. Retrieved November 4, 2005, from http://pubs.niaaa.nih. gov/publications/Social/Module10J families/Module10J.html

Negative Effects of Parental Drinking: Parental Drinking Affects Children's Behavior (2005). *About*. Retrieved November 7, 2005 from http://alcoholism.about.com/cs/tipsforparents/a/aa 000725a.htm

Parker, D.A. and T.C. Harford (1988, July). Alcohol-related problems, marital disruption and depressive symptoms among adult children of alcohol abusers in the United States. *Journal Stud. Alcohol*, 49:4. Retrieved November 1, 2005, from http://www.ncbi.nlm. nih.gov/entrez/query.fcgi?cmd=Retrieve&db=PubMed&list_uids =31 ...

Parsons, Tetana (2003, December). Alcoholism and Its Effect on the Family. *AllPsych Online*. Retrieved November 4, 2005m from http://allpsych.com/journal /alcoholism.html

Schuckit, M.D. and J. E. Tipp and E. Kelner. Are daughters of alcoholics more likely to marry alcoholics? (1990). *American Journal of Drug Alcohol Abuse*, 20:2. Retrieved November 1, 2005, from http://www.ncbi.nih.gov/entrez/ query.fcgi?cmd=Retrieve&db= PubMed&List_uids=80 ...

Silverstein, H. (1990). Alcoholism. New York: Franklin Watts.

The effect of parental substance abuse on young people (2004, October). *Joseph Rowntree Foundation 2005*. Retrieved November 7, 2005, from http://www.jrf.org.uk/knowledge/findings/ socialpolicy/064.asp

Tomison, Adam A. (1996). Child Maltreatment and Substance Abuse. *National Child Protection Clearinghouse*. Retrieved November 1, 2005, from http://www. aifs.gov.au/nch/discussion2.html

Vance, Eric and Horacio Sanchez (1998, February). Creating a Service System That Builds Resiliency. Retrieved October 30, 2005 from http://www.dhhs.state. nc.us/mhddsas/childandfamily/technicalassistance/risk_and_resilie ...

Werner, Emmy and Ruth Smith (1989). Vulnerable But Invincible. New York: Adams, Bannister, and Cox, 151–164.

Women, Girls, and Alcohol. *The Center of Alcohol Marketing and Youth.* Retrieved November 4, 2005, from http://camy.org/factsheets/index.php?Factsheet

CHAPTER 5: DANGERS OF EARLY DATING AND MATING

A Preventable Epidemic: Teen Dating Violence And its Impact on School Safety and Academic Achievement (2004, October). *California Attorney General's Office and California Department of Education.*

Atherton, Martin J. and James A. Metcalf (2004, September). Forced Sexual Intercourse Among American High School Students: Statistical Correlates from a National Survey. *Electronic Journal of Human Sexuality*, 7. Retrieved November 17, 2005 from http://www.ejhs.org/volume7/forcedsex.html

Austin, Elizabeth (2003, June). In Contempt of Courtship: Why we love to watch others date, but hate to do it ourselves. *Washington Monthly.* Retrieved November 16, 2005, from http://www/washingtonmonthly.com/features/2003/0306.austin.html

Baily, Beth L. (1988). From Front Porch to Back Seat: Courtship in Twentieth-Century America. Baltimore: The John Hopkins University Press.

Cere, Daniel (2001, Spring). Courtship Today: The View from Academia. *Public Interest*, 143, 53. Retrieved November 16, 2005, from EBSCOhost.

Dailard, Cynthia (2001, August). Recent Findings from the "Add Health" Survey: Teens and Sexual Activity. *The Guttmacher Report of Public Policy*, 1–3.

Feiring, Candice and Wyndol Furman (ed.) (2000, November). Victimization and Romantic Relationships in Adolescence. *Child Maltreatment*, 5:4.

Fisher, Bonnie and Francis Cullen and Michael Turner (2002, March). Being Pursued: Stalking Victimization in a National Study of College Women. *Criminology & Public Policy*, 1, 257–308.

Gardyn, Rebecca (ed) (2001, April). Top Lines: What a Girl (and Boy) Wants. *American Demographics*, 23:4, 10–11.

General References

Heibrun, Carolyn G. (1988). Writing a Women's Life. New York: Ballantine Books.

Howard, Donna E. and Min Qi Wang (2003, Spring). Risk Profiles of Adolescent Girls Who Were Victims of Dating Violence. *Adolescence*, 38:149. Retrieved November 15, 2005, from EBSCOhost.

Howard, Donna E., Kenneth Beck, Melissa Hallmark Kerr, and Teresa Shattuck (2005, Summer). Psychological Correlates of Dating Violence Victimization Among Latino Youth. *Adolescence*, 40:158. Retrieved November 15, 2005, from EBSCOhost.

Hurst, Marianne D. (2005, June). Dating Abuse. *Education Week*, 24:41, 16. Retrieved November 15, 2005 from EBSCOhost.

Kass, Amy (1999, September). A Case for Courtship. *Institute Annual Symposium*. Retrieved November 16, 2005, from http://americanvalues.org/html /2_kass_keynote.html

Kass, Leon R. (1997). The End of Courtship: Part 1 of 3. *Boundless Webzine*. Retrieved November 16, 2005, from http://www.boundless.org/2005/articles/a0001154.cfm

Kass, Leon R. (1997). The End of Courtship: Part 2 of 3 *Boundless webzine*. Retrieved November 16, 2005, from http://www.boundless.org/2005/articles/a0001158.cfm

Kass, Leon R. (1997). The End of Courtship: Part 3 of 3. *Boundless Webzine*. Retrieved November 16, 2005, from http://www.boundless.org/2005/articles/a0001161.cfm

Konieczny, Mary Ellen. Domestic Violence and Birth Control Sabotage: A Report from the Teen Parent Project. *Center for Impact Research*.

Kramer, Ilana (2004, January). Teen Sex That's "No Big Deal." *New York*, 28:4, 16. Retrieved November 15, 2005, from ProQuest.

Lickona, Thomas (1994). The Neglected Heart: The Emotional Dangers of Premature Sexual Involvement. *Catholic Educator's Resource Center*. Retrieved November 17, 2005, from http://www.catholiceducation.org/articles/sexuality.se0064.html

Lisante, Joan E. (2004, April). Getting Serious About Teen Relationship Abuse. *Connect for Kids*. Retrieved November 17, 2005, from http://connectforkids.org/node/562 ?tn=la/ra

McCabe, Martina (2005, May). Boys want sex, girls want commitment: Does this trade-off still exist? *Sexual and Relationships Therapy*, 20:2, 139–141. Retrieved November 15, 2005, from EBSCOhost.

Mendel, Sharron (2004, January). US Teens Fight Date Violence With Girl Power. *PanosLondon*. Retrieved November 17, 2005, from http://www.panos.org.uk/newsfeatures/featuredetails.asp?id=1098

Molidor, Christian, and Richard Tolman, and Jennifer Kober (2000, February). Gender and Contextual Factors in Adolescent Dating Violence. *The Prevention Researcher*, 7:1.

Morse, Anne (2000). The Dating Game: The Dangers of Cash-Based Courtship. *Boundless Webzine*. Retrieved November 15, 2005, from http://www.boundless.org/2000departments/beyond_buddies/a0000234.html

Pellegrini, Anthony D and Jeffrey D. Long (2003). A Sexual Selection Theory Longitudinal Analysis of Sexual Segregation and Integration in Early Adolescence. *Journal of Experimental Child Psychology*. Retrieved November 16, 2005, from MetaLib.

Peterson, Karen S. (2000, September). Wooing the Past: Courtship Flirts with a Comeback. *USA Today*. Retrieved November 15, 2005, from http://american values.org/html/a-wooing_the_post.html

Research Briefs: Aggressive Girls, Withdrawn Boys: A reaction to Forced Sex? Retrieved November 17, 2005, from http://focus.hms.harvard.edu/1998/ briefts.html

Room, Robin (1991, August). "Should I Surrender?—Women's Drinking and Courtship in American Movies. *American Psychological Association*. Retrieved November 15, 2005 from http://www.bks.no/surrendr.htm

Sessions Stepp, Laura (2003, October). Modern Flirting: Girls Find Old Ways Did Have Their Charms. *Washington Post*. Retrieved November 15, 2005, from http://www.washingtonpost.com/acz/wp_dyn/A32799-2003Oct15?language =printer

Silverman, Jay, Anita Raj, Lorelei Mucci, and Jeanne Hathaway (2001, August). Dating and Other Dangers for High School Girls. *Journal of American Medical Association*, 286:5, 572–579. Retrieved November 15, 2005 from http://www. center4research.rog/dating-dangers.html

Smith, Todd A. and James J. McEldrew III (2004, September). Sexual Harassment Never a Joke to Children. *Philadelphia Tribune*, 120:89. Retrieved November 15, 2005, from ProQuest.

Sombat, Windy (2000). Teenage Dating in the 1950's. Retrieved November 15, 2005 from http://www.honors.umd.edu/HONR269J/projects/sombat.html

Teitelman, Anne M. (2004). Girls' Perspectives on Family Scripts and Sex-Related Topics and Relationships: Implications for Promoting Sexual Health and Reducing Sexual Risk. *Journal of HIV/AIDS Prevention in Children and Youth*. Retrieved November 15, 2005 from MetaLib.

Tijaden, P. and Thoennes, N. (2000). Prevalence and consequences of male-to-female and female-to-male intimate partner violence as measured by the National Violence Against Women Survey. *Violence Against Women*, 6:2, 142–161.

Tolman, Deborah (1999,October). Asking Some Unasked Questions. *Wellesley Centers for Women*. Retrieved November 17, 2005, from http://www.wcwonline.org/p-reflections-questions.html

U.S. Department of Health and Human Services. (2000). *Healthy People 2010*. National Health Promotion and Disease Prevention Objectives. Washington, D.C.

Walton-Moss, Benita J. and Jacquelyn C. Campbell (2002). Intimate Parter Violence: Implications for Nursing. Nursing World. Retrieved November 17,2005, from http://www.nursingworld.org/ojin/topic/tpc17_5.htm.

Wekerle, C. and Wolfe. D. A. (1999). Dating Violence in mid-adolescence: Theory, significance, and emerging prevention initiatives. *Clinical Psychology Review*, 19:4, 435–456.

CHAPTER 6: MODELS AND MENTORS

Admas, Natalie G. (2005). Growing Up Female. NWSA Journal, 17.1, 206–211. Retrieved November 14, 2005, from http://muse.jhu.edu/journa ls/v017/17.11adams_n.html

Conroy, Mary (1989). Where have all the smart girls gone? *Psychology Today*, 23, 20.

Wright, Kathryn (2004). Search for the Techie Woman. Women Gamers. Retrieved December 14, 2005, from http://www.womengamers.com/doctork/womenIT.php

Glaser, Connie (2004, August). Male vs. Female: Which mentor is best? *The BizPlace*. Retrieved December 14, 2005, from http://www.biz.journals.com/bizwomen/c onsultants/winning_at_work/2004/08/23/column . . .

Bell, Ella L. J. E. and Stella M. Nkomo (2001). Careers of a Different Color. Retrieved from http://hbswk.hbs.edu/item.jhtml?id=2454&t=organizations

Allen, Tammy D. (2004). Factors related to mentor reports of mentoring functions provided: gender and relational characteristics. *Look Smart*. Retrieved November 14, 2005, from http://www.findarticles.com/p/articles/m1_m2294/is_1-2_50/ao_113419431/print

Sosik, J. J. and V. M. Godshalk (2000). The role of gender in mentoring: Implications for diversified and homogeneous mentoring relationships. *Journal of Vocational Behavior*, 57, 102–122.

Wallace, J. E. (2001). The benefits of mentoring for female lawyers. *Journal of Vocational Behavior*, 58, 366–391.

Falk, Joni and Brian Drayton (1998). Many Futures: Mentoring Middle School Girls. *TERC*, 21:1. Retrieved December 14, 2005, from http://www.terc.edu/h andsoIssues/s98/falk.html

Mack, Maureen D. The Psychological Features of Effective Mentors for Girls and Young Women.

Matkins, Jaunita Jo (1997). Women, Wife, Mommy, and Scientist: Helping Females see Themselves in Science. Retrieved December 15, 2005, from http://www.ed. psu.edu/ci/Journals/97pap23.htm

Matthews, D.J. and N. Steinhauer (1998). Giftedness, girls, others, and equity: Theory based strategies for the regular classroom. *Exceptionality Education Canada*, 8. Retrieved December 14, 2005, from http://www.hunter.cuny.edu/gifted-ed/articles/m&S-girls_regclass.shtml

Pearson, Joyce (2004). Women Helping Girls: A Mentoring Program Offers Many Ways to Make a Difference. *About . . . Time*, 32:2, 14. Retreived December 14, 2005, from ProQuest.

Warren-Sams, Barbara (2001). Mentors Confirm and Enhance Girls' Lives. *Women's Educational Equity Act Publishing Center Digest*. Retrieved December 14, 2005, from ProQuest.

Stefanik, Donna (2002). Program Builds Girls' Leadership: Series of Workshops uses mentoring discussion to enhance self-esteem. *The Skanner*,10:68, 1. Retrieved December 14, 2005, from ProQuest.

Russell, Bob (1998). SciTech Clubs for Girls. *Informal Learning Experiences, Inc.* Retrieved December 14, 2005, from http://www.infromallearning.com/archieve/1998-0102-b.htm

Perez, Christina (2001). What is Equity?: A Look into a reform math classroom. *TERC*. Retrieved December 23, 2005, from http://www.terc.edu/TEMPLATE/publica tions/item. cfm? PublicationsID=34

Warren, Beth and Ann S. Jasminebery. Equity in the Future Tense: Redefining Relationships Among Teachers, Students, and Science in Linguistic Minority Classrooms. *TERC*. Retrieved December 23, 2005, from http://www.terc .edu/TEMPLATE/publications/ item.cfm?PublicationID=5

Rubin, Andee and Nicola Yelland (eds.) (2002). Ghosts in the Machine: Women's Voices in Research and Technology. New York: Peter Lang.

Dicciani, Nance K. (2005). No Boundaries, Please. *New York Times*. Retrieved December 14, 2005, from ProQuest.

Arsenovic, Suzi, Timothy Smita and Zoleko Gladys (2005). Influences on Adolescent Females' Career Aspirations: Home Versus Public Schooling. *Goshen College Symposium Annual 2005*. Retrieved December 14, 2005, from http://72.14.203. 104/se arch?q= cache:SJJ2KpwOJpMJ:www.goshen.edu/cWtools/downl ...

Arnold, Karen D. (2002). What Role Do Elite Colleges Play. *About Campus*.

Arnold K. D. (1995). Lives of Promise: What Happens to High School Valedictorians? San Francisco: Jossey-Bass.

Whiston, Susan C. and Briana K. Keller (2005). Family Influences on Career Development: A North American Perspective. Retrieved December 14, 2005, from http://72.14.203.104/search?q= cache:quOfidjvyeEJ:www.aiospconference 2005.pt/full_wo ...

Whiston, S. C. and B. K. Keller (2004). The Influences on the family of origin on career developments: A review and analysis. *The Counseling Psychologist* 32, 493–568.

CHAPTER 7: SENSUALITY AND SEXUALITY

Abma, Joyce C., Gladys M. Martinez, William D. Mosher, and Brittany S. Dawson (2002). Teenagers in the United States: Sexual Activity, Contraceptive Use, and Childbearing, 2002.

An Explanation of the Circles f Sexuality. *Advocates For Youth.* Retrieved May 19, 2005, from http://www.advocatesforyouth.org/lessonplans/circlesofsexuality3.htm

Bullard, Jean, David G. Bullard, Ernest H. Jasminenbaum, and Isadora R. Jasminenbaum. Sexuality, Intimacy and Communications. *Cancer Supportive Care Programs.* Retrieved January 2, 2006, from http://www.cancersupportivecare.com/sexuality.html

Estes, Clarissa Pinkola (1992). Women Who Run with the Wolves: Myths and Stories of the Wild Woman Archetype. New York: Ballantine Books.

Gauntlett, David. More About More!: The Sexual Language of Young Women's Magazines. *Media, Gender and Identity.* Retrieved April 27, 2005, from http://theoryhead. com/gender/more.htm

Havrilesky, Heather (2002). Powerpuff Girls to the Rescue. *Salon.* Retrieved January 3, 2006, from http://www.alternet.org/story/13531/

Healy, Christopher (2004). A nation of little princesses. Retrieved January 3, 2006, from http://www.freepress.net/news/print.php?id=5557

Hayward, Chris, Joel D. Killen, and Darrell M. Wilson (1997, February). Psychiatric risk associated with early puberty in adolescent girls. *Journal of the American Academy of child and Adolescent Psychiatry*, 36, 255–262. Retrieved January 3, 2006 from MetaLib.

Hite, Shere (2005). What is a woman's 'sexual nature'? *Hite Research International.* Retrieved January 2, 2006, from http://www.hite-research.com/art_womensexnature.html

Hite, Shere (2005). Why is Female Masturbation Important to understand? *Hite Research International*. Retrieved January 6, 2006, from http://www.hite-research.com /artmasturbation.html

Into a New World: Young Women's Sexual and Reproductive Lives (2004). *The Alan Guttmacher Institute*. Retrieved April 27, 2005 from http://www.agi-usa.org/pubs/ new_world_engl.html

Kang, Melissa (2005, March). Age of consent laws: Puritan notions of right and wrong. Retrieved January 12, 2006, from http://www.onlineopinion.com.au/print.asp? article=3266

Kang, Melissa (2003, August). Protecting young women from sexual right and wrong. Retrieved January 12, 2006, from http://www.onlineopinion.com.au/print/asp?article=647

Kaplan, Elaine Bell (1997). Women's Perceptions of the Adolescent Experience. *Adolescence*, 32:127.

Katharine Dexter Mc Cormick Library (2003). The Heath Benefits of Sexual Expression. *Planned Parenthood Federation of America Inc.*

Koch, Patricia Barthalow (2001/2002). Women's sexuality as they age: The more things change, they more than stay the same. *Look Smart*. Retrieved May 10, 2005, from http://www. findarticles.com/p/articles/mi_qa3781/is_200112/ai_n9012863/print

Lifelong Sexuality (2005). *Help Guide*. Retrieved January 2, 2006, from http://helpguide. org/life/sexuality_aging.htm

Ogden, Gina (2001). Spiritual Passion and Compassion in Late-Life Sexual Relationships. *Electronic Journal of Human Sexuality*. Retrieved from http://ejhs.org/volume4/ Ogden.htm

Ogden, Gina (2002). Sexuality and Spirituality in Women's Relationships: Preliminary Results of an Exploratory Survey. *Wellesly Centers for Women*.

Satcher, David (2001). The Surgeon General's Call to Action to Promote Sexual Health and Responsible Sexual Behavior 2001. Rockville: Office of the Surgeon General.

Sensuality in Bomber Nose Art: Sensuality in form and design of WWII war bird nose art (2005). *Northstar Gallary*. Retrieved January 4, 2006, from http://northstargallery.com /Aircraft/ensuality.htm

Sex and Relationships in the Media (2005). *Media Awareness Network*. Retrieved January 2, 2006, from http://www.media-awareness.ca/english/issues/stereotyping/women_and_girls/women_sex ...

Simon, Clea (2001). Hooked. Ms. Magazine. Retrieved January 3, 2006, from http://msmaganze.com/jano1.html

Sprecher, Susan (2002). Sexual Satisfaction in Premarital Relationships: Associations with Satisfaction, Love, Commitment, and Stability. *The Journal of Sex Research*, 39:3, 190–196.

Walters, Andrew and Gail M. Williamson (1998). Sexual Satisfaction Predicts Quality of Life: A Study of Adult Amputees. *Sexuality and Disability*, 16:2, 103–115.

Weeks, David and Jamie James (1998). Secrets of the Superyoung. New York: Berkley Books.

Weiner, Bernard (1998, June). Initiation in Coming of Age: Theory and practice. Everyman, 31, 12. Retrieved from ProQuest.

CHAPTER 8: WOMEN AS ASSETS

Asinof, Richard. Strong, Fast, Smart: These Women Rock! *Jewish Telegraphic Agency*. Retreived August 29, 2005 from http://www.jewishexponent.com/ViewArticle.asp?ArtID=1114

Beard, Patricia. Good Daughters. Retrieved August 6, 2005, from http://www.twbookmark.com/books/92/0446523593/chapter_excerpt7927.html.

Beeferman, Larry W. (2003). Women and Assets: The Promise of Asset Development. Center for Hunger and Poverty.

Bix, Amy Sue (2004). From "Engineeresses" to "Girl Engineers" to "Good Engineers": A History of Women's U.S. Engineering Education. *NWSA Journal*, 16:1.

Colley, Linda (1992). Women and Political Power. *Wilson Quarterly*, 16:2. Retrieved January 14, 2006 from ProQuest.

Collins, Christopher (2003 April). Girls and Careers: Girls' education is essential in a knowledge based economy. New York: Girls Incorporated.

Conway, Margaret M. and David W. Ahern and Gertrude A. Stevernagel (1999). Women & Public Policy: A Revolution in Progress. *Congressional Quarterly Inc.*

Cox, Megan (2001). Why Women Can't Afford to Retire. Retrieved February 17, 2001 from http"//www.msnbc.com/news.528945.asp?cpl=7

Dingell, John D. and Carolyn B. Maloney (2003, October). GAD Congressional briefing: Analysis of the earnings Difference between men and Women.

Duggan, Lynn (2001). Retail on the 'Dole': Parasitic Employers and Women Workers. *NWSA Journal,* 13:3. Retrieved January 18, 2006, from EBSCOhost.

Dyer, Susan ed. (2004). Under the Microscope: A decade of gender equity projects in the sciences. Washington DC: American Association of University Women Educational Foundation.

El-Haj, T.R.A. (2003). Challenging the Inevitability of Difference: Young Women and Discourses and gender. *Curriculum Inquiry,* 33:4, 401–425.

Equity Initiatives (1999). *United States Department of Education.* Retrieved February 19, 2001 from http://www.ed.gov/offices/ODS/equity.html

Five Frequently Asked Questions About University and College Women. *American Association of University Women Educational Foundation.* Retrieved March 21, 2005 from http://www.aauw.org/print_page.cfml?Path_info=F:%5Cweb% Caauw%5Cresearch%5cs.

Francis, David R. (2005, March). The American Dream gains a harder edge. *The Christian Science Monitor.* Retrieved January 17, 2006, from http://www.csmonitor.com/2005/0523/p17s01-cogn.htm

Goldstein, Leslie Friedman (1979). The Constitutional Rights of Women. New York: Longman Inc.

Hawkins, Paula (2006). Where women are going wrong. *Times Online.* Retrieved January 14, 2006, from http://business.timesonline.co.uk/article/1,,8214-1971969,00.html

Hernandez, Donald, Arlene Saluter, and Catherine O'Brien (1993, September). We the American Children. U.S. Department of Commerce: Economics and Statistic Administration.

Holt, Evelyn R. (1990, March). Remember the Ladies—Women in the Curriculum. *ERIC Clearinghouse for Social Studies.* Retrieved

February 17, 2001 from http://www.ed.gov/databases/ERIC_Digests/ed319652.html

Huth, Mary M. Upstate New York and the Women's Rights Movement. Retrieved February 17, 2001, from http://www.lib.rochester.edu/rbk/women/women.htm

Kohlstedt, Sally Gregory (2004). Sustaining Gains: Reflections on Women in Science and Technology in 20th-Century United States. *NWSA Journal*, 16:1.

Mantilla, Karla (2005, January/February). Class Issues: The Bottom Line For Feminist Change? *off our backs*, 19–21.

Money Sense: Learning, Earning, Investing, Managing, Giving. *The National Coalition of Girl's Schools*. Retrieved January 14, 2006 from http://www.ncgs.org/type0.php?pid=134

Recent changes in U.S. Family Finances: Evidence from the 1998 and 2001 Survey of Consumer Finances. *Institute For Women's Policy Research*.

Robelen, Erik W. (2004 April). Administration Criticized on Girls' Education Issues. Education Week, 23:31. Retrieved October 21, 2004 from EBSCOhost.

Sadker, David. An Educator's Primer to the Gender War. Retrieved October 21, 2004 from http://www.sadkar.org/primer.htm

Silva, Javier. A Woman's (Net) Worth. *a Demos eJournal*. Retrieved January 14, 2006, from http://www.demos-usa.org/aroundthekitchentable.cfm?edition=013&article=assets

Social Security and Today's Woman (1999 October). *Social Security Administration*. Retrieved February 17, 2001 from http://www.ssa.gov/pubs/10127.html

Statistics About Girls, Non-traditional Careers, and STEM. *Puget Sound Center for teaching, learning, and technology*

Ten Hottest Careers for College Graduates: Experts Predict Where the Jobs Will be in 2012 (2006). College Board. Retrieved January 16, 2006, from http://www.collegeboard.com/article/0,3868,4-24-0-236,00.html

The President's High Growth Job Training Initiative examines what jobs are in demand as well as the fastest growing careers and nationally growing industries (2005). Retrieved January 16, 2006, from http://workforce3one.org/_fast_growing_careers.cfm

General References

The Status of Women in the States Overview. *Institute of Women's Policy Research*, IWPR# R250.

US Census Bureau (2000 December). Educational Attainment in the United States (Publication number 20-536). *US Department of Commerce*.

US Census Bureau (1990). Social Characteristics.

US Census Bureau (1993). Dynamics of Economic Well Being: Labor Force.

US Census Bureau (1998 October). Current Population Reports (Publication number 20515).

US Census Bureau (1999). Marital Status By Age for Women 15 to 50 years.

US Census Bureau (2000 November). Low Income Uninsured Children by State. Retrieved January 16, 2001 from http://www.census.gov/hhes/nlthins/lowinckid.html

US Census Bureau (2000 October). Who's Minding the Kids? Child Care Arrangements (Publication number 70-70).

US Department of Education (2003 March). Trends in Educational Equity of Girls and Women. Washington DC: National Center for Education Statistics.

Weiner, Bernard (1998, June). Initiation is Coming of Age: Theory and practice. *Everyman*, 31,12. Retrieved January 2, 2006 from ProQuest.

Wilby, Peter (1997, September). Now I am convinced: The monarchy is finished. Let them all rest in peace. *New Statesman*, 126:4350, 11. Retrieved January 14, 2006, from EBSCOhost.

Winning the Right to Vote (1998). *National Women's Hall of Fame*. Retrieved February 17, 2001 from http://www.greatwomen.org/lcvt.htm

Women and Assets: The Promise of Asset Development. *Asset Development Institute*. Waltham: Brandeis University

Women at Work (2003). *American Association of University Women*. Retrieved September 16, 2004 from http://www.aauw.org/research/womenatwork.cfm.

Wootton, Barbara H. (1997, April). Gender differences in occupational employment. *Monthly Labor Review*, 15–24.

CHAPTER 9: NEW AGE SCHOOLING

About the Author. *Little Women*. Retrieved September 15, 2005, from http://www.xroads.virginia.edu/~HYPER/ALCOTT/aboutla.html

A Profile of the American High School Sophomore in 2002: Initial results From the Base Year of the Education Longitudinal Study of 2002. *U.S. Department of Education*, NCES 2005-338.

Bauer, Karlin S. (2000). Promoting Gender Equity in Schools. *Contemporary Education*, 71:2. Retrieved November 16, 2004 from ECSCOhost.

Brenzel, Barbara M.(1983). History of 19th Century Women's Education: A Plea for Inclusion of Class, Race and Ethnicity. *Center for Research on Women*. Wellesley: Wellesley College.

Caine, Geoffrey (2004, winter). Getting it! Creativity, Imagination, and Learning. *Independent School*, 63:2. Retrieved October 21, 2004, from EBSCOhost.

Classroom Ideas for Teaching Women's History (2003). *National Women's Hall of Fame*. Retrieved February 17, 2001, from http://www.greatwomen.org/lcclrmid.htm.

Elliot, Jane and Christ Powell (1987). Young Women and Science: Do We Need More Science? *British Journal of Sociology and Education*, 8.3, 277–286.

Freeman, Catharine E. (2004, November). Trends in Educational Equity of girls & Women. *National Center for Educational Statistics*.

Gatto, John Taylor (1990). The Psychopathic School: The Failure of Modern Public School. Retrieved September 30, 2004, from http://www.sntp.net/educationnn/gatto.htm.

Ginorio, Angela B. and Janice Fournier and Katie Frevert (2004, February). The Rural Girls in Science Program. *Educational Leadership*, 61:5. Retrieved October 21, 2004, from EBSCOhost.

Girls in the Middle: Working to Succeed in School. (1996). *American Association of University Women*. Retrieved September 16, 2004, from http://www.aauw.org/rearch/girls_educaion/gim.cfm

Haar, Charlene K. and Emily Feistritzer (2005). Profile of Teachers in the U.S. in 2005. NCEI. Retrieved September 16, 2005, from http://www.ncei.com/POT O5PRESSREL3.htm

Helping Girls Succeed. *IPL Teenspace*. Retrieved September 16, 2004, from http://www.ipl.org/teen/esteem/bksodl.html

Klein, Susan Shurberg (1988, March). Sex Education and Gender Equity. *Educational Leadership*, 45:6, 69–76.

Mack, Maureen D. (1992, September). Changing Families-Changing Middle Schools. *Middle School Journal*.

Maher, Frances A (1999). Progressive Education and Feminist Pedagogies: Issues in Gender, Power, and Authority. *Teachers College Record*, 101.1, 35–60.

Marshall, Carol Sue and Judy Reinhartz (1997, July/August). Gender Issues in the Classroom. *Clearing House*, 70:6, 333–338.

Mayberry, Maralle and Margaret N. Rees (2001). Feminist Pedagoy, Interdisciplinary Praxis, and Science Education. *National Women's Studies Journal*, 9, 57–75.

McKee, Alice (1993, Summer). Hostile Hallways: The AAUW Survey on Sexual Harassment in America's Schools. *International Network News*, 19.3, 74–76.

Moses, Alexa (2005). Princess Power. *Fairfax Digital*. Retrieved September 6, 2005, from http://www.smh.com.au/news/tv—raido/princess/2005/08/04/112312 5839637.html

Owens, Sherry Lynn and Bobble C. Smothers and Fannye E. Love (2003, June). Are Girls Victims of Gender Bias in our Nation's Schools? *Journal of Instructional Psychology*, 30:2, 131–137.

Parsons, Sharon (1999). Feminisms and Science Education: One Science Educator's Exploration of her Practice. *International Journal of Science Education*, 21.9, 989 1005.

Peter, Katharine, Laura Horn, and C. Dennis Carroll (2005). Gender Differences in Participation and Completion of Undergraduate Education and How They Have Changed Over Time. *U.S Department of Education*, NCES 2005-169.

Preston, Jo Anne (1991). Gender and the Formation of a Women's Profession: The Case of Public Schoolteaching. *Center for Research on Women*. Wellesley: Wellesley College.

Saunders, Jo (1997). Teacher Education and Gender Equity. *ERIC Digest*. Retrieved February 17, 2001, from http://www.ed.gov/databases/ERIC_Digests/ed408277.html

Taylor, Linda E. (1995). Math Challenged? *Canada & The World Backgrounder*, 60:4, 20–22.

Tech-Savvy: Education Girls in the New Computer Age (2000). Washington, DC: American Association of University Women Educational Foundation.

The Careers of Public School Administrators: Policy Implications from an Analysis of State-Level Data. *RAND Corporation*. Retrieved September 16, 2005, from http://www.rand.org/publications/RB9054/

The Power of Promise of Girls' Education (2005). State of the Worlds' Mothers.

Thom, Mary (2002, January). Girls in Science and Technology: What's New, What's Next? *Education Digest*, 67:5, 17–25.

United States Census Bureau (1997, October). Computer Use in the United States.

Welty, Kenneth and Brenda Puck (2001). Modeling Athena: Preparing Young Women for Work and Citizenship in a Technology Society. *Wisconsin Department of Public Instruction.*

Whitney, Linda and Jasmine Marie Hoffman. (1998, Winter). Middle School Advisors: A Vehicle for Developing Students' Gender Self-Confidence. *Education*, 119:2. Retrieved November 16, 2004, from EBSCOhost.

Content Index

A

Activism, 122
Adaptability skills, 29
Adaptation, 50
Addiction, 18, 36–37, 41, 47
Administrators, xiii, 132–133
Advocates for Youth, 99–100
African American girls, 69
Agentic Characteristics of Independent Girls-Young Women, 79, 81
Alcohol in the family, 36, 38, 41
Alcohol in the family survey, 38, 41
Alcoholic Tight Rope, 44
Alcoholism, 38–39, 42–43
Alcoholism, family dynamics, 49
Alcott, Louisa May, 29
American Association of University Women, xiv, 85
American Medical Association, 68
Anxiety, 11, 15, 17, 19, 40–42, 45, 69, 103–104, 161
Aristocracy, 3
Arnold, Karen, 75
Asset Development Institute, Brandeis University, 114
Assets, 111, 114
Assets for Female Economic Well-Being, 114
Attachment, 5–7, 9–19

Attachment bonds, 10, 18
Attachment disorder, 19
Attachment wise, 9
Attributes of Sensuality, 100

B

Balance work and family life, 120
Barriers, 26, 30, 75, 77, 81, 125, 137, 149
Beard, Patricia, 6
Believing in self, xv
Belonging, 7, 9
Biological maturation, 59
Body Image, 100
Boiled frog theory, 37
Bomber Girls, 97
Bowen, Elizabeth, 3
Bowman, Katie, 129, 140
Brain, 2, 9, 28, 33, 44, 48, 56, 59, 96, 103–104, 106
Brain Research, 28
Brumberg, Joan, xi
Building an Asset Rich Female Kingdom, 17

C

California Attorney General and State Superintendent of Public Instruction, 68
Campbell, Joseph, 22, 30
Career goals, 75

Careers of Public School Administrators, 132
Cashflow, 126
Cere, Daniel, 62–63
Cherlin, Andrew, 62
Child Resiliency, 50
Choices, xi–xiii, xv, 8, 10, 12, 23, 33, 58, 60, 62, 72, 77, 80, 84, 89, 95–96, 102–103
Cinderella, 3, 24, 111–112
Civil Rights, 25
Close relationship pair bonds, 62, 66, 68
Codependent, 37
College, x, xvi, 41, 67
Coming-of-Age Ritual, 109
Communication, 143, 151
Computer communication, 87
Confidence, 2, 6, 36, 148, 173
Contributions women, xiii
Cost of Sexual Harassment to Girls and Boys, 143
Courting, rituals, 70
Courtship, 62–65
Cross-gender mentoring, 82
Current media representations of girls and women, 97
Curriculum, xii–xiii, 125
Curriculum of difference, 134

D

Dating, 58, 68, 71
Decision-making process, 133
Denial pattern, 42, 47
Denny, Terry, 74
Dependency, 8, 41–43, 46, 52
Dependent, 37, 43–44, 46, 52
Dependent Girl vs. Independent Girl, 127
Depression, 18–19
Diminished voice, 130
Dora the Explorer, 93–94
Dowry, 24
Dualism, 136

E

Eating Disorders, 22, 70
Economic independence, 25
Effect on a girl's academic participation and performance, xi
Effective Attachment Strategies, 14
Emotional sensitivity, 6–7, 18
Energy force, 104
Estes, Clarissa Pinkola, 96–97
Exchange Bargain, 63
Eyes to the future, 86

F

Family, 36, 41, 43, 50, 79
Family Systems, 38–39
Fastest Growing Occupations for College Graduates, 124
Father in Attachment, 11
Features of vibrant women's studies curriculum, 146
Feelings, xi, 8, 10, 15, 17, 20, 28, 45–46, 62, 96–97, 99, 103, 141
Female asset development, 114
Female brain, 28
Female Initiation Ceremony, 108
Female Leaders, 132
Female Mentors, 76
Feminist classroom, 147

Financial growth, 121
Flanagan, Anna Smalley, 72
Fourth stage mentor, 81, 83–84
Francis, David, 113
Friendships, 16–17

G

Gains of women, 118
Gallup International Millennium Survey, 34
Gender, 25, 34–35, 39, 42–43, 45, 72–73, 75, 82, 84, 114–115, 123, 129, 132, 134–135, 140
Gender Differences in Employment, 82, 123
Gender inclusive sex education, 140
Gender Research, 28
Gender Savvy, 157
Gender stereotypes, 25, 82
General Motors, 27
Genetic theory, 64
Girls and Women in the Box, 31
Girls Incorporated, 25
Godfrey, Joline, 124–125

H

Hammerstein II, Oscar, 58
Harder, Sarah, 129
Harris Survey, 25–26
Healing, 19, 51
Healthy Sexual Expression, 107
Helen in Briefing Time, 98
Hidden Agenda, 134
Hiring Practices, 133
Hispanic, xi, 69
Hite, Shere, 101–103
Home, xiii, 4, 6, 11, 18, 22, 24, 31, 46, 63, 70, 81, 96–97, 107, 118, 120–122, 131
Hostile hallways, xiv
Human capital, 122
Huxley, Julian, 3
Huxley, Juliette, 3

I

Identity, xv, 2, 7, 18, 22, 106
Impact on Children, 81
Incest, 36, 40, 42, 45
Independent women, 9, 79
Industries with Fastest Employment Growth, 124
Insecure Father Attributes, 13
Internalizing behaviors, 11

J

Johnson, James, 48
Jump Start Financial Smarts for Kids, 127

K

Kang, Melissa, 107–108
Kilbourne, Jean, 95
Kiyosaki, Robert, 126
Klein, Susan Shurberg, 141
Kohlstedt, Sally Gregory, 118
Koteliansky, S.S., 3

L

Language of Love, 70
Leadership, ix, 12, 16, 27, 60, 74–75, 78, 133, 142, 151, 157, 161
Legal rights, x
Liberticide, 25

Life Planning Education, 100
Little Women, 29
Loss of family, 4
Loss of home, 4
Low self regard, 18
Luttrell, Wendy, xii

M

Mainstream Media, 95, 97
Male mentors, 82
Marriage, marriages, x, 24, 66–67
Masturbation, 62, 103, 110, 140
Math, 77, 88, 141–142
McGraw, Phil, 23
Mentor, xv, 76, 78, 81–86, 88
Mentor Purposes, 84
Mentoring Stages, 84
Mentoring Strategies, 83
Mentors, 74
Mentorship Exemplars, 85
Message, xvi, 12, 22, 51, 81, 95, 98–99, 101, 105, 125–127, 133
Miller, Marcia, 5
Models, 74
Mother, xi–xii, xvi, 2–12, 14–15, 19–21, 28, 32, 35–38, 46–47, 50, 58, 60, 77–78, 80–82, 93, 120, 130–132, 134, 156–157
Mothering Capital, 5
Mothers as Mentors, 78
Movement, 105
Mr. Right, 71
My Father Drinks, 48

N

National Center for Education Information, 132

National Clearinghouse for Alcohol and Drug Information, 43
National Coalition of Girls', 11, 125
National Election Studies, 34
National Institute of Alcohol Abuse and Alcoholism, 49
Neutralizing gender, 140
Non-effective Attachment Strategies, 14

O

Of brain endorphins, 110
Ogden, Gina, 103
Orgasm, 100–101, 103, 110
Oxytocin, 103

P

Parenting, 13–14, 44, 47, 120, 131
Patriarchal status quo, 145
Physical appearance, 141
Physical attractiveness, 64, 67, 141
Pipher, Mary, 94, 103
Poor attachment, 7
Popular culture, 5
Positive Context for Expressing Sensual & Sexual Energy, 103
Potentially Disabling Factors in Girls & Women's Future Aspirations, 78
Primary Enabling Factors in Girls & Young Women Future Aspirations, 78
Primary types of bargains, 63
Prince, 24–25, 30
Princess, xviii, 3, 5, 22–25, 93–94, 111

Princess Diana, 23, 111–112
Princess message, 22
Profile of Teachers in the U.S., 132

R

Recognizing Redirecting and Releasing Sexual Energy, 109
Resilience, 50
Respect for students and their future, 144
Rethinking female sensuality, 101
Rethinking female sexuality, 101
Reviving Ophelia, 94, 146
Saving the Selves of Adolescent Girls, 94
Rich Dad Poor Dad, 126–127
Risks to women drinkers, 44
Romance, 26, 67, 72
Rules, 71
Rural teacher, 132

S

Sackville, Vita, 3
Sadker, Myra, 74
Salutatorians, 74
Sarton, Mary, 2–4
School, xi, xiv, 16–17, 26, 68–69, 85, 87–88, 111, 125, 127–128, 137, 154
Schools, one room, 131
Science, 77, 88
Science and Technology Interactive Center SciTech, 86
SciTech clubs for girls, 86
Secure attachment, 6, 9–10, 15, 17
Secure Attachment Father Attributes, 13
Secure attachment for fathers, 16
Secure attachment for mothers, 9
Secure Attachment in Girls and Young Women, 17
Self-pleasuring, 110
Self-worth, 11, 70, 72, 96, 102, 105–106
Sensory Building for Confidence and Pleasure, 105
Sensory Communication System, 104
Sensual portrayal, 94
Sensuality, 95
Separating students by gender, 140
Sex, xiv, 17, 62, 72, 75, 78, 100–103, 107–110, 133, 140–141
Sexist dualistic stereotypes, 136
Sexology research, 101
Sexual, xii, xiv–xv, 100, 109–110, 143–144
Sexual activity, 100, 103
Sexual harassment, xii, xiv–xv, 143–144
Sexual harassment violence, xii, xiv, 143
Sexual harassment in schools, 143
Sexual intercourse, 100
Sexual portrayal, 94
Sexuality, 100–101, 103
Sexually active, 100–101, 103
Sexy as a Princess, 94
Silencing of girls and women, ix
Silverstein, 46
Smart Girls, 74
So sensual, 99
Social Reconstruction, 65

Social Security, 116, 122
Softer Skills, 75
Stereotypical belief, 27
Stereotypical roles, 82
Strategies, 13, 51
Stress, 9, 40, 44, 46–47, 66, 83–84, 107, 157, 161

T
Tatar, Maria, 94
Teaching, 16, 122, 129–133, 136–138, 140, 145, 147, 153–154
Teaching methods, 132, 137–138, 140
Teaching of difference, 134
Technology, 77, 88
Teen dating violence, 68
The American Dream for Girls and Women, 113
The National Forum, 107
The responsibility for sexist traits, 138
The Rites of Passage Institute, 108
The Women's Report Card, 116
Third Stage Mentors, 83
Title IX, xiii, 59, 65

Touch, 105
Trauma, 1, 18, 70, 104–105, 107
Treatment programs, 36, 50

U
U.S. Department of Health and Human Services, 43
U.S. Department of Labor Women's Bureau, 119

V
Valedictorians, 74
Victimization, 68
Victorian, 22, 67
Vision, 28

W
Ways of Knowing, 19
Well-being of partner, 46
Whitaker, Martha, 131
Women helping girls, 83
Women Who Run with the Wolves, 96–97
Women As Assets, 111
Woolf, Virginia, 3
World War II, 6, 52, 56, 98–99